Inspiration for Servant-Leaders

Lessons from Fifty Years of Research and Practice

John C. Burkhardt & Jessica Y. Joslin, Editors

Greenleaf Center for Servant Leadership
2020

ISBN 13: 978-1-944338-12-1

Book design by Adam Robinson

Published by The Greenleaf Center for Servant Leadership
Seton Hall University
400 South Orange Avenue
South Orange, NJ 07079

www.greenleaf.org

Contents

Forward

"GREAT IDEAS...COME INTO THE WORLD AS GENTLY AS doves." With this Albert Camus quotation, Donald Frick's most authoritative biography of Robert Greenleaf opens its final chapter and sums up the contribution that Greenleaf made in his several influential essays on the subject of servant leadership. A half a century after the publication of his most important personal writings, we can point to the fact that many more words have been written to explore the dimensions of his thoughts on servants and leaders than Greenleaf produced during his own lifetime.

As executive director of the Robert K. Greenleaf Center, I take inspiration and pride in the publication of this new volume marking fifty years since "The Servant as Leader" was brought into the world. The Center's previous directors and trustees have consistently treated the concepts left to them by the founding spirit of Robert Greenleaf as an important and living trust. It was in that spirit of stewardship that this volume was prepared for use by scholars and practitioners. Readers will find a balance in the chapters which follow between the retrospective, the reflective and the stirringly expectant. Intergenerational teams of thoughtful writers—representing diverse backgrounds as academics and as practitioners—place Greenleaf's work in its deserving context and test it in terms of the many changes that have surrounded servant leadership in the decades that followed its first flight.

This book comes at a particularly challenging moment in our understanding of leadership. Many of our most important institutions seem threatened. There are moments when gaining and holding power takes precedence over putting others' highest priority needs first. Perhaps, this is no worse than what Greenleaf observed during his lifetime. Yet he was able to see beyond the mask of such discouragement in composing the uplifting, counter-intuitive and fundamentally revolutionary concept that he left to us.

I believe that to be so. Knowing that, I feel it completes the quotation that Camus provided us when he brought the metaphor of doves into the world. "But even in the midst of this... if we listen attentively, we shall hear, amid the uproar...a faint flutter of wings, the gentle stirring of life and hope."

I am grateful to the contributors to this book and to the PPC Foundation who provided financial support for its creation.

Patricia (Pat) Falotico
South Orange, New Jersey
2019

Preface

John C. Burkhardt

THIS BOOK HAS A LONG HISTORY AND OFFERS A NEW response to a challenge associated with the concept of servant leadership, one that has never been fully addressed since the term was coined by Robert Greenleaf a half century ago.

From the publication of his first essay, "The Servant as Leader" (1970), and throughout the remaining years of his life as he elaborated his ideas in dozens of essays and speeches, Greenleaf avoided placing strict boundaries on the concept he advanced. He frequently referred to servant leadership as an intellectual paradox and an aspiration for those hoping to practice it. Perhaps he felt that further limiting his seminal insight by placing it within strictures would only diminish it as an idea and not be of great benefit to those who otherwise understood and embraced the concept. If the absence of a more clearly stated definition caused a problem for scholars or made empirical validating tests difficult, he seemed to be less than concerned. He was speaking and writing for an audience of "seekers," not validators or judges.

As reported in this volume, the implications of this somewhat ascientific posture have been significant. They have contributed to acknowledgement and tolerance but otherwise inconsistent attention paid to Greenleaf's observations in some academic circles. This neglect may have something to do with the very way in which scholarly thought is customarily advanced, a process that honors formal theory construction, situated in previous scholarship, objective and generally repeated testing (using a limited set of methodologies) and cautious conclusions based on demonstrated proofs, generally asserted tentatively amidst numerous limitations.

Greenleaf's reticence may also reflect some humility on his part. He may have avoided sweeping claims for his concept knowing that he wrote within the context of his immediate time and place, each situated in a period of enormous social change. He was right. His ideas emerged just as many assumptions about our institutional, organizational, and community lives were being challenged. Given that his perspectives were grounded in experiences that had been shaped by the old orders, they might well have been discredited on that basis alone.

Nonetheless, the core concept of servant leadership has not disappeared; in fact, as one of the authors of this volume suggests, it has enjoyed several revivals and rediscoveries. It is presently in one of those periodic phases of heightened interest. It should be reassuring (if humbling to scholars) to know that important ideas survive even when they are not paying attention. All of us—and particularly scholars—should find security and inspiration in that.

Several years ago, members of the Robert K. Greenleaf board of directors discussed the problems arising from the fact that "servant leadership," while generally understood, was imprecisely applied to many situations and argued from intellectual constructs that did not seem entirely consistent or clear. It was suggested, pragmatically perhaps, that this drift in concept was unimportant and possibly even a good thing if it meant more people identified with the basic idea that Greenleaf had named without becoming entangled in details. Unfortunately, upon further discussion it became clear that even around our own table, servant leadership was being defined in terms of goodness (versus badness), caring (versus uncaring), easy (versus demanding), or saintly (versus selfish). Some of those adjectives would be preferable in describing almost anything—and that was the problem.

Through reflection and much discussion, we agreed then that one of the most important assets given to the Robert K. Greenleaf Center was the gift of Greenleaf's ideas and if we were to be stewards of that inheritance, we would need the courage to invest his thoughts in new ways. Recognizing that a relatively small but productive group of scholars had taken up the challenge of exploring servant leadership in their writings, we sought advice on how we might further grow the field of inquiry. Among the most emphatic suggestions we received was for a strategy to nurture new generations of servant leadership scholars, drawing them from diverse backgrounds, and giving them an opportunity to examine the concept of servant leadership within a wider range of contemporary environments.

In response, over the last ten years the Greenleaf Center has awarded annual fellowships for early-career individuals who propose studies of servant leadership drawing on their own disciplinary tools and shaped by the contexts of modern organizations and community life. The mechanics of this effort are not terribly important except to know that it was based within a university setting, engaged graduate students in organizing a review process, and drew upon a panel of international scholars as reviewers and occasionally as coaches to promising applicants. Not every study we have supported has resulted in findings that could be called groundbreaking. Not every study we have supported has even been published or even worth publishing. What we found was that the incentive of funding was attractive to rising scholars but often needed to be strengthened by more careful consideration of previous work in the field, nurtured through association with other authors, and offered in the context of a community of "seekers."

This book builds on what we learned. Each chapter reflects a collaboration between several contributors, established and emerging. Often the writing teams grouped around a senior scholar who served as convener, mentor, and goad. The authors as a group comprise a range of academic affiliations, ages and identities. The work that resulted is a true team effort, broadly informed, carefully and collectively developed, and edited in a participatory environment. Remarkably, each chapter holds its own and yet each contributes to the volume in complementary and even additive ways.

Beyond the distinction of process, what makes this approach particularly valuable? This book brings to life some of the most challenging and enduring insights of Robert Greenleaf's concept of servant leadership. In doing so it reclaims an idea that was first named and given voice by a white, male, organizationally bound, post-World War II American and holds it to the tests of a very different world. We hope this can be a book that will inform and inspire students, scholars, and practitioners and seem equally relevant to both young, aspiring leaders and to those who are trying to sort out many years of personal study and experience.

This is certainly not the first book to reflect on the idea of servant leadership. In fact, many famous academics and well-known leaders have done that over the last five decades. This will not be the last word on the subject either—unless we have failed in our approach. We do hope that this volume will be both a statement and an invitation for those who find these ideas intuitively familiar and want to dig deeper into their intellectual promise and while exploring the enormous benefits that follow from their realization.

John C. Burkhardt
Ann Arbor, Michigan
2019

Inspiration for Servant Leaders

LESSONS FROM FIFTY YEARS
OF RESEARCH AND PRACTICE

Chapter 1

Leadership and Servant Leadership: Understanding Both by Bridging the Past and Present

G. James Lemoine & Terry C. Blum

As society faces new challenges in the forms of increased globalization, corporate scandal, and ethical meltdowns, management scholars have increasingly recognized the inadequacy of the dominant and primarily goal-oriented approaches to leadership which have been their focus of study for decades (Avolio & Gardner, 2005; Bass & Steidlmeier, 1999; Nohria & Khurana, 2010). In need of a different lens of leadership which emphasizes cooperation and care for stakeholders over power and short-term gains, management researchers have rediscovered servant leadership (Greenleaf, 1970; van Dierendonck, 2011) as an approach which may better meet the needs of modern organizations and societies. And the results thus far have been promising, as evidence has emerged that servant leadership is related to a wide variety of positive outcomes, including subordinate performance, trust, psychological safety, positive climates, team potency, commitment, work engagement, and organizational citizenship behavior (Hu & Liden, 2011; Liden, Wayne, Liao, & Meuser, 2014b; Liden, Wayne, Zhao, & Henderson, 2008; Peterson, Galvin, & Lange, 2012; Schaubroeck, Lam, & Peng, 2011; van Dierendonck, Stam, Boersma, de Windt, & Alkema, 2013; Walumbwa, Hartnell, & Oke, 2010).

3

Although this body of evidence is both informative and encouraging, certain aspects of servant leadership crucial to its full understanding remain unexamined. Most pressingly, practitioners and researchers lack consensus on a simple, broadly accepted definition of servant leadership. Put another way, we have a general idea of behaviors engaged in by servant leaders, but we have less knowledge of how to answer the question, "What is servant leadership?" Research on leadership as a broad construct (rather than on servant leadership specifically) has similarly eluded precise and agreed-upon definition by both academics and practitioners (Yukl, 2010). Perhaps as a result, much research on servant leadership has focused on construct measurement and outcomes, providing limited insight as to what it actually entails and how it fits into broader understandings of leadership (Hunter et al., 2013). This represents a problem for practice of servant leadership if we cannot simply state what it is. The lack of a clear definition also poses issues for our ability to study servant leadership and the continuous development of a research base around it; after all, if we research a construct without first agreeing as to what exactly it is, we may or may not be studying the same thing. What is servant leadership?

Once we understand what servant leadership is, a second critical issue can be most directly addressed: Is servant leadership important, and why? How does it fit within the broader leadership phenomenon and literature? Hundreds of leadership approaches have emerged in the academic and practitioner press in the past decades (Avolio, Walumbwa, & Weber, 2009; Rost, 1991), and most have been accompanied by some evidence for their effectiveness. But relatively few of the authors of these approaches have considered other perspectives, nor considered how their chosen approach might be integrated into broader leadership theory (DeRue, Nahrgang, Wellman, & Humphrey, 2011; Nohria & Khurana, 2010; Rost, 1991). Altogether, it is worthwhile to examine what we really know about leadership, how it works, and what it should be. With this knowledge in mind, we are better equipped to understand why and whether servant leadership is important, and how appropriate it is for modern organizations.

The purpose of this chapter, then, is to review the current state of both leadership and servant-leadership research, determine how servant leadership fits within and builds upon extant research and thought on what leadership is and should be, and develop a core understanding of servant leadership that can guide its implementation in practice.

The conceptual vagueness of servant leadership

The idea of the "servant-as-leader" has since its conception been a difficult one to nail down. Although its originator, Robert Greenleaf, wrote in depth and frequently on the topic (Greenleaf, 1977, 1996a, b, 1998), he never explicitly defined servant leadership in a concise or theoretical manner. Indeed, he admits in an early collection of essays on servant leadership that such a clear definition would be very difficult (1977). What is clear in all of his writings, though, is that servant leadership is best viewed not as a loosely related group of characteristics, but rather as a set of connected behaviors emerging from an overall mindset of a manager, which leads him or her to engage in consistent activities. Greenleaf's most frequently cited description of servant leadership is one that is unfortunately dependent upon its outcomes:

> Do those being served grow as persons: do they, while being served, become healthier, wiser, freer, more autonomous, more likely themselves to become servants? And what is the effect on the least privileged in society; will she or he benefit, or at least, not be further deprived? (Greenleaf, 1977)

In a follow-up essay, Greenleaf (1996a) added one additional condition to servant leadership: that the servant leader's actions would not knowingly harm any others, directly nor indirectly. This requirement does not preclude a leader's use of discipline, accountability, or performance reviews which are sometimes considered "necessary evils" of leading people (Margolis & Molinsky, 2008); rather, it indicates a leader's cognizance of and responsibility for the consequences of his or her actions (Greenleaf, 1996a).

This provides a good idea of the servant leader's priorities, and servant leadership's intended outcomes, but remains somewhat vague as to what servant-leaders actually do. As a result of this, the scholarly body of work on servant leadership is plagued with numerous operationalizations for servant leadership with historically little agreement on meaning and theoretical frameworks (van Dierendonck, 2011). Although there is a surprisingly large body of research in which various authors propose new componential structures and accompanying measures (e.g. Barbuto & Wheeler, 2006; Liden et al., 2008; Russell & Stone, 2002; Sendjaya, Sarros, & Santora, 2008; Spears, 1995; van Dierendonck & Nuijten, 2010), several of which specifically reference need for measurement of the servant leadership "theory," relatively few authors have attempted to conceptually define the construct or explain what that theory might be. Indeed, in most of these papers, as well as subsequent reviews and empirical studies (e.g. Liden, Panaccio, Meuser, Hu, & Wayne, 2014a; Ng, Koh, & Goh, 2008; Owens & Hekman, 2012; van Dierendonck et al., 2013), it is exceedingly rare to encounter an explicit conceptual explanation of what servant leadership is.

More progress has been made in identifying competencies and behaviors used by servant-leaders (e.g. Barbuto & Wheeler, 2006; Laub, 1999; Sendjaya et al., 2008; van Dierendonck & Nuijten, 2010). As servant leadership has grown in prominence, some degree of consensus has arisen in the management literature around a model of behaviors developed by Liden and colleagues (2008) which considers servant leadership as being broadly represented by leader ethical behavior and prioritization of subordinate issues, breaking this down into seven categories of subordinate empowerment, subordinate development, ethical behaviors, conceptual skills, putting subordinates first, value creation for external stakeholders, and emotional healing, defined as empathy and sensitivity for the concerns of others (Liden et al., 2008).

In the following, we consider three important sources of information for developing a definition of servant leadership: facets of servant leadership agreed upon by subject-matter experts which should serve as examples of servant leadership; the writings of Greenleaf (as the original creator of the concept), who conceptualized the "servant" in some detail; and a more general understanding of what leadership, by itself, represents. We draw attention to the broader leadership literature in our investigation of servant leadership for two reasons. First, we propose that it is unreasonable to attempt to define any *approach* to leadership without first considering the composition of the core construct of leadership. Many authors have defined approaches to leadership along the lines of, "It is a form of leadership which…" without defining leadership itself, which is vague and unhelpful. Second, the review of what leadership itself broadly entails is also appropriate in order to better understand how servant leadership might best fit within the literature—in fact, our review indicates that servant leadership represents exactly what many scholars and practitioners have for decades been arguing that leadership needs to be.

What is leadership?

Leadership is somewhat unique among management and social psychological constructs such that in a field where clear definitions of our variables are of paramount importance to theory (Bono & McNamara, 2011), and despite massive attention to the topic, there is regardless little consensus as to what leadership actually is. It's not difficult to understand and define other organizational terms such as 'motivation,' 'commitment,' or 'creativity,' but leadership has uniquely defied easy description. As Stogdill (1974, p. 259) remarked several decades ago, there are "almost as many definitions of leadership as there are persons who have attempted to define the concept." For instance, early theorists defined leadership as a collection of extraordinary personality characteristics, empowering the leader to inspire others to action through their charisma rather than authority based on traditional or rational-legal systems (Bingham, 1927; Weber, Henderson, & Parsons, 1947). Scholars later concluded that such a definition of leadership was inadequate, however, as it did more to describe the leader him- or herself than the actual leadership behaviors which manifested.

Students of leadership in the mid 20th century turned to a behavioral focus, defining leadership generally as occurring when one individual altered the behaviors of another (Bass, 1960; Hemphill, 1949). The early management scholar Chester Barnard may have spurred this change in direction as he often argued for a more behavioral understanding of leadership, explaining it as "the act of creating awareness of and belief in an organization's purpose, without which there would be insufficient effort for the organization's survival" (Barnard, 1938). These behavioral approaches to leadership were most often measured through assessment of behaviors grouped into two categories: *consideration*, representing an orientation towards people; and *initiating structure*, representing an orientation toward task accomplishment (Fleishman, 1953b; Judge, Piccolo, & Ilies, 2004). The focus of this literature was explicitly on exploration of broad groups of behaviors which led to leadership effectiveness, rather than examination of why those behaviors might be effective (Fleishman, 1953b). Although initially fruitful, this general approach led to a flood of conflicting, insignificant, and unreliable studies, eventually contributing to a decline in interest in leadership and a corresponding belief that the concept was unimportant to organizations (Lombardo & McCall, 1978). It is likely that the move from leader personality to leadership behavior was a step in the right direction, but this purely behavioral approach suffered from two scientific flaws. First, understandings of leadership as the mere act of changing another's behavior were more consistent with the use of power than any definition of leadership (Bass, 1990). Second, and perhaps more importantly, there was little rationale as to why exactly any particular behaviors might lead to effectiveness; rather, leadership was a mysterious construct that could only be understood by its outcomes (Fleishman, 1953b; van Knippenberg & Sitkin, 2013). Without a logical explanation for leadership's effectiveness, scholars had no basis on which to ground expectations, and practitioners were understandably skeptical of predictions.

Modern approaches to leadership

Two significant approaches emerged attempting to deal with these quandaries: In the first, political scientist James MacGregor Burns introduced the concept of the 'transforming' leader (which would later evolve into the transformational leadership paradigm), and in the second, organizational scholars introduced the idea of leadership as a relationship, the quality of which might determine outcomes of interest. The latter idea, emerging from the theory of vertical dyad linkage (Dansereau Jr, Graen, & Haga, 1975), became the basis of Leader-Member-Exchange theory (LMX: Liden & Graen, 1980), which states that the quality of relationships between leaders and followers may differ among varying subordinates of the same leader, ranging from simple contractual arrangements to deeper dyadic ties.

An LMX approach defines leadership as representing the simple quality of relationship between a leader and each individual follower, and these relationships have been shown to be predictive of important organizational outcomes such as satisfaction and performance (Liden & Maslyn, 1998). The LMX paradigm, like those before it, has also been the subject of some criticism for its inattention to leader influence on overall groups (Cogliser & Schriesheim, 2000; Hogg, Martin, & Weeden, 2004), its lack of explanation of exactly what behaviors constitute leadership (Amabile, Schatzel, Moneta, & Kramer, 2004; Schriesheim, Castro, & Cogliser, 1999), and other measurement and methodological concerns (Avolio et al., 2009).

Concurrently, and building on Burns' (1978) idea of the 'transforming' leader and earlier work on leader charisma, Bass (1985) proposed the construct of transformational leadership. He envisioned transformational leadership as involving individual consideration, representing mentorship and subordinate skill development; intellectual stimulation, or encouragement of team members to create new solutions to existing problems; charismatic leadership (or idealized influence), in which the leader used his or her stimulating personality to infuse followers with a relevant sense of meaning; and inspirational motivation, a leader's passionate and effective communication of a future idea for the organization (Avolio & Bass, 1991; Hater & Bass, 1988). Transformational leadership rose to become so dominant in the field that it was to many scholars the very definition of effective leadership (Judge & Piccolo, 2004; Judge, Woolf, Hurst, & Livingston, 2006; van Knippenberg & Sitkin, 2013). However, this paradigm has been subject to at least as much scholarly criticism as its predecessors, leading to calls to reconsider it altogether (van Knippenberg & Sitkin, 2013; Yukl, 1999).

A relatively unique criticism of transformational leadership involves its morality: While the stated goal of transformational leadership is to increase individual performance through transforming subordinate priorities (Bass, 1985), there is nothing in the concept which speaks to ethical treatment of or concern for followers (Walumbwa et al., 2010). Transformational leaders owe their allegiance not to their subordinates but to the organization and its goals (Graham, 1991) and do not consider supporting followers to be a core component of their leadership responsibilities (Yukl, 1999). Further, some scholars have questioned the ethics of leadership behaviors which cause subordinates to alter their priorities to make work more relatively important than personal concerns, when that leadership is driven by improving the welfare of the organization rather than helping subordinates themselves (Stephens, D'Intino, & Victor, 1995). Even the transformational leadership component of individualized consideration is limited to mentoring followers and developing their skills, not for the benefit of the follower, but rather to enhance that individual's productivity. This led the individual most often credited with conceptualizing transformational leadership, Bernard Bass, to admit that the idea of transformational leadership as commonly understood could indeed lead to highly undesirable and unethical consequences for individuals and organizations (Bass & Steidlmeier, 1999).

The lack of theoretical basis for most of these leadership approaches (Hackman, 2002; Kerr & Jermier, 1978; Morgeson, DeRue, & Karam, 2010; Yukl, 2010) should serve as a cautionary tale for individuals interested in leadership; both practitioners and academics have defined leadership by its outcomes, rather than its processes, for decades. In other words, if it drove results, and it was implemented by a person of some power, we assume it must have been "leadership." But if *everything* is leadership, then we really don't understand anything about what leadership is. Such vagueness has led to doubts as to whether leadership meaningfully exists or if it is a 'romantic myth' invented by individuals to rationalize team performance (Meindl, Ehrlich, & Dukerich, 1985; Miner, 1975).

What should leadership be?

Yukl (2010), in his review of the academic treatment of the subject, concludes that the only thing the many definitions of leadership have in common is their view of it as a process of influence. Yukl avoids the outcome-as-definition trap in that he views the specific influence *behaviors* as comprising leadership, rather than the successful influence outcome (i.e. Yukl & Tracey, 1992). Others, such as those focused on the Leader-Member-Exchange (LMX) and emerging followership paradigms, contend that the root of all understandings of leadership is the idea of a relationship among a leader and a 'follower' or subordinate (e.g. Scandura & Graen, 1984; Uhl-Bien, Riggio, Lowe, & Carsten, 2013). Both positions seem reasonable—in the process of leadership, a leader exerts influence on another individual over the course of some relationship (even if the relationship is one sided, as might be the case with a well-known charismatic leader and a distant follower). It is also suggested by much of the literature on leadership, or at least strongly implied, that the process involves a focus on developing others, and simultaneously increasing subordinate motivations to engage in certain desired behaviors or reach particular goals (Burns, 1978; Lord & Brown, 2001; Yukl, 2010). The key to understanding leadership may be in viewing it as influential but noncoercive behaviors enacted within relationships in order to build the motivation of others to accomplish certain tasks and goals, developing them as appropriate.

However, another possible criteria, not for what leadership *has been* but for what leadership *should* be, has arisen in the aftermath of the widespread corporate scandals of the 21st century (Fortune, 2009): Leadership behaviors should help subordinates and the larger organizational and community contexts, rather than harm them. Leadership is not alone among fields of organizational study for which this call has been made; there are growing calls for both more attention to positive experiences and institutions throughout research on organizational behavior and psychology, and the need to understand and teach practices which increase the well-being of both individuals within organization, and the communities in which those organizations reside (e.g. Cameron, Dutton, & Quinn, 2003; Rucci, 2008). Perhaps no call for the promotion of more beneficial and positive approaches to leadership is more apt than that of Nohria and Khurana, who introduced their *Handbook of Leadership Theory and Practice* by referencing

> a time when societies around the world are crying out for more and better leadership, when our current leaders (especially in business, but also in government and other spheres of public life) have lost legitimacy, questions are being asked, sometimes angrily, of the institutions that school these leaders: What kinds of leaders are these institutions developing that have caused so much hardship for so many? ... What is the vision or model of leadership that animates the curriculum and developmental models [of current leadership approaches taught in institutions]? If there is such a model, does it need to be revisited, reexamined, and revised in light of the widespread failures of leadership? Do we really understand what it takes to develop better leaders? (Nohria & Khurana, 2010, p. 3)

Those authors, mirroring the aforementioned criticism of the dominant transformational approach to leadership, concluded that they cannot answer those questions with any confidence. Although many scholars historically considered leadership an ethically neutral affair (Bass, 1985; Rost, 1991; Thompson, 1956), a growing body of both researchers and practitioners have come to believe the opposite. Although we may struggle to precisely determine leadership's definition, our understanding and instruction of leadership should include some consequentialist component of behavior which helps, or at least does not harm, followers and society (Padilla, Hogan,

& Kaiser, 2007; Podolny, Khurana, & Besharov, 2010; Treviño, Brown, & Hartman, 2003).

If we cannot agree on the semantics of what leadership is, perhaps a more useful approach to leadership may be to consider what it *should* be, for both practical meaningfulness and value in a modern context. We propose consistent with the literature that there are several themes which should be included in a modern understanding of leadership, including established components such as influencing behaviors (Yukl, 1971) and quality relationships (Liden & Graen, 1980; Uhl-Bien et al., 2013), as well as this newer emphasis on stakeholder well-being (de Luque, Washburn, Waldman, & House, 2008).

Beyond performance

As described above, there is a growing consensus that a modern understanding of leadership must be infused with some sense of stakeholder values, involving behaviors geared toward help-ing rather than harming stakeholders and societies (Cameron, 2008; Nohria & Khurana, 2010; Rosenthal, 2011), in addition to profit and mission concerns. This argument is similar at the organizational level to stakeholder theory (Laplume, Sonpar, & Litz, 2008), an approach to organizational priorities which argues that firms should consider the interests of all stakeholders (including employees, communities, customers, environment, diversity, and mission/profit concerns) rather than prioritizing shareholders alone. Freeman (1984) build this argument based on the observation that other organizational theories could not account for the rapidly changing business environment, includ-ing progress in globalization, information transparency, and consumer action. This idea is in stark contrast to the predomi-nant stockholder-focused idea that a firm exists only to generate shareholder wealth (Friedman, 1982). Critics of the stakeholder approach draw on agency theory (Eisenhardt, 1989) to argue that stakeholder theory is itself unethical, as it redirects owner resources away from profit-creation (or mission-achievement) uses without owner consent (Jensen, 2010). Proponents of stakeholder theory have rebutted this by suggesting that stakeholder concern boosts profits and mission accomplishment in the long term by improving firm-stakeholder relations and building organizational legitimacy, credibility, and attractiveness. And indeed, tests of the theory have confirmed that firms which prioritize stakeholders tend to enjoy greater business performance over time (de Luque et al., 2008; Margolis & Walsh, 2003). To some, this represents an unintuitive paradox: The research shows that spending less resources on profitability, and more on stakeholders, is actually the most profitable solution for modern organizations.

Another criticism asks how such stakeholder concern aligns with organizational goal accomplishment and performance, given that these are the traditional measures of leader success (cf. Andersen, 2009; Giampetro-Meyer, Brown, Browne, & Kubasek, 1998; Rost, 1991). There are at least three avenues of rebuttal to this criticism. First, leadership must not be defined and constrained merely by an expected performance outcome. Second, leadership might be understood as a collection of behaviors oriented most proximally toward the creation of meaning and positive change in others, rather than immediate performance goals. Finally, there is growing theoretical and conceptual evidence that this stakeholder concern may serve as a meaningful antecedent to more instrumental measures of team and organizational performance. Each of these arguments will be reviewed in turn below.

First, an immediate performance/profit outcome cannot be a necessary condition of leadership, as this comes dangerously close to defining the construct by its outcomes (van Knippenberg & Sitkin, 2013). Practically speaking, if anything that could boost performance is leadership, then we would need to enlarge our understanding of leadership to include things like sales, paychecks, technology purchases, etc. It would be like arguing that good salesmanship is anything that increases sales, or that the secret to creativity is generating a new idea. Both statements may be true, but they don't help us at all in understanding how to sell or be creative. Clearly, there are many things a firm can do to build profits which are not "leadership." Further, it is arbitrary and atheoretical to assume that the sole aim of leadership is performance (Avolio & Gardner, 2005; Podolny et al., 2010) in the absence of formal, accepted, and tested theory and rationale establishing that this is the case. No other construct in the management literature, to our knowledge, is claimed to exist only if it has a measurable impact on immediate performance. Creativity researchers, for instance, do not maintain that behaviors cease to be creative unless they immediately boost organizational performance; rather, creative behaviors generate ideas that are both novel and useful (George, 2007). Similarly, characterization of a behavior as fair and just is not predicated on immediate positive efficiency boosts; rather, justice is a perception of fairness (Colquitt, Conlon, Wesson, Porter, & Ng, 2001). In this manner, it seems unreasonable to mandate that something must benefit immediate performance to be termed 'leadership'; perhaps behaviors which benefit immediate performance gains might more accurately describe the concept of 'management' (Bennis & Nanus, 1985; Zaleznik, 1977).

Follower well-being

As Podolny and colleagues (2010) have pointed out, scholarly interest in understanding leadership first developed not because of interest in efficiency, but because it created well-being and purpose in the lives of followers, a stakeholder of primary importance. Typologies going back to the Leader Opinion Questionnaire (Fleishman, 1953a) have recognized that leadership behaviors are geared toward both people and goals, and

Burns' (1978) original basis for the transforming leader was one who could "arouse, engage, and satisfy the motives of followers" (p. 18). It is likely that the fundamental and proximal desired outcome of leadership is not merely performance, but rather an innate transformation of those being led, increasing their motivations and abilities to assist the organization in its goals (Bass, 1985), increasing their own capabilities and confidence (Liden et al., 2008), or driving moral growth (Mayer, Kuenzi, Greenbaum, Bardes, & Salvador, 2009). It is plausible that leadership most effectively drives performance and other outcomes through giving followers a sense of meaning and purpose (Podolny et al., 2010). Empirical evidence has supported the idea that such meaning-driven leadership, even without a performance focus, can significantly drive performance both at the individual (Judge et al., 2004; Walumbwa et al., 2011) and organizational (de Luque et al., 2008; Ogden & Watson, 1999) levels.

This idea that leadership may most effectively enhance performance through its emphasis on improving the lives and abilities of others is not a new one. The groundbreaking early 20th century scholar Henri Fayol, for instance, emphasized the importance of creating satisfaction and a sense of fairness in a leader's subordinates, saying specifically that, "For the personnel to be encouraged to carry out its duties with all the devotion and loyalty of which it is capable it must be treated with kindliness, and equity results from the combination of kindliness and justice" (Fayol, 1949, p. 38). It is important to note that while Fayol saw kindliness and justice as worthy ends unto themselves, they were not the end of his causal chain. It was through this caring that subordinates were motivated to perform at their highest levels via a mechanism of reciprocation (Gouldner, 1960), with a level of effort, consistency, and persistence that could not be inspired through incentives or punishments.

The primal importance of a positive leader-follower relationship serves as the basis for more modern theories such as LMX (Liden & Graen, 1980) and the emerging literature on leadership co-creation by leaders and followers (Shamir, 2007) and leader and follower identities (DeRue & Ashford, 2010). Beyond these specific approaches, even simple displays of manager humility (Owens & Hekman, 2012) or treating all group members equally (Wu, Tsui, & Kinicki, 2010) can have meaningful positive effects on performance outcomes. Therefore, we argue that leadership behaviors may be oriented toward a variety of results, but follower growth and improvement may serve both as primary outcomes, and as mechanisms through which other ends are accomplished.

Broader stakeholder concerns

Evidence is also accumulating that effective leadership 'should' include an emphasis on stakeholders beyond the traditional subordinates, team, and organization. This emphasis on working for the good of society, alongside a focus on profits and performance, is a growing expectation of modern leaders (Nohria & Khurana, 2010; Rosenthal, 2011; Servaes & Tamayo, 2013). Many business authors, however, as well as management scholars, generally ignore any responsibility for societal good, focusing instead on organizational performance, employee satisfaction, and more recently, general ethical behaviors as important outcomes (Judge & Piccolo, 2004; Mayer et al., 2009). As organizations become more transparent and the activities of leaders become increasingly visible both within and outside of organizations, attention and scrutiny to management activities has grown exponentially and in correspondence with growing demands that organizational leaders help, or at least not harm, external stakeholders. However, this is not an idea that is well captured in modern theories such as transformational leadership, which contains no emphases on outcomes beyond organizational performance (Bass, 1985; Bass & Steidlmeier, 1999). Even the idea of "ethical leadership," as it's usually discussed, has no focus on outcomes for any external stakeholders, instead prioritizing compliance by managers and employees to prevailing norms and standards, in the interest of avoiding costly lawsuits (Brown & Treviño, 2006; Treviño, Hartman, & Brown, 2000). A recent review of 'moral' approaches to leadership such as ethical and authentic leadership (Lemoine, Hartnell, & Leroy, 2019) concluded that only one approach to leadership encompassed stakeholder priorities: that of servant leadership.

Research has confirmed the importance of external stakeholder orientation, with an especially large and growing body of work on firm performance. Organizations led and guided by concern for stakeholders such as communities, customers, and the natural environment encounter easier access to capital (Cheng, Ioannou, & Serafeim, 2014) and quality employees (Greening & Turban, 2000), learning and innovation capabilities (Sharma & Vredenburg, 1998), higher product quality (Agle, Mitchell, & Sonnenfeld, 1999), and greater financial performance (de Luque et al., 2008). Individuals exhibit preferences to work for leaders who prioritize stakeholder concerns, providing competitive recruiting advantages to such organizations (Agle et al., 1999), and once employed develop relatively strong organizational commitment (Maignan, Ferrell, & Hult, 1999) and high levels of performance (Jones, 2010). To be clear, we do not argue nor feel that financial performance should be the only 'bar' by which the effectiveness of leadership is measured. However, the fact that stakeholder concern boosts such performance, as well as other outcomes such as follower well-being, learning, and commitment, provides evidence for its importance in the modern organizational reality.

The attractive outcomes of stakeholder orientations in and of themselves do not mandate their inclusion in a definition of leadership. But in a discussion of what leadership *should* be, it seems apparent that concern for stakeholders, and behaviors oriented toward them, are consistent with both the process of leadership and its outcome orientations. If we consider the process of leadership as playing out through influence behaviors, leader attention to stakeholder needs may aid this process as it increases members' trust, commitment, and engagement with the leader (Shamir, House, & Arthur, 1993). And if leadership behaviors are conducted in order to improve the development and well-being of followers and enhance organizational performance, stakeholder concern would seem to contribute to these outcomes by, respectively, infusing the leadership with meaning (Podolny et al., 2010), and creating a positive context for long-term approaches to performance gains (de Luque et al., 2008; Freeman & Gilbert, 1988).

Positive organizational change

The achievement of future positive, meaningful change implies the existence of a communicable and motivating vision, an idea which occurs frequently in the literature on leadership and is related to both effectiveness and leader capacity to implement change (Grant, 2012; Larwood, Falbe, Kriger, & Miesing, 1995; Westley & Mintzberg, 1989). Although this idea would be outside of the classic distinction of leadership behaviors as oriented toward consideration or structure (Judge et al., 2004), the idea of driving change through vision has been a vital component of many leadership paradigms, most visibly charismatic leadership (Conger & Kanungo, 1987) and the intellectual stimulation and inspirational motivation dimensions of transformational leadership (Avolio & Bass, 1991). This outcome is not disconnected from the stakeholder-oriented approach outlined above; on the contrary, research indicates that a stakeholder emphasis may lay the groundwork for meaningful, positive organizational change by building the motivation and open mindedness necessary for creative outcomes (Amabile, 1996; Maignan et al., 1999; Sharma & Vredenburg, 1998).

Leadership and servant leadership

Altogether, a useful understanding of leadership might be one in which behaviors are directed toward multiple outcomes, including follower development and well-being, task/goal accomplishment, meaningful and positive organizational change, and helping (or at least not harming) *all* stakeholders. Organizational owners and stockholders would certainly be prevalent among these stakeholders, but not necessarily most proximal and certainly not the only stakeholders of importance. Even if they were considered to be of foremost importance, evidence is growing that the most effective way to reach organizational and stockholder goals is through caring for and developing subordinates (Bass & Steidlmeier, 1999) and stakeholders (de Luque et al., 2008), infusing the organization with meaning and transforming it into a powerful institution (Selznick, 1957). Is there any approach to leadership, then, from which we can derive a more direct and concise understanding, to represent what practitioners and academics alike agree that leadership *should* be? Burns' (1978) original conceptualization of the 'transforming' leader aligns surprisingly well with ideas of performance, change, and follower and stakeholder orientation, but modern models of charismatic and transformational leadership as we currently discuss and study them do not fit these criteria.

We propose that an understanding of the concept of servant leadership, as it was originally theorized (Greenleaf, 1970), aligns quite well with all of these criteria for what leadership 'should' be. Servant leadership is unique among all of these approaches to leadership in that it is the only one that was not developed by an academic. Robert K. Greenleaf (1904-1990) was a businessman, consultant, and philosopher who served as AT&T's first director of management research. During his time there, he developed the core idea of the leader-as-servant: the premise that organizational leadership positions, when held by people with motivations and values directed at serving others, could benefit not only their own organizations but also broader institutions and society (Greenleaf, 1977). To aid in the advocacy of this new approach to management, he founded in 1964 a nonprofit "Center for Applied Ethics," which operates today as the Robert K. Greenleaf Center for Servant Leadership.

Greenleaf considered the servant-as-leader as a response to his concerns that people and society were becoming increasingly devoid of hope, a characteristic he considered necessary for fulfilling and quality life (Greenleaf, 1998). He believed society, through its guiding institutions, was losing a degree of care for both individual and common good, and that this degeneration could only be corrected by installing leaders in those institutions who thought of themselves more as servants than as leaders (Greenleaf, 1977, 1998). This is often misinterpreted to indicate a weak leader or one who is subject to the whims of his subordinates (Johnson, 2001). This was emphatically not the case in Greenleaf's writings, however, as he frequently mentions the need for a servant-leader to push subordinates to higher performance levels (Greenleaf, 1977), to keep a "tough attitude" to get things done (Greenleaf, 1998), and "to say 'Do it now!' instead of 'Do it tomorrow, it'll be easier!'" (Greenleaf, 1996a). Being a servant, at least in the Greenleaf sense, entails neither a leader struggling with self-esteem, nor an abandonment of the power needed to gain the respect of co-workers (van Dierendonck, 2011). Rather, he wrote that a servant approaches leadership as an opportunity to enhance the lives of others—a commitment to the improvement of those being led, the greater organization, and society as a whole (Reinke, 2003). Whereas hierarchies mandate service to those *above*, the servant-as-leader is also interested in serving those *below*; not because she is required to, but because she prefers to and sees it as a way to improve others. This core motivation, perhaps conceptualized as a motivation to serve (Ng et al., 2008), was theorized by Greenleaf as preventing the power of management from corrupting the servant-as-leader, and acting as the root driver of related servant behaviors. Such a servant, he posited, would be resistant to arrogance and care little for power, happy to share it as appropriate for the good of the team and organization (Greenleaf, 1998).

In addition, Greenleaf never mentioned any limits to the beneficiaries of this leader service, as he wrote about the importance of prioritizing others (beyond the leader him or herself) including subordinates, communities, families, society, and the employing organization (Greenleaf, 1977, 1996a, 1998). The stereotypical view of servant leadership is that in its emphasis on serving subordinates and stakeholders, it does not consider achieving organizational objectives to be important (Andersen, 2009; Heskett, 2013; Johnson, 2001). This is wholly inconsistent with Greenleaf's model of servant leadership. While he did strongly emphasize the importance of enhancing the well-being and development of followers, he also saw the role of the servant-leader as one who "initiates, provides the ideas and the structure, and takes the risk of failure along with the chance of success" (Greenleaf, 1977, p. 29). Such a leader would always be prepared to communicate the team or organization goal and persuade any who were unsure of it as to why it needed to be done. Without an emphasis on organizational performance and growth, the organization would fail, an outcome that would be counter to the best interests of all stakeholders (Greenleaf, 1998). The servant leader, Greenleaf argued, took the organization's successes and failures very personally, and as a result would consistently and carefully examine routine processes within the organization, alongside his or her team, to determine how they could be made better (Greenleaf, 1996a). Vision and support for creative follower ideas to improve processes were named particularly important attributes of the servant-leader (Greenleaf, 1977, 1996b): "An essential part of servant leadership is vision - it's required to open us to willingness to use what we know and to work to extract hard reality from a dream" (Greenleaf, 1998). The servant-leader would not let his or her team or organization fail, because to do so would be to eliminate opportunities for subordinates to grow, and opportunities for the team and organization to serve other internal and external constituents.

On servant leadership and religion

It is worth mentioning that whereas the concept of servant leadership has often been linked with spirituality and the Christian faith, both in academia (e.g. Ng et al., 2008; Page & Wong, 2000) and in the popular press (e.g. Agosto, 2005; Blanchard & Hodges, 2003), it was not at all Greenleaf's intent that servant leadership be considered a predominantly spiritual exercise nor limited to those of any particular belief (Frick, 2004). Rather, he saw servant leadership as an approach to organizational stewardship that was beneficial for both the organization itself and society at large. While the concept has proven popular within religious institutions worldwide (Blanchard & Hodges, 2003; Fryar, 2001; Hale & Fields, 2007), the core belief that positive organizational practices are desirable is hardly unique to any one philosophy or religion. The idea that positive relationships exist between treating others well and desirable organizational outcomes is prevalent throughout management scholarship as well, such as within the research on justice (Colquitt et al., 2001), psychological safety (Edmondson, 1999), and the positive organizational behavior literature (Cameron et al., 2003).

Greenleaf's Christian faith guided the development of the servant-as-leader idea (Frick, 2004), and Jesus Christ is often cited as the primary exemplar of servant leadership (Sendjaya et al., 2008). But Greeleaf's exemplar of leader service was no religious figure: rather, he took inspiration for the concept from Hesse's *Journey to the East*. The servant concept, while well represented in Christianity, is hardly unique to it; the importance of those in power remaining humble and serving others is an idea found in virtually all major world religions, as well as nonreligious philosophies of life (Kurth, 2003). For instance, centuries before Christ's birth, Laozi (also known as Lao Tzu), the Chinese philosopher and founder of Taoism, wrote in the *Dao De Jing* of the humble and empowering leader:

> The highest type of rule is one of whose existence the people are barely aware. Next comes one whom they love and praise... The Sage is self-effacing and scanty of words. When his task is accomplished and things have been completed, all the people say, 'We ourselves have achieved it!' (quoted in Rae & Witzel, 2004)

The founder of the Sikh religion, Guru Nanak Dev Ji, established service to others, especially service enacted by those in power toward those of lower status, as a core pillar of this faith. The guru emphasized this idea of service through the values of *Vand Chhakna* and *Seva* (sharing and community service), respectively: "In the midst of this world, do selfless service, and you shall be given a place of honor in the Court of the Lord." - *Sri Guru Granth Sahib*, p. 26, lines 1-2. Similarly, an analytical study comparing servant leadership with Islamic leadership (as proposed by Muslim scriptures) found the two approaches matched quite well, especially in their mutual influence on ethical leader behaviors, empowerment, and service to others (Sarayrah, 2004). This is a representative but not exhaustive comparison of servant leadership with religion and philosophy; servant leadership does have connections with various religious and secular beliefs, just as other positive management concepts do, but servant leadership is itself neither inherently spiritual nor religious in nature. Indeed, Greenleaf himself wrote most frequently and most emphatically of the need for servant leadership in large businesses and institutions, and empirical research has found servant leadership to be particularly effective at driving performance and profitability in nonreligious contexts (see Lemoine et al., 2019, for a review).

What is servant leadership?

If we want to understand the core of what servant leadership is, can its founder's writings lend clarity? Greenleaf insists that a servant-leader is one who creates better followers, grows communities, improves organizations and institutions, and does no harm to others (Greenleaf, 1996a). He wrote that servant leadership emphasizes persuading followers—but not coercing them—through words and deeds, of the value of service to community, employer, and each other (Greenleaf, 1998). Such behavior would revolve around what he called "seeking," or looking for a new vision and a better way of running things, while staying humble, exhibiting care for all around the leader, and keeping an open mind to the prospect of personal learning and change, thus exhibiting and managing to a sense of foresight (Greenleaf, 1998).

It is striking how similar Greenleaf's idea of servant leadership is to modern thought on how our understanding of effective leadership needs to evolve. Both involve vision and an orientation toward meaningful, positive organizational change (Greenleaf, 1996b; Yukl, 2010); both involve prioritization of getting things done (Giampetro-Meyer et al., 1998; Greenleaf, 1998; Posner & Kouzes, 1988) through subordinate development and the creation of meaning (Greenleaf, 1977; Hackman, 2010; Selznick, 1984); both involve behaviors that demonstrate concern for multiple stakeholders (Greenleaf, 1977; Nohria & Khurana, 2010); and both view stakeholder ethics as essential to sustainable performance (Bass & Steidlmeier, 1999; Greenleaf, 1977). The original concept of servant leadership aligns quite well with modern thought on what leadership needs to be.

How have we attempted to conceptually and concisely describe servant leadership in the past? One of the earlier attempts at a definition emerged in Laub's (1999) dissertation on the topic, wherein he suggested that servant leadership is "an understanding and practice of leadership that places the good

of those led over the self-interest of the leader." Other authors
have expanded on this definition, such as Hale and Fields'
(2007) addition that it "emphasizes leader behaviors that focus
on follower development, and de-emphasizing glorification of
the leader." Adapting from Greenleaf, Ehrhart (2004, p.
68) suggested that the basis of servant leadership is that such a leader
would acknowledge "his or her moral responsibility not only to
the success of the organization but also to his or her subordinates,
the organization's customers, and other organizational
stakeholders." Schaubroeck and colleagues (2011) explained
servant leadership as "a group-oriented approach to leadership
that emphasizes serving others, building a sense of community,
emphasizing teamwork, and sharing power." Although useful,
these definitions are inconsistent on several key points, and still
remain vague in their use of general terms such as "practice of
leadership."

Although interest in servant leadership has waxed and waned
over the years, research on servant leadership was revitalized
by the introduction of a 7-dimensional model which captures
the elements of servant leadership described throughout this
chapter, and explains outcomes beyond that which is attributed
to other leadership approaches (Liden et al., 2008). The servant-
leader grows performance through a mastery of *conceptual
skills* and *helping subordinates grow and succeed.* Servant-leaders
promote positive organizational change by granting power and
decision-making authority to those in lower roles (captured
in the *empowerment* dimension) and by interacting openly
and fairly with others (captured in the *behaving ethically*
dimension), which should precipitate psychological safety and
creativity (Edmondson, 1999). They put people before profits
and grow profits through people by being sensitive to their
personal concerns (*emotional healing*) and *putting them first,*
and demonstrate their stakeholder priorities through *creating
value for the community.* Further, this operationalization of
servant leadership has provided promising evidence for its

effectiveness, as related in the first paragraph of this chapter. This understanding of servant leadership predicts desirable outcomes ranging from engagement and trust to individual and firm financial performance (e.g. Chen, Zhu, & Zhou, 2015; Hu & Liden, 2011; Liden et al., 2014b; Liden et al., 2008; Peterson et al., 2012; Schaubroeck et al., 2011).

A proposed definition

How, then, can servant leadership be defined in a useful manner (cf. Parris & Peachey, 2013)? That is, how can we define servant leadership such that it is defined not by its antecedents nor by its outcomes, yet is defined parsimoniously, clearly, and distinctly from other approaches to leadership? Integrating Greenleaf's original theory-in-use (Greenleaf, 1977, 1996a) with current academic understandings of the construct (Ehrhart, 2004; Liden et al., 2014a; van Dierendonck & Nuijten, 2010), while considering current thought on what leadership might and should be overall (Avolio & Gardner, 2005; Nohria & Khurana, 2010; Yukl, 2010), we leverage existing scholarship to propose the following definition:

> Servant leadership is composed of influence behaviors, manifested humbly and morally within relationships, oriented towards continuous and meaningful improvement for all stakeholders. These stakeholders include, but are not limited to, those being led, communities, customers, and the leader, team, and organization themselves.

It is the influence behaviors within relationships that forms the leadership itself, rather than the stakeholder outcomes toward which they are directed. This influence may represent a form of power or come from a basis of power, but it is a specialized type of power in that individuals follow not because they are forced to, but because they are persuaded to. This definition is similar to those proposed by others (Hale & Fields, 2007; Laub, 1999; Schaubroeck et al., 2011) in several respects, but augments them in two ways. First, it does not use the term "leadership" to define an approach to leadership, reducing vagueness and confusion. Second, it adds the leader's team, organization, and society to the list of stakeholders toward which servant leadership behaviors are aimed, explicitly allowing performance-oriented components. It also adds the leader him or herself as a possible beneficiary of leadership, as the servant-leader is interested in learning and developing herself as well as her followers, seeking wisdom and positioning herself to better serve others. Servant-leaders learn alongside their teams, not separate from nor instead of them, and are open to learning and influence from those ranked above and below them (Graham, 1991; Greenleaf, 1970).

Although concern with more performance-centric organizational goals (*in addition to*, but not *replacing*, concerns for followers and other stakeholders) is not present in the definitions cited above, its inclusion within a definition of servant leadership is far from unprecedented in the recent literature on the topic. Most prevalent dimensional structures of servant leadership, for instance, include conceptual skills relevant to the organization and the team's tasks (Ehrhart, 2004; Liden et al., 2008), or a system of accountability to ensure that goals are accomplished (van Dierendonck & Nuijten, 2010). Servant-leaders feel a moral responsibility for organizational success (Ehrhart, 2004), push subordinates to envision new ways to more effectively and efficiently achieve goals (Graham, 1991), and strengthen a promotion-focus in those around them toward growing the organization (Neubert, Carlson, Roberts, Kacmar, & Chonko, 2008). Although some researchers have claimed that servant leadership is opposed to such organizational performance initiatives (Andersen, 2009; Whetstone, 2002) or that this approach to leadership focuses on maintaining the current status quo of organizational operations (Smith, Montagno, & Kuzmenko, 2004), these stances are not supported by research. On the contrary, the conceptualization of servant leadership described here, which weights it as focused more on stakeholder concerns rather than performance, has repeatedly related to organizational growth and profitability (e.g. Liden et al., 2014b; Peterson et al., 2012).

It might be argued that such a definition, focused on follower transformation, empowerment, and positive organizational change, has much in common with the dominant approach of transformational or charismatic leadership (Bass, 1985; Judge et al., 2006). Indeed, if the term were not already in use, one would be tempted to call servant leadership a 'transformational' form of leadership, and it has much in common with Burns' (1978) original concept of the transforming leader. The differences between these approaches have been well documented (Bass, 2000; Graham, 1991; Liden et al., 2008; Schaubroeck et al., 2011) and remain relevant when considered alongside the conceptual additions made by this proposed definition. First is the issue of the leader's allegiance: Transformational leaders' first and only obligation, as measured and conceptualized, is to their employing organizations, whereas servant-leaders feel strong obligations toward all stakeholders, and especially those whom they have power over (Bass, 2000; Liden et al., 2008; Parolini, Patterson, & Winston, 2009). The transformational leader aligns follower motivations with the needs of the organization (a leadership of 'ends over means'; Nohria & Khurana, 2010), whereas a servant-leader models a focus on the needs of many groups (Graham, 1991). Several scholars have claimed that transformational leadership has little theoretical basis holding its component behaviors together beyond their impact on organizational performance (e.g. van Knippenberg & Sitkin, 2013; Yukl, 1999); servant leadership behaviors, on the other hand, are connected by their root service motivation and their orientation toward creating opportunities to have positive impacts on stakeholders. Servant leadership behaviors such as developing followers, promoting volunteerism, and building sustainably successful institutions that create meaning for followers are all linked by core values aimed at improving organizations and communities (Graham, 1991; Greenleaf, 1970; Liden et al., 2008).

Conclusion

Even when servant leadership is defined in research or practice, it is usually explained as either "a style of leadership which...", leaving its true meaning somewhat vague, or it is defined by its outcomes, as is the case with Greenleaf's popular definition of servant leadership as creating others who are "healthier, wiser, freer", etc. (Greenleaf, 1970). By proposing servant leadership as influence behaviors, manifested humbly and ethically within relationships and oriented toward continuous and meaningful improvement for all stakeholders, we hope to contribute to ongoing debates as to what leadership in general, and servant leadership specifically, represent. This proposed definition of servant leadership is not the first to be proposed, and we hold no illusions that it will be the last, but we hope it contributes to practical, theoretical, and integrative examinations of the concept, allowing for more fruitful research. Specifically, the definition positions servant leadership as unique within the leadership literature, as no other popular theory of leadership includes its stakeholder emphasis. Neither transformational, nor ethical, nor authentic (Walumbwa, Avolio, Gardner, Wernsing, & Peterson, 2008) approaches to leadership mandate concern for communities and stakeholders, as will be described in the following chapter; in this manner, the servant leadership approach is meaningfully distinct.

This conceptual definition answers calls from the broader leadership literature (Nohria & Khurana, 2010) for attention to stakeholder issues, while providing an element of a theory of servant leadership from which we can develop hypotheses and research questions which will, in turn, allow a greater understanding of why and how the servant leadership approach can meet the challenges and opportunities of contemporary organizations and societies.

Chapter 1 References

Agle, B. R., Mitchell, R. K., & Sonnenfeld, J. A. (1999). Who Matters to CEOs? An Investigation of Stakeholder Attributes and Salience, Corporate Performance, and CEO Values. *The Academy of Management Journal, 42*(5), 507-525.

Agosto, E. (2005). *Servant leadership: Jesus & Paul.* St. Louis, MO: Chalice Press.

Amabile, T. M. (1996). *Creativity in context.* Boulder, CO: Westview Press.

Amabile, T. M., Schatzel, E. A., Moneta, G. B., & Kramer, S. J. (2004). Leader behaviors and the work environment for creativity: Perceived leader support. *Leadership Quarterly, 15*(1), 5-32.

Andersen, J. A. (2009). When a servant-leader comes knocking. *Leadership & Organization Development Journal, 30*(1), 4-15.

Avolio, B., & Bass, B. M. (1991). *The full range of leadership development: Basic and advanced manuals.* Binghamton, NY: Bass, Avolio, & Associates.

Avolio, B. J., & Gardner, W. L. (2005). Authentic leadership development: Getting to the root of positive forms of leadership. *The Leadership Quarterly, 16*(3), 315-338.

Avolio, B. J., Walumbwa, F. O., & Weber, T. J. (2009). Leadership: Current Theories, Research, and Future Directions. *Annual Review of Psychology, 60*, 421-449.

Barbuto, J. E., & Wheeler, D. W. (2006). Scale Development and Construct Clarification of Servant Leadership. *Group & Organization Management, 31*(3), 300-326.

Barnard, C. I. (1938). *The functions of the executive.* Cambridge, MA: Harvard University Press.

Bass, B. M. (1960). *Leadership, psychology, and organizational behaviour.* New York, NY: Harper.

Bass, B. M. (1985). *Leadership and Performance Beyond Expectations.* New York, NY: The Free Press.

Bass, B. M. (1990). *Bass and Stogdill's handbook of leadership*. New York, NY: Free Press.

Bass, B. M. (2000). The Future of Leadership in Learning Organizations. *Journal of Leadership & Organizational Studies, 7*(3), 18-40.

Bass, B. M., & Steidlmeier, P. (1999). Ethics, character, and authentic transformational leadership behavior. *The Leadership Quarterly, 10*(2), 181-217.

Bennis, W. G., & Nanus, B. (1985). *Leaders: The Strategies for Taking Charge*. New York, NY: Harper & Row.

Bingham, W. V. (1927). Leadership. In H. C. Metcalfe (Ed.), *The psychological foundations of management*. New York, NY: Shaw.

Blanchard, K. H., & Hodges, P. (2003). *The servant leader: Transforming your heart, head, hands and habits*. Nashville, TN: J. Countryman.

Bono, J. E., & McNamara, G. (2011). From the editors: Publishing in AMJ - Part 2: Research design. *Academy of Management Journal, 54*, 657-660.

Brown, M. E., & Treviño, L. K. (2006). Ethical leadership: A review and future directions. *Leadership Quarterly, 17*(6), 595-616.

Burns, J. M. (1978). *Leadership*. New York, NY: Harper & Row, Publishers, Inc.

Cameron, K. S. (2008). *Positive Leadership: Strategies for Extraordinary Performance*. San Francisco, CA: Berrett-Koehler Publishers.

Cameron, K. S., Dutton, J. E., & Quinn, R. E. (2003). Foundations of Positive Organizational Scholarship. In K. S. Cameron, J. E. Dutton, & R. E. Quinn (Eds.), *Positive Organizational Scholarship*(pp. 3-27). San Francisco, CA: Berrett-Koehler Publishers.

Chen, Z., Zhu, J., & Zhou, M. (2015). How does a servant-leader fuel the service fire? A multilevel model of servant leadership, individual self identity, group competition climate, and customer service performance. *Journal of Applied Psychology, 100*(2), 511-521.

Cheng, B., Ioannou, I., & Serafeim, G. (2014). Corporate social responsibility and access to finance. *Strategic Management Journal, 35*(1), 1-23.

Cogliser, C. C., & Schriesheim, C. A. (2000). Exploring Work Unit Context and Leader-Member Exchange: A Multi-Level Perspective. *Journal of Organizational Behavior* (5), 487.

Colquitt, J. A., Conlon, D. E., Wesson, M. J., Porter, C. O. L. H., & Ng, K. Y. (2001). Justice at the millennium: a meta-analytic review of 25 years of organizational justice research. *Journal of Applied Psychology, 86*(3), 425.

Conger, J. A., & Kanungo, R. N. (1987). Toward a behavioral theory of charismatic leadership in organizational settings. *Academy of Management Review, 12*(4), 637-647.

Dansereau Jr, F., Graen, G., & Haga, W. J. (1975). A Vertical Dyad Linkage Approach to Leadership within Formal Organizations. A Longitudinal Investigation of the Role Making Process. *Organizational Behavior & Human Performance, 13*(1), 46-78.

de Luque, M. S., Washburn, N. T., Waldman, D. A., & House, R. J. (2008). Unrequited Profit: How Stakeholder and Economic Values Relate to Subordinates' Perceptions of Leadership and Firm Performance. *Administrative Science Quarterly, 53*(4), 626-654.

DeRue, D. S., & Ashford, S. J. (2010). Who will lead and who will follow? A social process of leadership identity construction in organizations. *Academy of Management Review, 35*(4), 627-647.

DeRue, D. S., Nahrgang, J. D., Wellman, N., & Humphrey, S. E. (2011). Trait and behavioral theories of leadership: An integration and meta-analytic test of their relative validity. *Personnel Psychology, 64*(1), 7-52.

Edmondson, A. (1999). Psychological safety and learning behavior in work teams. *Administrative Science Quarterly, 44*(2), 350-383.

Ehrhart, M. G. (2004). Leadership and Procedural Justice Climate as Antecedents of Unit-Level Organizational Citizenship Behavior. *Personnel Psychology, 57*(1), 61-94.

Eisenhardt, K. M. (1989). Agency Theory: An Assessment and Review. *Academy of Management Review, 14*(1), 57-74.

Fayol, H. (1949). *General and Industrial Management.* London, UK: Sir Isaac Pitman & Sons, Ltd.

Fleishman, E. A. (1953a). The description of supervisory behavior. *Journal of Applied Psychology, 37*(1), 1-6.

Fleishman, E. A. (1953b). The measurement of leadership attitudes in industry. *Journal of Applied Psychology, 37*(3), 153-158.

Fortune. (2009). *Scandal! Amazing Tales of Scandals that Shocked the World and Shaped Modern Business.* New York, NY: Fortune Books.

Freeman, R. E. (1984). *Strategic management: A stakeholder approach.* Boston, MA: Pitman.

Freeman, R. E., & Gilbert, D. R., Jr. (1988). *Corporate strategy and the search for ethics.* Englewood Cliffs, NJ: Prentice Hall.

Frick, D. M. (2004). *Robert K. Greenleaf: A life of servant leadership.* San Francisco, CA: Berrett Koehler.

Friedman, M. (1982). *Capitalism and freedom.* Chicago, IL: University of Chicago Press.

Fryar, J. L. 2001. *Servant Leadership: Setting Leaders Free.* St. Louis, MO: Concordia Publishing House.

George, J. M. (2007). Creativity in organizations. *Academy of Management Annals, 1*(1), 439-477.

Giampetro-Meyer, A., Brown, T., Browne, M. N., & Kubasek, N. (1998). Do We Really Want More Leaders in Business? *Journal of Business Ethics, 17*(15), 1727-1736.

Gouldner, A. W. (1960). The norm of reciprocity: A preliminary statement. *American Sociological Review, 25*(2), 161-178.

Graham, J. W. (1991). Servant-leadership in organizations: Inspirational and moral. *The Leadership Quarterly, 2*(2), 105-119.

Grant, A. M. (2012). Leading with Meaning: Beneficiary Contact, Prosocial Impact, and the Performance Effects of

Transformational Leadership. *Academy of Management Journal,* 55(2), 458-476.

Greening, D. W., & Turban, D. B. (2000). Corporate Social Performance as a Competitive Advantage in Attracting a Quality Workforce. *Business & Society, 39*(3), 254.

Greenleaf, R. K. (1970). The servant as leader. Newton Centre, MA: The Robert K. Greenleaf Center.

Greenleaf, R. K. (1977). *Servant Leadership: A journey into the nature of legitimate power and greatness.* Mahwah, NJ: Paulist Press.

Greenleaf, R. K. (1996a). *On becoming a servant leader: The private writings of Robert K. Greenleaf.* Jossey-Bass: San Francisco, CA.

Greenleaf, R. K. (1996b). *Seeker and servant: reflections on religious leadership.* San Francisco, CA: Jossey-Bass.

Greenleaf, R. K. (1998). *The power of servant leadership.* San Francisco, CA: Berrett-Koehler.

Hackman, J. R. (2002). *Leading teams: Setting the stage for great performances.* Boston, MA: Harvard Business School Press.

Hackman, J. R. (2010). What Is This Thing Called Leadership? In N. Nohria, & R. Khurana (Eds.), *Handbook of Leadership Theory and Practice.* Boston, MA: Harvard Business Press.

Hale, J. R., & Fields, D. L. (2007). Exploring Servant Leadership across Cultures: A Study of Followers in Ghana and the USA. *Leadership, 3*(4), 397-417.

Hater, J. J., & Bass, B. M. (1988). Superiors' evaluations and subordinates' perceptions of transformational and transactional leadership. *Journal of Applied Psychology, 73*(4), 695-702.

Hemphill, J. K. (1949). The leader and his group. *Journal of Educational Research, 28*, 225-229; 245-246.

Heskett, J. (2013). *Why Isn't 'Servant Leadership' More Prevalent?* Retrieved 2/20/2014, from http://hbswk.hbs.edu/item/7207. html.

Hogg, M. A., Martin, R., & Weeden, K. (2004). Leader-member relations and social identity. In D. van Knippenberg (Ed.),

Leadership and Power: Identity Processes in Groups and Organizations (pp. 18-33). London, UK: Sage.

Hu, J., & Liden, R. C. (2011). Antecedents of team potency and team effectiveness: An examination of goal and process clarity and servant leadership. *Journal of Applied Psychology, 96*(4), 851-862.

Hunter, E. M., Neubert, M. J., Perry, S. J., Witt, L. A., Penney, L. M., & Weinberger, E. (2013). Servant-leaders inspire servant followers: Antecedents and outcomes for employees and the organization. *The Leadership Quarterly, 24*(2), 316-331.

Jensen, M. C. (2010). Value Maximization, Stakeholder Theory, and the Corporate Objective Function. *Journal of Applied Corporate Finance, 22*(1), 32-42.

Johnson, C. E. (2001). *Meeting the ethical challenges of leadership.* Thousand Oaks, CA: Sage.

Jones, D. A. (2010). Does serving the community also serve the company? Using organizational identification and social exchange theories to understand employee responses to a volunteerism programme. *Journal of Occupational & Organizational Psychology, 83*(4), 857-878.

Judge, T. A., & Piccolo, R. F. (2004). Transformational and Transactional Leadership: A Meta-Analytic Test of Their Relative Validity. *Journal of Applied Psychology, 89*(5), 755-768.

Judge, T. A., Piccolo, R. F., & Ilies, R. (2004). The Forgotten Ones? The Validity of Consideration and Initiating Structure in Leadership Research. *Journal of Applied Psychology, 89*(1), 36-51.

Judge, T. A., Woolf, E. F., Hurst, C., & Livingston, B. (2006). Charismatische und transformationale Führung: Ein Überblick und eine Agenda für zukünftige Forschungsarbeiten. *Zeitschrift für Arbeits- und Organisationspsychologie, 50*(4), 203-214.

Kerr, S., & Jermier, J. M. (1978). Substitutes for leadership: Their meaning and measurement. *Organizational Behavior & Human Performance, 22*(3), 375-403.

Kurth, K. (2003). Spiritually renewing ourselves at work: Finding meaning through serving. In R. A. Giacalone, & C. L. Jurkiewicz

(Eds.), *Handbook of Workplace Spirituality and Organizational Performance*. New York, NY: M.E. Sharp.

Laplume, A. O., Sonpar, K., & Litz, R. A. (2008). Stakeholder Theory: Reviewing a Theory That Moves Us. *Journal of Management, 34*(6), 1152-1189.

Larwood, L., Falbe, C. M., Kriger, M. P., & Miesing, P. (1995). Structure And Meaning Of Organizational Vision. *Academy of Management Journal, 38*(3), 740-769.

Laub, J. A. (1999). Assessing the servant organization: Development of the Organizational Leadership Assessment (OLA) model. *Dissertation Abstracts International, 60*(02),308A (UMI No. 9921922).

Lemoine, G. J., Hartnell, C. A., & Leroy, H. (2019). Taking Stock of Moral Approaches to Leadership: An Integrative Review of Ethical, Authentic, and Servant Leadership. *Academy of Management Annals, 13*(1), 148-187.

Liden, R. C., & Graen, G. (1980). Generalizability of the vertical dyad linkage model of leadership. *Academy of Management Journal, 23*(3), 451-465.

Liden, R. C., & Maslyn, J. M. (1998). Multidimensionality of Leader-Member Exchange: An Empirical Assessment through Scale Development. *Journal of Management, 24*(1), 43-72.

Liden, R. C., Panaccio, A., Meuser, J. D., Hu, J., & Wayne, S. J. (2014a). Servant leadership: Antecedents, processes, and outcomes. In D. V. Day (Ed.), *The Oxford handbook of leadership and organizations*. Oxford, UK: Oxford University Press.

Liden, R. C., Wayne, S., Liao, C., & Meuser, J. (2014b). Servant leadership and serving culture: Influence on individual and unit performance. *Academy of Management Journal, 57*(5), 1434-1452.

Liden, R. C., Wayne, S. J., Zhao, H., & Henderson, D. (2008). Servant leadership: Development of a multidimensional measure and multi-level assessment. *The Leadership Quarterly, 19*(2), 161-177.

Lombardo, M. M., & McCall, M. W. (1978). Leadership. In M. W. McCall, & M. M. Lombardo (Eds.), *Leadership: Where else can we go?* (pp. 3-12). Durham, NC: Duke University.

Lord, R. G., & Brown, D. J. (2001). Leadership, values, and subordinate self-concepts. *Leadership Quarterly, 12*(2), 133.

Maignan, I., Ferrell, O. C., & Hult, G. T. M. (1999). Corporate Citizenship: Cultural Antecedents and Business Benefits. *Journal of the Academy of Marketing Science, 27*(4), 455.

Margolis, J. D., & Molinsky, A. (2008). Navigating The Bind of Necessary Evils: Psychological Engagement and The Production of Interpersonally Sensitive Behavior. *Academy of Management Journal, 51*(5), 847-872.

Margolis, J. D., & Walsh, J. P. (2003). Misery Loves Companies: Rethinking Social Initiatives by Business. *Administrative Science Quarterly, 48*(2), 268-305.

Mayer, D. M., Kuenzi, M., Greenbaum, R., Bardes, M., & Salvador, R. (2009). How low does ethical leadership flow? Test of a trickle-down model. *Organizational Behavior and Human Decision Processes, 108*(1), 1-13.

Meindl, J. R., Ehrlich, S. B., & Dukerich, J. M. (1985). The romance of leadership. *Administrative Science Quarterly*, 78-102.

Miner, J. B. (1975). The uncertain future of the leadership concept: An overview. In J. G. Hunt, & L. L. Larson (Eds.), *Leadership Frontiers* (pp. 197-208). Kent, OH: Kent State University Press.

Morgeson, F. P., DeRue, D. S., & Karam, E. P. (2010). Leadership in teams: A functional approach to understanding leadership structures and processes. *Journal of Management, 36*(1), 5-39.

Neubert, M. J., Carlson, D. S., Roberts, J. A., Kacmar, K. M., & Chonko, L. B. (2008). Regulatory Focus as a Mediator of the Influence of Initiating Structure and Servant Leadership on Employee Behavior. *Journal of Applied Psychology, 93*(6), 1220-1233.

Ng, K. Y., Koh, C. S.-K., & Goh, H.-C. (2008). The heart of the servant leader: Leader's Motivation-to-Serve and Its Impact on LMX and Subordinates' Extra-Role Behaviors. In G. Graen,

& J. A. Graen (Eds.), *Knowledge-Driven Corporation: Complex Creative Destruction* (pp. 125-144). Charlotte, NC: Information Age.

Nohria, N., & Khurana, R. (2010). Advancing Leadership Theory and Practice. In N. Nohria, & R. Khurana (Eds.), *Handbook of Leadership Theory and Practice.* Boston, MA: Harvard Business Press.

Ogden, S., & Watson, R. (1999). Corporate performance and stakeholder management: Balancing shareholder and customer interests in the U.K. privatized water industry. *Academy of Management Journal, 42*(5), 526-538.

Owens, B. P., & Hekman, D. R. (2012). Modeling how to grow: An inductive examination of humble leader behaviors, contingencies, and outcomes. *Academy of Management Journal, 55*(4), 787-818.

Padilla, A., Hogan, R., & Kaiser, R. B. (2007). The toxic triangle: Destructive leaders, susceptible followers, and conducive environments. *Leadership Quarterly, 18*(3), 176-194.

Page, D., & Wong, P. T. P. (2000). A conceptual framework for measuring servant leadership. In S. Adjibolosoo (Ed.), *The human factor in shaping the course of history and development.* Boston, MA: University Press of America.

Parolini, J., Patterson, K., & Winston, B. (2009). Distinguishing between transformational and servant leadership. *Leadership and Organization Development Journal, 30*(3), 274-291.

Parris, D., & Peachey, J. (2013). A Systematic Literature Review of Servant Leadership Theory in Organizational Contexts. *Journal of Business Ethics, 113*(3), 377-393.

Peterson, S. J., Galvin, B. M., & Lange, D. (2012). CEO servant leadership: Exploring executive characteristics and firm performance. *Personnel Psychology, 65*(3), 565-596.

Podolny, J. M., Khurana, R., & Besharov, M. L. (2010). Revisiting the meaning of leadership. In N. Nohria, & R. Khurana (Eds.), *Handbook of Leadership Theory and Practice.* Boston, MA: Harvard Business Press.

Posner, B. Z., & Kouzes, J. M. (1988). Development and validation of the Leadership Practices Inventory. *Educational and Psychological Measurement, 48*(2), 483-496.

Rae, I., & Witzel, M. (2004). *Singular and Different: Business in China Past, Present, and Future.* London, UK: Palgrave Macmillan.

Reinke, S. J. (2003). Does the form really matter? Leadership, trust, and acceptance of the performance appraisal process. *Review of Public Personnel Administration, 23,* 23-27.

Rosenthal, S. A. (2011). National Leadership Index 2011: A National Study of Confidence in Leadership. Cambridge, MA: Center for Public Leadership, Harvard Kennedy School, Harvard University.

Rost, J. C. (1991). *Leadership for the twenty-first century.* New York, NY: Praeger Publishers.

Rucci, A. J. 2008. I/O Psychology's "Core Purpose": Where science and practice meet. Closing keynote address to the 23rd Annual Conference of the Society for Industrial and Organizational Psychology: San Francisco, CA.

Russell, R. F., & Stone, A. G. (2002). A review of servant leadership attributes: Developing a practical model. *Leadership & Organization Development Journal, 23*(3), 145-157.

Sarayrah, Y. K. (2004). Servant Leadership in the Bedouin- Arab Culture. *Global Virtue Ethics Review, 6*(3), 58.

Scandura, T. A., & Graen, G. B. (1984). Moderating effects of initial leader–member exchange status on the effects of a leadership intervention. *Journal of Applied Psychology, 69*(3), 428-436.

Schaubroeck, J. M., Lam, S. S. K., & Peng, A. C. (2011). Cognition-Based and Affect-Based Trust as Mediators of Leader Behavior Influences on Team Performance. *Journal of Applied Psychology, 96*(4), 863-871.

Schriesheim, C. A., Castro, S. L., & Cogliser, C. C. (1999). Leader-member exchange (LMX) research: A comprehensive review of theory, measurement, and data-analytic practices. *Leadership Quarterly, 10*(1), 63.

Selznick, P. (1957). *Leadership in Administration: A Sociological Interpretation.* Berkeley, California: University of California Press.

Selznick, P. (1984). *Leadership in administration: A sociological interpretation.* Berkeley, CA: University of California Press.

Sendjaya, S., Sarros, J. C., & Santora, J. C. (2008). Defining and Measuring Servant Leadership Behaviour in Organizations. *Journal of Management Studies, 45*(2), 402-424.

Servaes, H., & Tamayo, A. (2013). The Impact of Corporate Social Responsibility on Firm Value: The Role of Customer Awareness. *Management Science, 59*(5), 1045-1061.

Shamir, B. (2007). From passive recipients to active co-producers: The roles of followers in the leadership process. In B. Shamir, R. Pillai, M. Bligh, & M. Uhl-Bien (Eds.), *Follower-Centered Perspectives on Leadership: A Tribute to JR Meindl.* Greenwhich, Connecticut: Information Age Publishing.

Shamir, B., House, R. J., & Arthur, M. B. (1993). The motivational effects of charismatic leadership: A self-concept based theory. *Organization Science, 4*(4), 577-594.

Sharma, S., & Vredenburg, H. (1998). Proactive corporate environmental strategy and the development of competitively valuable organizational capabilities. *Strategic Management Journal, 19*(8), 729.

Smith, B. N., Montagno, R. V., & Kuzmenko, T. N. (2004). Transformational and Servant Leadership: Content and Contextual Comparisons. *Journal of Leadership & Organizational Studies (Baker College), 10*(4), 80-91.

Spears, L. C. (1995). *Reflections on leadership: How Robert K. Greenleaf's theory of servant-leadership influenced today's top management thinkers.* New York, NY: John Wiley.

Stephens, C. U., D'Intino, R. S., & Victor, B. (1995). The Moral Quandary of Transformational Leadership: Change for Whom? *Research in Organizational Change and Development, 8*, 123-143.

Stogdill, R. M. (1974). *Handbook of leadership: A survey of theory and research.* New York, NY: Free Press.

Thompson, J. D. (1956). On Building an Administrative Science. *Administrative Science Quarterly, 1*(1), 102-111.

Treviño, L. K., Brown, M., & Hartman, L. P. (2003). A Qualitative Investigation of Perceived Executive Ethical Leadership: Perceptions from Inside and Outside the Executive Suite. *Human Relations, 56*(1), 5-37.

Treviño, L. K., Hartman, L. P., & Brown, M. (2000). Moral Person and Moral Manager: How Executives Develop a Reputation for Ethical Leadership. *California Management Review, 42*(4), 128-142.

Uhl-Bien, M., Riggio, R. E., Lowe, K. B., & Carsten, M. K. (2013). Followership theory: A review and research agenda. *The Leadership Quarterly* (in press).

van Dierendonck, D. (2011). Servant leadership: A review and synthesis. *Journal of Management, 37*(4), 1228-1261.

van Dierendonck, D., & Nuijten, I. (2010). The Servant Leadership Survey: Development and Validation of a Multidimensional Measure. *Journal of Business and Psychology*, 1-19.

van Dierendonck, D., Stam, D., Boersma, P., de Windt, N., & Alkema, J. (2013). Same difference? Exploring the differential mechanisms linking servant leadership and transformational leadership to follower outcomes. *The Leadership Quarterly*, in press.

van Knippenberg, D., & Sitkin, S. B. (2013). A critical assessment of charismatic-transformational leadership research: Back to the drawing board? *Academy of Management Annals, 7*(1), 1-60.

Walumbwa, F. O., Avolio, B. J., Gardner, W. L., Wernsing, T. S., & Peterson, S. J. (2008). Authentic leadership: Development and validation of a theory-based measure. *Journal of Management, 34*(1), 89-126.

Walumbwa, F. O., Hartnell, C. A., & Oke, A. (2010). Servant Leadership, Procedural Justice Climate, Service Climate, Employee Attitudes, and Organizational Citizenship Behavior: A Cross-Level Investigation. *Journal of Applied Psychology, 95*(3), 517-529.

Walumbwa, F. O., Mayer, D. M., Wang, P., Wang, H., Workman, K., & Christensen, A. L. (2011). Linking ethical leadership to employee performance: The roles of leader–member exchange, self-efficacy, and organizational identification. *Organizational Behavior and Human Decision Processes*, *115*(2), 204-213.

Weber, M., Henderson, A. M., & Parsons, T. (1947). *The theory of social and economic organization (1st Amer. ed.)*. New York, NY US: Oxford University Press.

Westley, F., & Mintzberg, H. (1989). Visionary leadership and strategic management. *Strategic Management Journal*, *10*(S1), 17-32.

Whetstone, J. T. (2002). Personalism and moral leadership: the servant-leader with a transforming vision. *Business Ethics: A European Review*, *11*(4), 385-392.

Wu, J. B., Tsui, A. S., & Kinicki, A. J. (2010). Consequences of differentiated leadership in groups. *Academy of Management Journal*, *53*(1), 90-106.

Yukl, G. (1971). Toward a behavioral theory of leadership. *Organizational Behavior and Human Performance*, *6*(4), 414-440.

Yukl, G. (1999). An evaluation of conceptual weaknesses in transformational and charismatic leadership theories. *The Leadership Quarterly*, *10*(2), 285-305.

Yukl, G. (2010). *Leadership in organizations* (7th ed.). Englewood Cliffs, NJ: Prentice Hall.

Yukl, G., & Tracey, J. B. (1992). Consequences of influence tactics used with subordinates, peers, and the boss. *Journal of Applied Psychology*, *77*(4), 525-535.

Zalezink, A. (1977). Managers and leaders: Are they different? *Harvard Business Review*, *55*(3), 67-78

Chapter 2

The State of the Art in Academic Servant Leadership Research: A Systematic Review

Haoying (Howie) Xu, Meng Zhong, & Robert C. Liden

SERVANT LEADERSHIP IS A PEOPLE-CENTERED AND SERV-
ing-oriented leadership approach (Liden, Panaccio, Meuser,
Hu, & Wayne, 2014a; van Dierendonck, 2011). Unlike other
leadership approaches (e.g., transformational leadership), servant leadership is centered around the view that effective leaders should lead by selflessly serving others (Greenleaf, 1970):
Servant-leaders not only serve each follower by prioritizing their
needs, but also extend beyond organizations to serve multiple
stakeholders, including customers, communities, and society as
a whole (Liden, Wayne, Zhao, & Henderson, 2008). Capturing
these core characteristics, a recent systematic and integrative
review touches upon the motive, mode and mindset of being
a servant leader, and accordingly, defines servant leadership
as "an (1) other-oriented approach to leadership [motive], (2)
manifested through one-on-one prioritizing of follower individual needs and interests [mode], (3) and outward reorienting
of their concern for self towards concern for others within the
organization and the larger community [mindset]" (Eva, Robin,
Sendjaya, van Dierendonck, & Liden, 2019: 114). Through
behavioral modelling of serving others, an important mission
of servant leadership is to nurture followers into servant-leaders
(Greenleaf, 1970).

With almost two decades of theoretical development, researchers have established the legitimacy of servant leadership, and provided widely accepted scales; more importantly, academic research on servant leadership related to its antecedents and consequences has witnessed a marked increase. The purpose of our chapter is to provide a comprehensive review of servant leadership. We first review how servant leadership is distinct from other leadership approaches and provide a brief summary of the existing servant leadership scales. Then we provide a detailed and systematic review of antecedents, consequences, boundary conditions, and theoretical bases of servant leadership. In the antecedent section, we categorize the existing research into two categories: the nature perspective wherein researchers focus on unchangeable or stable predictors, and the nurture perspective wherein researchers focus on more malleable predictors. In the consequence section, we not only review the benefits of servant leadership, but also discuss its potential harm. In the boundary condition section, we categorize the moderators (i.e., variables that influence the relationships between servant leadership and outcomes) into three types: follower characteristics, leader characteristics, and contextual characteristics. We also explain how and why each moderator works. Finally, we provide an independent section for the theoretical bases of servant leadership, elaborating on how each theory is applied in servant leadership research. We close our chapter by providing six promising research avenues for researchers and four recommendations for practitioners. Figure 1 on the next page provides an integrated summary of our review.

Antecedents
1. *Nature perspective*
   - Demographic characteristics
   - Narcissism
   - Agreeableness
   - Extraversion
   - Core self-evaluation
   - Mindfulness
2. *Nurture perspective*
   - Emotional intelligence
   - Organizational identification
   - Servant leadership of higher-level managers

Servant Leadership

Boundary Conditions
1. *Follower characteristics*
   - Attributions about servant leadership
   - Collectivism & Extraversion
   - Ideal leader prototype/desire for servant leadership
   - Proactive personality
   - Positive reciprocity beliefs
   - Sensitivity to others' favorable treatment
   - Selfless and self-serving motive
   - Tenure
   - Trust in supervisor
2. *Leader characteristics*
   - Leader sex
   - Organizational embodiment
   - Political skill
3. *Contextual characteristics*
   - Environmental uncertainty
   - Organizational climate
   - Organizational structure
   - Team power distance

Mediating Mechanisms
1. Social learning
2. Social exchange
3. Social identity
4. Self-determination
5. Conservation of resources

Benefits
1. *Employees*
   - Psychological well-being
   - Personal and professional growth
   - Work-life balance
2. *Groups or teams*
   - Justice climate
   - Service climate
   - Serving culture
   - Team potency
   - Team performance
   - Team service-oriented OCB
   - Team innovation
3. *Leaders*
   - Leader-directed OCB
   - Follower gratitude
4. *Organizations*
   - Organizational commitment
   - Task performance
   - Prosocial/proactive behaviors
   - Creativity
   - Organizational performance
5. *Communities or society*
   - Community citizenship behaviors
   - Corporate social responsibility
6. *Customers*
   - Customer-focused citizenship behavior
   - Service performance
   - Service quality

Potential Harm
1. *Employees*
   - Leadership avoidance
   - Be manipulated by leaders
2. *Leaders*
   - Role stressors
   - Emotional exhaustion
   - Work-to-family conflict
   - Discontinue leadership engagement
3. *Organizations*
   - Hurt organizations' financial goals

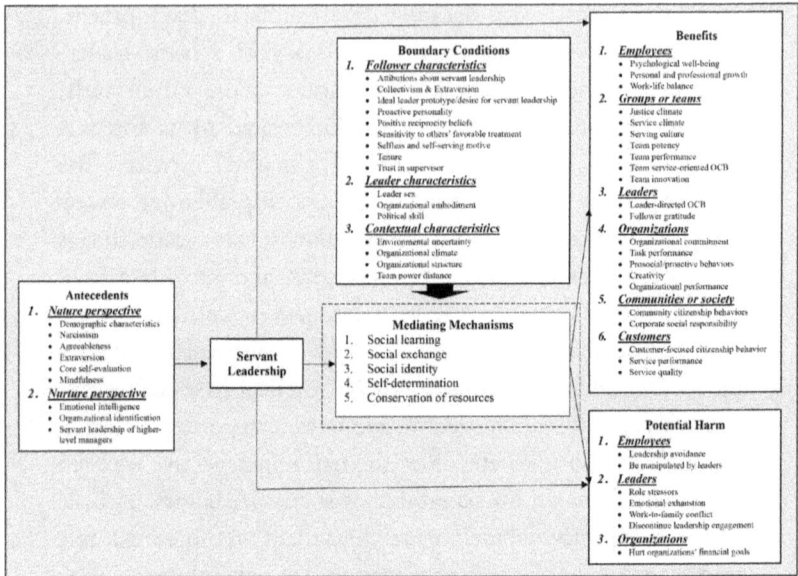

Figure 1. An Integrative Summary of Academic Servant Leadership Research

Distinctiveness of servant leadership: conceptual and empirical evidence

Parsimony, or explaining as much as possible with the fewest variables, is a hallmark of scientific research. Unfortunately, leadership research strays from parsimony, as at least 66 approaches to leadership have appeared since 2000 in the top academic journals (Dinh, Lord, Gardner, Meuser, Liden, & Hu, 2014). With the parsimony principle in mind, when servant leadership was first introduced to the academic community, it was necessary for researchers to determine whether the theory of servant leadership possesses features that are unique relative to the many other approaches to leadership. Thus, a first step in the study of servant leadership was to test its theoretical and empirical distinctiveness. Researchers have conceptually compared servant leadership with many existing leadership approaches, including transformational leadership, authentic leadership, ethical leadership, Level 5 leadership, empowering leadership, spiritual leadership, and self-sacrificing leadership (see Eva et al., 2019; Lemoine, Hartnell, & Leroy, 2019; van Dierendonck, 2011). It has been concluded that although servant leadership has similarities and areas of overlap with the other leadership approaches (also see Banks, Gooty, Ross, Williams, & Harrington, 2018), it is distinct from these approaches in some important ways. For example, different from transformational leadership, which focuses primarily on the achievement of organizational goals, servant leadership emphasizes serving followers through prioritizing and satisfying their needs (Parolini, Patterson, & Winston, 2009; Smith, Montagno, & Kuzmenko, 2004; Stone, Russell, & Patterson, 2004). Distinct from authentic leadership, servant leadership includes other core characteristics that authentic leadership does not explicitly incorporate (e.g., empowering followers, taking into account multiple stakeholders, and providing direction to followers; van Dierendonck, 2011). Servant leadership is also different from ethical leadership by placing more emphasis on the development of followers, rather than normative behaviors (Lemoine et al., 2019).

Empirical research has also demonstrated the distinctiveness of servant leadership by showing that servant leadership explains additional variance in important individual, team, and organization outcomes, beyond the two dominant leadership approaches—transformational leadership and leader-member exchange (or LMX) (Chen, Zhu, & Zhou, 2015; Ehrhart, 2004; Liden et al., 2008; Peterson, Galvin, & Lange, 2012; Schaubroeck, Lam, & Peng, 2011). For example, Liden et al. (2008) showed that, at the *individual* level, the seven dimensions of their SL-28 scale serve as unique predictors of community citizenship behaviors, organizational commitment, and in-role performance beyond transformational leadership and LMX. At the *team* level, Schaubroeck and his colleagues (2011) found that servant leadership is related to team performance, explaining an additional 10% of the variation in team performance beyond that explained by transformational leadership. At the *organizational* level, Peterson et al. (2012) found that servant leadership is positively related to firm performance (measured as return on assets), after controlling for CEOs' transformational leadership behaviors. Providing further support, a meta-analysis by Hoch, Bommer, Dulebohn, and Wu (2018) showed that servant leadership on average explains 12% more variance in employee overall outcomes beyond that explained by transformational leadership. More recently, the incremental predictive validity over other leadership approaches (e.g., authentic- and ethical leadership) was demonstrated in another meta-analysis (Lee, Lyubovnikova, Tian, & Knight, in press). Of note, the two meta-analyses are based almost exclusively on research conducted using a global measure of servant leadership, combining all servant leadership dimensions. Besides demonstrating discriminant validity and incremental criterion-related validity, two studies showed how servant leadership is distinct from transformational leadership in terms of influencing mechanisms (Schaubroeck et al., 2011; van Dierendonck, Stam, Boersma, de Windt, & Alkema, 2014). Specifically, Schaubroeck et al. (2011) showed that transformational leadership elicits team *cognition-based* trust in leaders, which in turn indirectly influences team performance through team potency and psychological safety, whereas servant leadership elicits team *affect-based* trust in leaders, which subsequently influences team performance through team psychological safety. van Dierendonck et al. (2014) showed that while transformational leadership positively influences employees' organizational commitment and work engagement via employees' perceived leadership effectiveness, servant leadership works through employees' need satisfaction.

Measures of servant leadership

The development of a psychologically sound scale to measure servant leadership was another research priority of the early academic research on servant leadership (e.g., Barbuto & Wheeler, 2006; Dennis & Bocarnea, 2005; Dennis & Winston, 2003; Ehrhart, 1998, 2004; Laub, 1999; Liden et al., 2008; Liden, Wayne, Meuser, Hu, Wu, & Liao, 2015; Page & Wong, 2000; Reed, Vidaver-Cohen, & Colwell, 2011; Sendjaya & Cooper, 2011; Sendjaya, Sarros, & Santora, 2008; van Dierendonck & Nuijten, 2011; for a systematic review, see Eva et al., 2019). Ehrhart (2004) was the first to offer a widely accepted measure for servant leadership (Eva et al., 2019; Liden et al., 2014a). Based on his review of the literature, Ehrhart identified seven dimensions of servant leadership (form relationships with followers, empower followers, help followers grow and succeed, behave ethically, have conceptual skills, put followers first, and create value for those outside of the organization) and developed a 14-item scale to capture the identified dimensions. Following Ehrhart's (2004) study, a number of servant leadership scales have been developed, including but not limited to the scales by Liden and his colleagues (2008, 2015), by Sendjaya and his colleagues (2008, 2019), and by van Dierendonck and his colleagues (2011, 2017). Specifically, Liden and his colleagues (2008) identified seven key dimensions of servant leadership: behaving ethically, emotional healing, putting followers first, helping followers grow and succeed, empowering, creating value for the community, and conceptual skills. Later, a corresponding short version of the measure was developed showing high internal consistency reliability and validity with the original full measure (Liden et al., 2015). Van Dierendonck and Nuijten (2011) identified eight core dimensions, including empowerment, standing back, accountability, forgiveness, courage, authenticity, humility, and stewardship. Based on the identified dimensions, they developed and validated a 30-item scale, followed by a shortened,

18-item version that reflects cross-cultural factorial stability (van Dierendonck et al., 2017). Sendjaya and his colleagues (2008) developed the servant leadership behavioral scale (SLBS) that captures six dimensions (i.e., voluntary subordination, authentic self, covenantal relationship, responsible morality, transcendental spirituality, and transforming influence) with 35 items, and a shortened version containing 6 items (SLBS-6) was provided later (Sendjaya, Eva, Butar-Butar, Robin, & Castles, 2019).

In terms of application in empirical research, Ehrhart's (2004) 14-item scale and Liden et al.'s (2008, 2015) SL-28 and SL-7 are the most widely-adopted scales (e.g., Chen et al., 2015; Hunter, Neubert, Perry, Witt, Penney, & Weinberger, 2013; Hu & Liden, 2011; Liden, Wayne, Liao, & Meuser, 2014b; Neubert, Hunter, & Tolentino, 2016; Neubert, Kacmar, Carlson, Chonko, & Roberts, 2008; Schaubroeck et al., 2011; Walumbwa, Hartnell, & Oke, 2010). As more rigorous research is required, we anticipate a surge in the use of the three scales recommended by Eva and his colleagues (2019) in the near future (i.e., Liden et al., 2008, 2015; Sendjaya et al., 2008, 2019; van Dierendonck, 2011; van Dierendonck et al., 2017). Of note, which of the three should be used depends on the specific research topic, as explained by Eva and his colleagues (2019).

Antecedents:
Nature perspective versus nurture perspective

With the distinctiveness of servant leadership established and multiple psychologically sound scales developed, there is a surge of research delving into antecedents and consequences of servant leadership. Regarding antecedents, there are two prevailing perspectives, both focusing on leader characteristics. The first perspective identifies the predictors that are unchangeable or relatively stable (*Nature perspective*), focusing on antecedents, such as leader demographics (e.g., sex, position tenure) and personality (e.g., extraversion, conscientiousness, and narcissism). Conversely, the other perspective focuses on the factors that are more malleable (*Nurture perspective*), such as emotional intelligence, organizational identification, and role modelling of higher-level leaders. Below, we summarize the key empirical findings.

Nature perspective

Some research results have indicated that leaders' demographic characteristics may be predictors of servant leadership behaviors. For example, Beck's (2014) exploratory study found that the more time leaders have been in a leadership role, the higher their level of servant leadership engagement. Another important demographic variable is sex. Specifically, Fridell, Belcher, and Messner (2009) surveyed 445 public-school principals and found that female leaders exhibit significantly higher levels of servant leadership than male leaders. However, Barbuto and Gifford's (2010) results indicated that males and females equally and effectively utilize both communal (e.g., altruistic calling, emotional healing, and organizational stewardship) and agentic (e.g., wisdom and persuasive mapping) servant leadership dimensions. These contradictory findings suggest that it may be gender difference (masculinity and femininity) rather than sex difference (male versus female) that is more salient with respect to practicing servant leadership. Specifically, males and females who score higher on feminine qualities, such as caring, empathy, and support, are more likely to engage in servant leadership than people who are characterized by masculine traits, such as competitiveness and aggression.

Leaders' personality and other stable traits are also examined. For example, Peterson et al. (2012) found that CEOs who scored lower on narcissism are more likely to engage in servant leadership. Hunter et al. (2013) reveal that leaders who are more agreeable or less extraverted exhibit more servant leadership behaviors. More recently, Flynn, Smither, and Walker (2016) demonstrated that leaders' core self-evaluation (CSE) is positively related to followers' perceptions of leaders' servant leadership behaviors. Finally, Verdorfer (2016) demonstrated that leaders' dispositional mindfulness predicts both servant attitudes (e.g., a non-self-centered motivation to lead) and actual servant leadership behaviors (e.g., humility, standing back).

Nurture perspective

Emotional intelligence has been regarded as an important precursor to servant leadership behaviors (Liden et al., 2014a). Roark (2013) found a positive relationship between leader self-rated emotional intelligence and self-rated servant leadership, with a sample of 42 leaders in two U.S. servant-led companies. This positive relationship was replicated with evidence from 75 civic leaders and 401 of their followers (Barbuto, Gottfredson, & Searle, 2014). However, slightly different from Roark (2013), Barbuto and colleagues (2014) suggested that emotional intelligence is not a good predictor of leaders' actual servant leadership behaviors as rated by their followers. Given the conflicting insights, we recommend additional research examining the role of leader emotional intelligence in predicting servant leadership. Beyond emotional intelligence, positive attitudes towards organizations can also predict servant leadership. For example, Peterson et al. (2012) suggested that CEOs with high organizational identification see less distinction between their own and the organizations' needs, and thus become more other-oriented and put more emphasis on employees' growth and development.

Grounded in the nurture perspective, another important line of research has explored the trickle-down effect of servant leadership, which examines servant leadership of high-level leaders as an antecedent. This area of research corresponds with a central tenet of servant leadership—the cultivation of servant leadership among followers through the role-modeling process (Greenleaf, 1970). Ling, Lin, and Wu (2016) demonstrated that top-level managers' servant leadership has a positive effect on middle-level managers' servant leadership. The trickle-down effect was demonstrated again in a recent study (Wang, Xu, & Liu, 2018).

Consequences: Benefits of servant leadership

Thus far, servant leadership has been demonstrated to be beneficial for a wide range of employee, group, organization, customer, and community outcomes. In the following section, we review the benefits of servant leadership to different beneficiaries.

Benefits to employees

One salient benefit of servant leadership concerns the enhancement of employees' psychological well-being. Research has shown that servant leadership fulfills employees' basic psychological needs for competence, relatedness, and autonomy (Chiniara & Bentein, 2016; Mayer, Bardes, & Piccolo, 2008; van Dierendonck et al., 2014), lowers their stress (Jaramillo, Grisaffe, Chonko, & Roberts, 2009b), and increases job satisfaction (e.g., Chan & Mak, 2014; Donia, Raja, Panaccio, & Wang, 2016; Jaramillo et al., 2009b; Mayer et al., 2008) and eudaemonic well-being (Chen, Chen, & Li, 2013).

Servant leadership is also conducive to employees' family outcomes. For instance, Zhang, Kwan, Everett, and Jian (2012) reported that when managers perceived higher levels of servant leadership exhibited by their leaders, they were more likely to feel that their experience in the work role helps improve the quality of their family life. Further, Yang, Zhang, Kwan, and Chen (2018) demonstrated that servant leadership perceived by employees bolsters employees' organization-based self-esteem (OBSE); employees with higher OBSE increase their attention to family members' needs and invest more effort to fulfill their family duties, thus resulting in the higher family satisfaction and quality of family life reported by their spouses. More recently,

Wang, Kwan, and Zhou (2017) demonstrated the benefits of servant leadership for employees' family life again. Specifically, servant leadership first elicits employees' leader identification; the psychological resources generated by the identification with leaders further positively spill over to employees' family domain, culminating in their work-family balance.

Benefits to groups/teams

Servant leadership has also been shown to be positively related to team outcomes. For example, Ehrhart's (2004) results revealed that servant-leader behaviors are positively related to procedural justice climate (i.e., the shared perception of fairness in decisions made regarding employees); the procedural justice climate in turn leads employees to reciprocate by engaging in unit-level organizational citizenship behaviors (OCBs), a concept that captures employees going the extra mile to help out others (Organ, 1988). Following Ehrhart's study, Schaubroeck and his colleagues (2011), in a study of a multinational bank conducted in Hong Kong and the U.S., found that servant leadership leads to team performance through its positive influence on affect-based trust, which was shown to provide psychological safety to team members. When employees feel psychologically safe, they are willing to take risks associated with being creative and challenge the status quo (which leads to better decision making), and are motivated to perform well as a way of reciprocating for fair treatment by the leader. Another team level study found servant leadership to be positively related to team potency (i.e., team confidence in its ability to perform well) and subsequent team performance (Hu & Liden, 2011). A noteworthy finding of Hu and Liden's investigation is that servant leadership positively influences the relationship between goal clarity and team potency. Not only did the findings show that goal clarity is more positively related to team potency when servant leadership is higher, but it was also discovered that for those teams with leaders exhibiting low levels of servant leadership, the clearer their goals, the lower the team potency and subsequent performance. Evidently, it was frustrating for employees to clearly understand their goals, but not get the leader support required to accomplish the goals. Furthermore, scholars have found that servant leadership can contribute to a service climate of a team, which benefits team performance. For example, service climate in a retail store was found to mediate the effects of servant leadership on store employees' sales behaviors, organizational citizenship behaviors, and turnover intentions (Hunter et al., 2013). In line with Greenleaf's (1970) core contention that servant-leaders instill in followers a desire to serve others, servant leadership enhances employees' serving behaviors by creating a serving culture, which in turn leads to high store performance, especially as measured by customer satisfaction and other objective service performance indices (Liden et al., 2014b). More recently, scholars revealed another underlying mechanism through which servant leadership translates into team performance. Specifically, Chiniara and Bentein (2018) found that servant leadership is negatively related to within-team LMX differentiation—i.e., the extent to which leaders develop leader-member relationships of varying quality with their followers (Liden, Erdogan, Wayne, & Sparrowe, 2006), which in turn increases team cohesion and finally helps teams achieve higher team performance. Not surprisingly, servant-leaders tend to form mostly (or all) high-quality relationships with followers, whereas non-servant-leaders differentiate considerably between followers, such that there is a range from low to high in the quality of relationships that they form with followers. Another key finding of Chiniara and Bentein's (2018) investigation pertains to the positive relationship between servant leadership and team service-oriented OCB—team members' support for other teams. Furthermore, it was revealed that servant leadership enhances team overall performance by facilitating team members' collective thriving at work, and subsequently, elevating team members' collective organizational commitment (Walumbwa, Muchiri, Misati, Wu, & Meiliani, 2018).

Beyond team performance and OCB, researchers have also examined the positive influence that servant leadership has on team innovation (Yoshida, Sendjaya, Hirst, & Cooper, 2014) and group social capital (Linuesa-Langreo, Ruiz-Palomino, & Elche-Hortelano, 2018). Using a two-nation sample of 154 teams, Yoshida and colleagues (2014) found that servant leadership increases team innovation through promoting the collective prototypicality with leaders—the extent to which leaders are perceived to embody team norms, values, and beliefs (van Knippenberg, 2011; van Knippenberg & van Knippenberg, 2005). Servant leadership also helps to build groups' internal social capital (Linuesa-Langreo et al., 2018), "the set of resources made available to a group through members' social relationships within the social structure of the group" (Oh, Labianca, & Chung, 2006: 569). This positive relationship is mediated by team members' engaging in group citizenship behavior, a team-level behavior that helps to produce stronger social relationships among team members.

Benefits to leaders

Scholarship also points out the potential benefits of engaging in servant leadership to leaders themselves. In particular, in their chapter regarding servant leadership and well-being, Panaccio and colleagues (2015a) contend that servant leadership engagement may help servant-leaders achieve self-actualization and obtain a sense of personal fulfillment. Their contention is based on self-determination theory (Ryan & Deci, 2000). The major point is that because servant-leaders are well equipped to provide personal and professional help to followers, build high-quality relationship with followers characterized by high levels of mutual respect, mutual trust, and mutual understanding, and feel able to authentically act on their endorsed values, they may satisfy their own personal needs for competence, relatedness, and autonomy. In addition, servant-leaders can also be benefited by growing their followers as servant employees, who may reciprocate by providing assistance and help to the leaders. To date, we found only two investigations offering direct or indirect empirical support for the benefits of servant leadership for leaders. Adopting conservation of resources theory as overarching framework and collecting data from diverse industries in China, Xu and Wang (2018) found that servant leadership is beneficial for leaders' workplace and family outcomes by reducing leaders' psychological resource loss and increasing their psychological resource gain. Although the research by Bavik, Bavik, and Tang (2017) did not provide direct support of the benefits brought by servant leadership to leader's well-being, it found that servant leadership increases followers' OCBs directed toward leaders. These OCBs are believed to help reduce leaders' workload, thus having positive influence on leaders' well-being.

Benefits to organizations
One benefit of servant leadership is increasing followers' positive attitudes and perceptions. These positive attitudes and perceptions include organizational commitment (Jaramillo, Grisaffe, Chonko, & Roberts, 2009a; LaPointe & Vandenberghe, 2018; Liden et al., 2008; van Dierendonck et al., 2014), organizational identification (Zhang et al., 2012; Zhao, Liu, & Gao, 2016), work engagement (de Clercq, Bouckenooghe, Raja, & Matsyborska, 2014; de Sousa & van Dierendonck, 2014; Ling, Liu, & Wu, 2017), psychological contract fulfillment (Panaccio, Henderson, Liden, Wayne, & Cao, 2015b). Servant leadership also reduces negative attitudes, such as turnover intentions (Hunter et al., 2013; Jaramillo et al., 2009a; Liden et al., 2014b; Zhao et al., 2016) and job cynicism (Bobbio, van Dierendonck, & Manganelli, 2012). These happen through underlying mechanisms such as the creation of a serving culture (Liden et al., 2014b), the building of a trust climate (Ling et al., 2017), the increased perception of person-organization fit (Jaramillo et

al., 2009a), and the satisfaction of psychological needs (Van Dierendonck et al., 2014).

Another salient benefit of servant leadership to organizations pertains to enhancing employees' performance and creativity (e.g., Chiniara & Bentein, 2016; Jaramillo et al., 2009b; Liden et al., 2014b; Ling et al., 2017; Neubert et al., 2008; Neubert et al., 2016). Specifically, employees working with leaders who score higher on servant-leaders are more creative and achieve higher task performance. Existing literature has shown that servant leadership enhances employees' task performance through satisfying their psychological basic needs for autonomy, competence, and relatedness (Chiniara & Bentein, 2016), and increasing employees' work engagement, and subsequently organizational commitment (Ling et al., 2017). Neubert et al. (2008) indicated that servant leadership first evokes employees' promotion focus—the orientation towards seeking pleasure, such as growth, gains, and attainment of aspiration and ideas (Higgins, 1997)—which in turn enhances employees' creativity. Liden and his colleagues (2014b) demonstrated that servant leadership contributes positively to employees' task performance and creativity through creating a serving culture, and subsequently increasing employees' identification with their group.

Servant leadership also benefits organizations by increasing employees' altruistic prosocial behaviors and proactive behaviors and reducing antisocial behaviors. One of the most-examined prosocial behaviors is employees' OCB. Followers led by servant-leaders exhibit higher levels of OCB primarily because they tend to imitate servant leaders' serving-oriented behaviors and/ or they want to reciprocate for the servant leaders' good treatment by doing good deeds for colleagues, leaders, and the organization. Research abounds regarding these positive relationships (e.g., Bavik et al., 2017; Chiniara & Bentein, 2016; Donia et al., 2016; Neubert et al., 2008, 2016; Newman, Schwarz, Cooper, & Sendjaya, 2017; Walumbwa et al., 2010; Zhao et al., 2016; Zou, Tian, & Liu, 2015). For example, Walumbwa and colleagues (2010) found that servant leadership encourages OCBs by enhancing self-efficacy (i.e., individuals' self-confidence in their ability to perform specific tasks well), creating a service climate at work, and establishing a fair workplace. The research findings of Newman et al.'s (2017) investigation revealed that LMX mediates the positive effect of servant leadership on employees' OCB. More recently, Bavik and colleagues (2017) provided a more comprehensive picture by demonstrating the positive relationships between servant leadership and employees' OCB directed toward customers and coworkers, which are mediated by employees' job crafting. Beyond that, servant leadership helps reduce employees' antisocial behaviors. For example, there is research demonstrating that servant leadership is negatively related to employees' deviant behavior (Sendjaya et al., 2019; Verdorfer, Steinheider, & Burkus, 2015). In addition, servant leadership increases followers' proactive behaviors. For example, servant leadership is positively related to employees' voice behavior (Chughtai, 2016; Duan, Kwan, & Ling, 2014; LaPointe & Vandenberghe, 2018), one well-recognized form of proactive behaviors. When employees feel psychologically safe, which tends to be the case under servant leaders, they are comfortable voicing ideas for positive changes, or identifying problem areas that need correction.

Finally, two studies provide direct support for the positive implications of servant leadership for corporate performance. Specifically, Peterson et al. (2012) found that company performance, as measured by return on assets, is higher in companies led by CEOs who engage in servant leadership. Similarly, within the hotel context, Huang, Li, Qiu, Yim, and Wan (2016) found a positive relationship between CEO servant leadership and firm performance. They further revealed that the relationship occurs because of the building of service climate.

Benefits to communities/society

A unique characteristic of servant leadership is that the leadership approach addresses the welfare of the entities outside the organization (Liden et al., 2008). One of the most important entities is communities where the servant-leaders and employees led by the leaders are living or working (Liden et al., 2008). Indeed, servant leadership is positively related to followers' community citizenship behaviors (Liden et al., 2008). Beyond the surrounding communities, employees led by servant-leaders also care about the well-being of the broader society—particularly, the least privileged in the society. This is evidenced by a recent empirical investigation by Grisaffe, VanMeter, and Chonko (2016), which revealed that servant leadership leads to salespersons' heightened concern for corporate social responsibility (CSR).

Benefits to customers

Although there is no direct evidence that customers' well-being is enhanced by servant leadership, research hints that the customer is one beneficiary, because the frontline employees under the supervision of servant-leaders tend to provide higher-quality service. For example, Wu, Tse, Fu, Kwan, and Liu (2013) found that servant leadership first enhances leaders' LMX relationships with their followers, which further positively influence hotel employees' customer-oriented organizational citizenship behavior—also known as customer-focused citizenship behavior (Chen et al., 2015) or extra-role service performance (Wang et al., 2018), which refers to an employee's discretionary behaviors in serving customers that extend beyond the formal job requirements (Bettencourt & Brown, 1997). Liden and his colleagues (2014b) found that store-level servant leadership increases employees' customer service behaviors by creating a serving culture within a store and subsequently, eliciting employees' identification with the store. The research by Chen and his colleagues (2015) demonstrated that servant leadership positively affects service employees' self-efficacy and group identification, which in turn leads to their superior service performance rated by customers, in the form of higher levels of service quality, customer-focused citizenship behaviors, and customer-focused prosocial behaviors. Further extending the prior investigations, Ling et al. (2016) and Wang et al. (2018) revealed that besides servant leadership of low-level supervisors, servant leadership by high-level managers also exhibits a positive effect on frontline employees' in-role and extra-role performance directly or indirectly. Of note, there is also unique research by Neubert and colleagues (2016) that demonstrated the benefits of servant leadership to patients within a hospital setting. Specifically, based on the data collected from 1,485 staff nurses and 105 nurse managers at nine hospitals, Neubert and colleagues (2016) found that servant leadership of nurse managers is positively related to patient satisfaction through nurse job satisfaction.

Consequences:
Potential harm of servant leadership

Although researchers have alluded to the potential dark sides of servant leadership, empirical research has not kept pace with the relevant theoretical development—to date, the potential harm has remained largely underexplored. Below, we provide an overview of the dark sides primarily based on the work by Liden et al. (2014a) and Panaccio et al. (2015a). Moreover, we enrich this section by providing relevant empirical evidence available from the existing empirical studies for each potential negative consequence.

Potential harm to employees
According to implicit leadership theories (Offermann, Kennedy, & Wirtz, 1994) and the literature on leader prototype (Lord, Foti, & De Vader, 1984), followers may vary in their reactions to

leadership behaviors. Accordingly, not all followers or organizations regard servant leadership as an ideal or effective leadership approach. For example, followers with a high-power-distance orientation may feel uncomfortable with the close relationship that servant-leaders build with them. Those followers who do not desire servant leadership may benefit less from this leadership style or are even hampered by servant leadership. For example, Meuser, Liden, Wayne, and Henderson (2011) found that when employees' desire for servant leadership is low, servant leadership undermines their in-role performance and helping behaviors. A more recent investigation suggested that servant leadership has a positive *direct* effect on followers' leadership avoidance —followers' inclination to be skeptical and averse to assuming leadership responsibilities (Lacroix & Verdorfer, 2017). A possible reason is that followers working with servant-leaders may view "the standards of being a leader as highly demanding and, to some degree, even daunting" (Lacroix & Verdorfer, 2017: 8).

In addition, it has been suggested that employees may be manipulated by pseudo servant leadership, "the persons who seek to be servant leaders, but have poor motives" (Stone et al., 2004: 358). Pseudo servant-leaders exhibit servant leadership behaviors primarily for manipulative purposes. They take advantage of their followers by prompting them to reciprocate acts of service. Once employees' felt obligation to reciprocate is induced, pseudo servant-leaders can manipulate them for achieving some self-interested (or even unethical) ambitions and goals. Although intuitively compelling, empirical research remains silent on examining this possibility. One issue of particular interest is the sustainability of pseudo servant leadership, as it seems probable that such a leader's true motives would be discovered in a short period of time.

Potential harm to leaders

Servant leadership may expose leaders to a number of risks as well. Panaccio and her colleagues (2015a) pointed out that practicing servant leadership may increase leaders' role conflict, role ambiguity, role overload, emotional exhaustion, and work-to-family conflict, which further poses harm to their life, work, and well-being. The reason why servant-leaders may experience role conflict, role ambiguity, and role overload can be informed by role theory (Kahn, Wolfe, Quinn, Snoek, & Rosenthal, 1964). Role theory suggests that role conflict occurs when individuals receive incompatible expectations and demands from others. As servant-leaders serve multiple stakeholders (e.g., organizational owners, employees, and social communities) who have different desires or needs, they may simultaneously face different demands or requests, and in turn, experience role conflict (Liden et al., 2014a; Panaccio et al., 2015a). Servant-leaders may also experience role ambiguity with stakeholders, who for various reasons are reluctant to reveal their needs, making it unclear to the leaders how they might serve these followers. In addition, when multiple stakeholders require the leaders' assistance at the same time, leaders may experience role overload because they only have limited amount of resources (e.g., time, energy, physical, or psychological resources), and sometimes, these resources are insufficient to meet the demands from multiple stakeholders. Further, Liden et al. (2014a) and Panaccio et al. (2015a) pointed out that servant-leaders may experience emotional exhaustion and inter-role conflict, such as work-to-family conflict.

In the worst scenario, leaders may discontinue their servant leadership engagement, because they have exhausted their psychological resources, and failed to obtain external resources to maintain this emotionally, logistically, and physically taxing leadership style. Liao, Lee, Johnson, and Lin (2017) suggested that the leaders who engage in daily servant leadership behaviors may experience self-control depletion, and subsequently disengage from their leadership roles (cf. Johnson, Lin, & Lee, 2018). Interestingly, servant-leaders who are skilled in perspective taking are not only less likely to suffer from self-control depletion, but experience recovery, because these leaders are better at empathizing with others and understanding their needs, which in turn makes their effortful servant leadership behaviors become less depleting (cf. Johnson et al., 2018).

Potential harm to organizations

Although servant-leaders care about the well-being of organizations, they also put high emphasis on enhancing the well-being of other stakeholders. In an extreme case, servant-leaders may view addressing community or societal issues as part of their responsibilities and address the issues without considering the organizations' financial bottom line. For instance, when organizations face a financially difficult situation, they may need to fire employees to reduce their labor cost and maintain their daily operation. This may be especially traumatic for servant leaders, who may feel hard pressed to lay off employees, for fear that the job loss would not only undermine the well-being of the terminated employees, but also those who are retained. Indeed, because servant-leaders attempt to satisfy the desires, interests, and needs of all stakeholders, they may experience internal conflict when forced to make decisions regarding whose (organizations vs. other stakeholders) desires, interests, and needs should be put first, especially when the desires, interests, and needs of one side conflict with those of the other side. These facts give rise to the concern over the potential harm of servant leadership practice for organizations (Anderson, 2009; Panaccio et al., 2015a).

Boundary conditions of servant leadership

The beneficial or harmful influence of servant leadership is constrained or enhanced by several boundary conditions. Below, we categorize them into three types: follower, leader, and contextual characteristics. We also elaborate on how each boundary condition works to moderate the relationship between servant leadership and the corresponding outcomes.

Follower characteristics

The influence of servant leadership varies across different followers. Below, we elaborate on the moderating effects of eleven follower characteristics: attributions for servant leadership, collectivism, desire for servant leadership, extraversion, ideal leader prototype, positive reciprocity beliefs, proactive personality, sensitivity to others' favorable treatment, selfless and self-serving motive, tenure, and trust in leader.

Attributions for servant leadership. According to attribution theory (Heider, 1958; Kelley, 1967, 1973; Weiner, 1985), followers' attributions about the reasons why a leader engages in servant leadership behaviors plays a critical role in determining their responses to the leader. This has been demonstrated by a recent study by Sun, Liden, and Ouyang (2019), who found that servant-leaders are not always appreciated by their followers. Specifically, when servant leadership behaviors of the leader are attributed to a high-quality relationship, servant leadership is less likely to induce followers' gratitude. In contrast, when followers do not attribute servant leadership to the relationship with the leader, the positive features of servant leadership are perceived as being unexpected, resulting in an elevated sense of gratitude.

Collectivism and extraversion. Grounded in substitutes for leadership theory (Kerr & Jermier, 1978), the work by Panaccio et al. (2015b) argue that followers' collectivism and extraversion may substitute for the positive effect of servant leadership on employees' psychological contract fulfillment. Specifically, extraverts are sociable and are better than introverts at building network connections with those who are able to help them with the fulfillment of perceived organizational promises; collectivists spend more time and energy than individualists developing relationships with their colleagues, who can assist with their fulfillment of psychological contract. As such, extroverts and collectivists may rely less on servant leadership in fulfilling their psychological contracts.

Ideal leader prototype and desire for servant leadership. Follower prototypes of ideal leaders are salient follower characteristics in determining the effect of servant leadership (Liden et al., 2014a; Panaccio et al., 2015a). Literature on implicit leadership theories and its accompanying study of leadership prototypes (Lord et al., 1984) is the most-invoked framework for arguing the potential negative effects of servant leadership on followers. Implicit leadership theories are stored in individuals' memory and are defined as "cognitive structures or prototypes specifying the traits and abilities that characterize leaders" (Epitropaki, Sy, Martin, Tram-Quon, & Topakas, 2013, p. 859). These implicit theories can be activated when followers interact with leaders, and subsequently, serve as a cognitive basis for their understanding of and responses to leadership behaviors. When a certain set of leadership behaviors fit followers' implicit leadership theories and ideal leadership prototype, followers respond positively to their current leaders; otherwise, employees respond negatively. Drawing from these theoretical insights, servant leadership may not be desired and may backfire for some employees. Research has provided initial empirical support by finding that servant leadership leads to decreased OCB and task performance among the employees whose desire for servant leadership is low (Meuser et al., 2011). A recent investigation provides further support by finding that servant leadership leads to decreased leadership avoidance only among those whose ideal leader prototype is congruent with servant leadership (Lacroix & Verdorfer, 2017). Followers with a low desire for servant leadership may have had bad experiences with previous leaders, making them skeptical of the leader's intent.

Proactive personality. Prior research has demonstrated that proactive employees are more likely to be influenced by servant leadership (Newman et al., 2017; Rodríguez-Carvajal, Herrero, van Dierendonck, de Rivas, & Moreno-Jiménez, 2018). Newman and colleagues (2017) found that the relationship between servant leadership and extra-role or citizenship behaviors is stronger for proactive followers, because those followers are more inclined to develop high-quality LMX relationships with servant-leaders and take greater advantage of the benefits and opportunities provided by them, which in turn enables them to achieve higher extra-role performance. For similar reasons, proactive followers are more likely to experience meaningfulness in their lives when working with servant-leaders (Rodríguez-Carvajal et al., 2018). On the other hand, there is also research grounded in substitutes for leadership theory (Kerr & Jermier 1978), suggesting that followers' proactive personality weakens the positive effects of servant leadership on some desirable outcomes. Because proactive followers tend to take initiatives to improve their situations and thus are more likely to experience psychological contract fulfillment, Panaccio et al. (2015b) argue that followers' proactive personality may weaken the positive effect of servant leadership on their psychological contract fulfillment. However, they did not find support for this moderating effect.

Positive reciprocity beliefs/sensitivity to others' favorable treatment. A social exchange perspective of servant leadership theorizes that followers exhibit positive attitudes and behaviors to return the servant leaders' serving behaviors. In reality, this contention does not always hold; it depends on followers' reciprocity beliefs and sensitivity to others' favorable treatment. Research has revealed that when followers hold high positive reciprocity beliefs (i.e., willingness of reciprocity), they are more likely to build high-quality LMX relationships with servant-leaders (Wu et al., 2013; Zou et al., 2015).

Selfless and self-serving motive. The influence of servant leadership also differs across followers with different motives. Based on implicit leadership theories (Offermann et al., 1994), Donia et al. (2016) argue that the positive effect of servant leadership on followers' job satisfaction and OCB is stronger among those with a high level of prosocial values, and weaker among those with a high level of impression management motive. The major reasoning is that the serving orientation of servant leadership fits the ideal leadership prototype of those with high prosocial values, but not those with high impression management motives. Donia and colleagues' (2016) investigation provides empirical support for the moderating effect of impression management motives on the relationship between servant leadership and job satisfaction. Interestingly, although their results did not support the moderating effect of prosocial motives, they found that servant leadership reduces the OCB-I (i.e., OCBs which benefit specific individuals such as colleagues) for those whose prosocial motive is low.

Tenure. Followers' tenure has been shown to moderate the positive relationships between servant leadership and follower trust in leader, and between servant leadership and followers' job satisfaction (Chan & Mak, 2014). It was found that the positive relations are stronger when followers have short-tenure than when they have long-tenure. This is because short-tenure followers tend to be more motivated to contribute to organizations and more eager to develop their careers than their long-tenure counterparts; therefore, when they are led by servant-leaders who show concern for them and meet their needs, they are more likely to trust in the leader and develop high job satisfaction.

Trust in leader. Trust in leader has also been identified as a follower factor that influences the functioning of servant leadership. For example, Jaramillo, Bande, and Varela (2015) showed that trust in leader moderates the negative relationship between servant leadership and the unethical peer-behavior dimension of ethical work climate, and the positive relationship between servant leadership and ethical responsibility and trust dimension of ethical work climate. When followers have high trust in the leader, they have high identification with servant leaders' actions and the consequences of these actions, such that the influence of servant leadership is strengthened.

Leader characteristics

There are several leader characteristics that act to qualify servant leadership's impact on follower outcomes, including leaders' sex, organizational embodiment, and political skill.

Leader sex. Politis and Politis (2018) showed that leaders' sex moderates the relationship between servant leadership and agency problems. These authors reason that as females are more ethical and less likely to get involved in highly risky financial matters than males, the relationship between servant leadership and agency problems is more negative when leaders are females than males.

Leader organizational embodiment. Grounding their research in social learning theory, Wang et al. (2018) demonstrated the moderating effect of organizational embodiment, which refers to the extent to which followers perceive leaders as embodying the organization (Eisenberger, Karagonlar, Stinglhamber, Neves, Becker, Gonzalez-Morales, & Steiger-Mueller, 2010), in the trickle-down effect of servant leadership. When low-level supervisors perceive high-level managers as the embodiment of their organizations, they are more likely to imitate the managers' servant leadership behaviors. Likewise, the more frontline employees perceive low-level supervisors as embodying the organization, the more likely they are to imitate the supervisors' serving-oriented behaviors and achieve superior in-role and extra-role service performance. These moderating effects are thought to happen for the following two social learning-based reasons. First, organizational embodiment can serve as an important cue of leaders' power, status and competence, thus making followers more likely to view them as role models. Second, organizational embodiment can convey a message that leaders' behaviors are congruent with the organization's rules and norms, thus making it more appropriate and acceptable for followers to imitate their leaders' values and behaviors.

Leader political skill. Researchers have also found that servant-leaders with higher political skill are better equipped to evoke followers' workplace spirituality. Specifically, politically skilled servant-leaders are better at building and influencing social network connections, which in turn enhances followers' sense of meaningful work and personal fulfillment (Williams, Randolph-Seng, Hayek, Haden, & Atinc, 2017).

Contextual characteristics
The context under which servant leadership takes place also plays a critical role in shaping its effects. Below, we review the moderation effects of four contextual characteristics: environmental uncertainty, organizational climate, organizational structure, and team power distance.

Environmental uncertainty. Earlier theoretical insights suggested that servant leadership, which focuses on satisfying followers' personal needs and interests, and which seems less heroic and charismatic, may be less effective in times of uncertainty (e.g., during economic crises; Smith et al., 2004). The reasons are that (1) during the times of uncertainty, followers focus more on groups or organizations than themselves for comfort and safety; and (2) when times are uncertain, followers seek leaders who can use unconventional approaches to address problems and achieve goals. As a response to the theoretical insights, an investigation by van Dierendonck et al. (2014) empirically tested whether servant leadership is less positively related to followers' need satisfaction and perceived leadership effectiveness when environmental uncertainty is high. However, inconsistent results were shown across three studies, leading the authors to conclude that "[the] findings regarding the moderation of environmental uncertainty are uncertain at best."

Organizational climate. Organizational climate also serves as an important boundary condition in shaping servant leadership effects. Organizational climate can take many forms (e.g., justice climate, service climate, and ethical climate; Kuenzi & Schminke, 2009). Service climate has been argued to strengthen the positive effect of high-level and middle-level servant-leaders on employees' service-oriented behaviors; the reason is that a strong service climate fits the serving-oriented characteristics of servant leadership and complements servant-leader behaviors by providing a strategic focus on delivering high-quality service (Ling et al., 2016). Interestingly, these researchers obtained paradoxical findings. Specifically, they found that although service climate accentuates the positive effect of middle-level servant leadership on frontline employees' service-oriented behaviors, it attenuates the positive effect of upper-level servant leadership on the same outcome. The authors attribute the latter, unexpected findings to the greater distance between upper-level servant-leaders and frontline employees, which results in the relatively weak influence of upper-level servant leadership on employees' behaviors. As such, it makes sense that strong service climate acts as a substitute for upper-level servant leadership in terms of providing behavioral guidelines for high-quality service.

Work-family climate is another important contextual boundary condition. In a study investigating the impact of servant leadership on followers' work-to-family enrichment, Zhang et al. (2012) identified work climate for sharing family concern as a moderator and argued that it attenuates the positive influence of servant leadership. Specifically, these researchers contended that when working in a situation where they can share their family concerns with their colleagues and obtain useful feedback on developing strategy to effectively manage their work and family roles, followers are more likely to identify with their organizations and achieve enhanced work-to-family enrichment. As such, the beneficial effects of servant leadership on followers' organization identification and work-to-family enrichment become less salient.

Other researchers have examined the moderating effect of caring ethical climate—an important dimension of ethical climate, which indicates the extent to which organizational members care about the well-being of others when making decisions and actions. It was argued that the positive relationship between servant leadership and salespeople's customer value-enhancing sales performance is stronger when the perception of caring ethical climate is high, because employees receive consistent information from both the leaders and organizations that helping others is important (Schwepker & Schultz, 2015). Results demonstrated the argument.

Organizational structure. Organizational structure is also identified as an important contextual moderator in shaping the influence of servant leadership (Neubert et al., 2016). Mechanistic organizational structure provides formalized prescriptions, rules, and procedures regarding how one relates to another (e.g., who reports to whom), how tasks are supposed to be completed, and how decisions should be made (Donaldson, 1996). In contrast, organic organizational structures tend to be flatter, less rule-oriented and more flexible, and thus better suited to servant leadership's goals of bringing out the full potential of followers through the provision of support and empowerment. Neubert and colleagues (2016) found followers to be more creative, the less structured and more organic the structure. As the degree of structure increases (towards a mechanistic structure), servant leadership is somewhat successful in buffering the stifling effect that structure has on employee creativity.

Team power distance. Team power distance captures "group members' shared values that authorities should be shown deference and can rightfully dictate to those in subordinate positions" (Yang, Mossholder, & Peng, 2007: 682). Yang, Liu, and Gu (2017) suggest that team power distance attenuates the positive relationship between servant leadership and team efficacy. When teams are characterized by high power distance, team members believe that they should follow the routine in organization, leading to less interaction with leaders. Less interaction with servant-leaders renders followers to perceive the leaders as less effective, further resulting in their low trust in the ability of the team.

Theoretical bases of servant leadership

In the preceding sections, we have discussed the effects of servant leadership on a wide variety of outcomes. In order to better inform researchers and practitioners about how these effects occur, we proceed to introduce the theoretical base upon which researchers explain how servant leadership positively or negatively influences key outcomes. Social learning theory (Bandura, 1977), social exchange theory (Blau, 1964), self-determination theory (Ryan & Deci, 2000), and social identity theory (Tajfel, 1978) are the dominant theoretical frameworks that have been used to explain the positive effects of servant leadership on follower, group, and organization outcomes; conservation of resources theory (Hobfoll, 1989) is used to explain the implications of servant leadership for leader outcomes.

Social learning theory

A social learning perspective of servant leadership proposes that servant leadership influences followers through leaders' role modeling and followers' direct and vicarious learning (Graham, 1991; Greenleaf, 1970; Liden et al., 2014b). Compared with other leadership approaches, servant-leaders have several key characteristics that make the role modeling process more likely to happen. First, servant leadership is tied less to leaders' position power compared to other leadership approaches (e.g., transformational or empowering leadership). It is more about serving others (Liden et al., 2008; Smith et al., 2004; Stone et al., 2004). Indeed, as pointed out by Greenleaf (1970), when leaders provide tangible and emotional support to followers and assist them in fulfilling their needs, followers will naturally see them as role models and spontaneously imitate their behaviors. Second, some unique characteristics of servant leadership make followers more willing to model servant leaders' behaviors. Servant-leaders actively assist their followers in achieving personal growth goals on their path toward the fulfillment of their full potential, treat followers in an egalitarian way, and put followers' needs and interests as first priority (Liden et al., 2008; Chen et al., 2015; Mayer et al., 2008; Smith et al., 2004; Stone et al., 2004). These practices suggest that servant-leaders interact with followers in a more intimate manner. This close and supportive interaction with followers provides followers with opportunities to observe and imitate the leaders' serving behaviors (Bandura, 1977). Also, servant-leaders strive to provide professional guidance and emotional support to ensure followers' successful modeling of servant behaviors (Laub, 1999). For instance, when followers face setbacks during the modeling process, servant-leaders express empathy and offer emotional healing to them (Barbuto & Wheeler, 2006; Liden et al., 2008). These unique characteristics increase followers' willingness and opportunities to imitate leaders' servant leadership behaviors. Through the social learning process, followers are developed into servant leaders, and a serving culture thus emerges (Greenleaf, 1970, 1977).

Social exchange theory

A social exchange perspective of servant leadership posits that followers tend to return favors to servant leaders, because they always put followers' interests and needs above their own and try their utmost to satisfy those interests and needs. Through the social exchange lens, scholarship has demonstrated that servant-leaders gain trust from their followers and build high-quality and long-term LMX relationships with them. In return, followers reciprocate to the leaders and the organization with positive attitudes and important behaviors, such as task performance, and OCB (Schaubroeck et al., 2011; Walumbwa et al., 2010; Wu et al., 2013). The social exchange perspective can also act as a supplement to social learning theory and provide an additional explanation for why followers tend to imitate servant leaders' values, attitudes, and behaviors. Specifically, Liden et al. (2014b) argued that followers reciprocate to servant-leaders by modeling their servant leadership behaviors. Of note, although servant-leaders are inclined to develop high-quality social exchange relationships with *all* of their followers (Anand, Hu, Liden, & Vidyarthi, 2011), the "currencies" exchanged within each social exchange with each follower may differ. Servant-leaders provide different resources to each follower based on their needs and desires via high-quality leader-member relationships. For example, for followers who are highly skilled and motivated but lack opportunities, servant-leaders provide them with the chance to leverage their skills and motivation. In contrast, servant-leaders provide followers who have weaker ability with training opportunities to help them to improve.

Self-determination theory

Drawing on the key insight from servant leadership theory that servant-leaders prioritize the fulfillment of followers' needs, some researchers have grounded their investigations in self-determination theory. According to this theory, psychological needs for autonomy, competence, and relatedness are innate and essential for psychological growth, internalization, and well-being (Ryan & Deci, 2000). To the extent that the three psychological needs are satisfied, individuals are optimally motivated and experience a high level of well-being (Ryan & Deci, 2000). A self-determination perspective proposes that servant leadership helps to fulfill followers' basic psychological needs, thus motivating them to exhibit desired behaviors and enhance their psychological well-being. Multiple characteristics of servant leadership help satisfy followers' basic psychological needs. For example, servant-leaders utilize empowerment to manage their followers, so that they can have the freedom and power to determine how and when to finish their tasks; servant-leaders care about the personal and professional development of their followers and provide training opportunities for them so that their potential can be developed to the fullest extent (Liden et al., 2008, 2014a, 2014b). These may contribute to followers' satisfaction of need for autonomy and competence (Chiniara & Bentein, 2016; Panaccio et al., 2015a). In addition, servant-leaders build high-quality relationships with followers, helping to fulfill followers' need for relatedness (Panaccio et al., 2015a). Empirically, Mayer et al. (2008) and van Dierendonck et al. (2014) demonstrated the positive effect of servant leadership on followers' overall need satisfaction, in both experimental and field studies. Furthermore, Chiniara and Bentein (2016) demonstrated that servant leadership is positively associated with employees' needs for autonomy, competency, and relatedness, which then leads to employees' in-role and extra-role performance.

Social identity theory

The central tenet of social identity theory is that the behaviors of individuals in a group arise from a shared sense of social category membership (Tajfel, 1978). Specifically, a person's sense of who they are partly depends on the groups to which they belong. According to the social identity lens, an essential element in the way employees view themselves is to identify with their servant leaders, and develop a strong sense of identification with the work group that is managed by their servant leaders. That sense of identification leads employees to engage in behaviors that are favorable to leaders, work groups, and organizations. Research has shown that, under the supervision of servant leaders, employees are more inclined to voice, show negative feedback seeking behaviors, and experience work-to-family enrichment, because their identification with the *organization* is enhanced (Chughtai, 2016). In addition, servant leadership is positively associated with followers' positive identification with the work *groups*, which enhances the quality of employees' service delivery (Chen et al., 2015). Similarly, Liden et al. (2014b) suggest that employees' *group* identification mediates the effects of serving culture, resulting from servant leadership, on employees' in-role performance, creativity, customer service behaviors, and turnover intentions). Servant leadership also contributes to employee creativity by increasing employees' identification with *leaders* (Yoshida et al., 2014).

Conservation of resources theory
The core tenet of conservation of resources theory is that people strive to obtain, retain, and protect resources, which are defined as the things that people value or that can help them attain what is valued (Hobfoll, 1989; Hobfoll, Halbesleben, Neveu, & Westman, 2018). This theory recognizes that people face many situations that may tax their resources, but it also posits that people can accumulate resources through resource investing. Protecting their remaining resources when facing resource loss enables them to maintain their resource account balance (Hobfoll, 1989; Hobfoll et al., 2018). It is an appropriate theory for capturing the effects of servant leadership on leaders. On the one hand, servant leadership is resource depleting to the leaders

(Liden et al., 2014a). On the other hand, it also helps leaders gain psychological resources (e.g., achieving self-actualization). Capturing these resource loss and resource gain mechanisms can help researchers obtain a balanced understanding of implications of servant leadership engagement for leaders.

Future research directions

Although available research on servant leadership has been highly supportive, much additional work is needed to better understand servant leadership. We highlight six important future research avenues designed to further develop servant leadership theory.

Explore antecedents of servant leadership
Whereas much evidence has accumulated showing the consequences of servant leadership for followers, their groups, and organizations, much less is known about the antecedents of servant leadership. Of the limited body of literature, most examine leader characteristics (e.g., demographic characteristics and personalities), assuming that some individuals are born to be servant leaders, while others are not. Recent studies have sought to identify contextual factors, such as higher-level managers' servant leadership (Wang et al., 2018) as facilitators of servant leadership. But this line of research is still in its infancy, requiring more research attention from academics. Future research can examine contextual antecedents, such as organizational stressors. Based on conservation of resources theory, it is likely that the stressed leaders, despite their strong desire to serve others, decrease their engagement in servant leadership behaviors, because they lack sufficient psychological resources to adopt this emotionally, logistically, and physically taxing leadership style.

Beyond leader and contextual characteristics, follower characteristics may also play an important role in influencing leaders' engagement in servant leadership. This is due to the fact that leaders may pay special attention to followers' needs, desires, and potential, and accordingly, tailor their leadership behaviors to each follower (Liden et al., 2014a). Liden and his colleagues (2014a) have identified three follower characteristics: proactive personality, CSE, and servant-leader prototype. They argue that for the followers higher in proactive personality, CSE, and servant-leader prototype, leaders are more inclined to engage in servant leadership behaviors. Given that these propositions have not yet been empirically examined, we recommend that future researchers test these ideas.

For a comprehensive understanding of the antecedents of servant leadership, future research can go further to integrate contextual, leader, and follower characteristics. In particular, we recommend future research that assesses the relative importance of contextual, leader, and follower characteristics as antecedents of servant leadership. Researchers also need to investigate how the three factors interact to influence leaders' exhibition of servant leadership.

Explore how serving culture emerges

Research is also needed to investigate how serving culture emerges at the group and organizational levels. While the leader-driven process suggested by Liden and colleagues (2014b) is plausible, it still needs to be integrated with an employee-driven process to provide a complete understanding. For example, employees' prosocial identity, the extent to which employees identify themselves as caring persons (Grant, Dutton, & Rosso, 2008), or prosocial motivation—employees' desire to benefit others or expand effort out of concern for others (Grant, 2008)—may be two important drivers of serving culture. Future research can examine the extent to which this culture is driven by servant leadership (a leader-driven process) versus the impetus of employee prosocial identity/motivation (an employee-driven process). Beyond that, researchers are also recommended to investigate how the employee-driven processes interact with the leader-driven processes to shape serving culture.

Investigate potential dark sides of servant leadership

Servant leadership does not come without cost (Liden et al., 2014a; Panaccio et al., 2015a). However, almost no empirical research touches upon this research topic. The lack of research constrains our balanced understanding of servant leadership theory. Besides continuing to document the positive features of servant leadership, researchers should start to empirically examine potential dark side of servant leadership. For example, because servant-leaders serve followers by prioritizing their desires, interests, and needs, and trying the utmost to satisfy them, the followers working with them may perceive that they are entitled to what others provide, and subsequently exhibit undesirable attitudes and behaviors, such as heightened job frustration and increased deviance behavior (Harvey & Dasborough, 2015). Researchers should also identify the factors that buffer the potential harm of servant leadership. For example, as researchers have realized the emotionally, logistically, and physically taxing nature of servant leadership engagement (Liden et al., 2014a; Panaccio et al., 2015a), researchers should examine the moderators that may weaken the harm of servant leadership engagement to leaders. Organizational culture is an important contextual factor. When servant-leaders work in an organization featuring a serving culture, they would be less likely to experience emotional exhaustion, because they can obtain a high level of support to compensate for their resource loss resulting from serving others. Follower factors play a critical role as well. For instance, followers' OCB toward leaders may help buffer the emotional exhaustion or self-control depletion resulting from servant leadership engagement.

Uncover the implications of servant leadership outside organizations

As servant leadership theory develops, there is increasing need to understand how servant leadership changes the society (Liden et al., 2014a). One potential way that servant leadership changes the society is through the prosocial behaviors of their followers, such as volunteering behaviors. Employees' volunteering behavior refers to "[employees'] giving time or skills during a planned activity for a volunteer group" (Rodell, 2013: 1274). According to the literature, employees' volunteering can be further categorized into two forms: personal volunteering—volunteering conducted on employees' own personal time—and corporate volunteering— volunteering conducted through corporate initiatives (Rodell, Breitsohl, Schröder, & Keating, 2016). Because servant-leaders instill prosocial values in their followers, the followers are more likely to engage in both personal and corporate volunteering. Following this line of thinking, another important question relates to *how* servant leadership is translated into volunteering behaviors. Affective intermediate processes offer one potential mechanism. For example, servant leadership may incur followers' gratitude emotion, which in turn leads to their volunteering behaviors outside the workplace.

Test the generalizability of servant leadership findings across countries/cultures
Research is also needed to explore servant leadership across a wider range of cultures. The majority of available research studies have relied on samples taken from the U.S. (Ehrhart, 2004; Hunter et al., 2013; Liden et al., 2008; Liden et al., 2014b; Peterson et al., 2012), Canada (Chiniara & Bentein, 2016; Lapointe & Vandenberghe, 2018), China (Chen et al., 2015; Han, Kakabadse, & Kakabadse, 2010; Hu & Liden, 2011; Schaubroeck et al., 2011; Wang et al., 2018), Africa (Hale & Fields, 2007; Walumbwa et al., 2010) and Europe (De Sousa & van Dierendonck, 2014; van Dierendonck et al., 2014). Although research to date has shown highly consistent results supporting the efficacy of servant leadership across national cultures, to enhance generalizability (see Zhang, Zheng, Zhang, Xu, Liu, & Chen, in press), research on servant leadership is needed in other parts of the world, including South America, Central America (e.g., Mexico), and parts of Asia beyond China, such

as India, Indonesia, and Malaysia. We also suggest that researchers compare servant leadership findings across countries/culture.
Some researchers have taken the lead. For example, Hale and
Fields (2007) have compared the U.S. sample and Ghana sample
in terms of servant leadership experience and the relationship
between servant leadership dimensions and leadership effectiveness. They found that the Ghana sample reported less servant
leadership experience, but the relationship between the vision
dimension of servant leadership and leader effectiveness in the
Ghana sample is stronger. Mittal and Dorfman (2012) showed
that the egalitarianism and empowering dimensions of servant
leadership are considered more important in Nordic/European
culture, while empathy and humility are more important in
Asian culture. These interesting studies indicate that it would be
useful for additional research to be conducted focused on other
potential cross-cultural differences.

Consider a within-person approach to studying servant leadership

Previous research has presented a static picture of leadership
phenomena, assuming that a leader's leadership behaviors are
fixed to a certain leadership style. However, recent research
has taken a more dynamic perspective, suggesting that a leader's leadership behaviors may vary on a daily basis (e.g., Barnes,
Lucianetti, Bhave, & Christian, 2015; Courtright, Gardner,
Smith, McCormick, & Colbert, 2016; Johnson, Venus, Lanaj,
Mao, & Chang, 2012; Lin, Scott, & Matta, 2019). In light of
this research trend, it may be theoretically meaningful to investigate whether there is within-person variance in servant leadership behaviors as well. We contend that within-person variance
of servant leadership could exist, but may be smaller compared
with the variance in other leadership behaviors (e.g., abusive
supervision). The reason is that servant leadership theory suggests that servant-leaders are intrinsically motived to serve others and thus may act in a consistent and stable manner in their

treatment of all followers (Greenleaf, 1970). It is likely though, that some daily contextual factors may influence levels of servant leadership behaviors. If the within-person variance of servant leadership behaviors is demonstrated, the critical next step is to build the nomological network of daily servant leadership behavior fluctuation by investigating its antecedents and consequences. A focus on the daily fluctuation of servant leadership also opens the door to the generation of many theoretically meaningful concepts, such as servant leadership tendency (i.e., the mean level of daily servant leadership behaviors) and servant leadership variability (i.e., the standard deviation of daily servant leadership behaviors).

Notwithstanding the promising research directions, researchers should be cautioned against reaching the conclusion that the importance of adopting the within-person approach to servant leadership outweighs the traditional between-person approach. We contend that both the within-person and between-person approaches contribute to the servant leadership field, as they reveal different aspects of the servant leadership theory—the between-person approach focuses on how the servant leadership behaviors vary from leader to leader, while the within-person approach focuses on how a leader's servant leadership behaviors vary from time to time. Researchers can consider a potential integration of the within-person and between-person approaches to servant leadership. For example, research designs may include a traditional survey combined with the collection of within-person event sampling data on a daily basis (e.g., Sun et al., 2019).

Recommendations for practitioners

Servant leadership has become a research topic of growing importance to practitioners, as an increasing number of great companies espouse servant leadership practices within their organizations (e.g., Aflac, PPC Partners, Southwest Airlines, Starbucks, FedEx,

Synovous, TDIndustries, and The Container Store). As the world is experiencing a shift from manufacturing-based economies to knowledge- and service-based economies (Grant & Parker, 2009), we expect servant leadership will gain even more relevance and popularity in the future. Thus, it is important for practitioners to understand what practitioners can learn from the existing scientific insights on servant leadership theory. Below, we offer four recommendations, which we believe can help practitioners better leverage the benefits of endorsing and embracing servant leadership.

Facilitate the beneficial effects of servant leadership

It has been demonstrated that servant leadership can bring diverse benefits to multiple stakeholders inside and outside organizations (i.e., employees, groups/teams, organizations, customers, leaders, and community/society). We recommend that practitioners pay special attention to how they can maximize the benefits of servant leadership. In doing so, the research investigating the boundary conditions of servant leadership seems especially helpful. For example, practitioners can consider promoting servant leaders' organizational embodiment in the eye of followers, so that servant-leaders are more likely to be viewed as role models to be imitated by their followers (Wang et al., 2018). Service organizations can consider building a service climate within organizations to amplify the positive influence of servant leadership on employees' service outcomes (Ling et al., 2016).

Select and cultivate servant leaders

Now that the benefits of servant leadership are well documented, practitioners are in a position to increase servant leadership practices within their organizations through *selecting* and *cultivating* servant leaders. The research focused on the antecedents of servant leadership provides useful practical insights for addressing both selection and development. For selecting servant leaders, practitioners can seek insights from the "*nature* perspective" of the antecedent research. For instance, as individuals' agreeableness is positively associated with their servant leadership behavior (Hunter et al., 2013), organizations can consider selecting leaders based on their level of agreeableness. On the other hand, organizations should avoid selecting narcissistic individuals as leaders, because narcissism has been demonstrated to be negatively related to servant leadership (Peterson et al., 2012). For cultivating servant leaders, practitioners can gain insights from the "*nurture* perspective" of the antecedent research. For instance, organizations can offer training to leaders for elevating their emotional intelligence. Leaders from upper levels of organization hierarchies should set an example for mid- and lower-level managers in terms of servant leadership, so that the trickle-down effect of servant leadership occurs. In addition, organizations should also try to increase leaders' organizational identification, so that their servant leadership behaviors increase correspondingly.

Develop serving culture within organizations
The long-term goal of the servant leadership-endorsed practitioners is to embed serving culture within their organizations. In organizations characterized by high levels of serving culture, leaders and employees across all levels of the organization engage in servant leadership behaviors (Liden et al., 2014b). The building of a serving culture is important, as previous research has demonstrated serving culture as the critical driver of key employee and group outcomes, including group performance, employee creativity, and employee service-oriented behavior (Liden et al., 2014b). For developing a serving culture, organizations should not only insist on servant leadership training, but also ensure that most of the employees being selected and hired are high on prosocial identity and prosocial motivation, as the cultivation of serving culture may require the concerted effort from both leaders and employees.

Be mindful of the potential dark sides of servant leadership
Although very little empirical research has been conducted on potential dark sides of servant leadership, negative outcomes to employees and organizations are possible (e.g., Meuser et al., 2011). Leaders need to be mindful of the potential harm that servant leadership may bring to the followers who have low desire for this leadership style. For those employees, leaders can first determine what their ideal leadership style may be. Equipped with this knowledge, leaders can consider complementing servant leadership behaviors with the ideal leadership behaviors that the followers desire. Also, as engaging in servant-leaders is taxing on the leaders (Liden et al., 2014a; Panaccio et al., 2015a), we recommend that organizations continually replenish servant leaders' tangible and intangible resources, so that they can sustain their servant leadership behaviors. For example, organizations can periodically give official recognition that rewards "star" servant leaders. In the long run, organizations should build a serving culture wherein servant-leaders can get substantial support.

Conclusion

During the past 15 years, research has shown a consistent pattern that affirms the veridicality of servant leadership and its promise for the future. The goal of our chapter was to provide scholars and practitioners with a comprehensive account of the state-of-the-art of academic servant leadership research by summarizing the existing theoretical and empirical insights on the antecedents, benefits and potential harm, boundary conditions, and theoretical bases of servant leadership. On the basis of our literature review, we also provide several promising research directions for researchers, as well as recommendations for practitioners. In the quest for the best possible leadership practices, we hope that this chapter stimulates greater interest in servant leadership from both research and practice communities.

Chapter 2 References

Anand, S., Hu, J., Liden, R. C., & Vidyarthi, P. R. (2011). Leader–member exchange: Recent research findings and prospects for the future. In A. Bryman, D. Collinson, K. Grint, B. Jackson, & M. Uhl-Bien (Eds.), *Sage handbook of leadership* (pp. 311–325). Thousand Oaks, CA: Sage.

Anderson, J. A. (2009). When a servant-leader comes knocking. *Leadership and Organizational Development Journal, 30*, 4–15.

Bandura, A. (1977). *Social learning theory.* Englewood Cliffs, NJ: Prentice-Hall.

Banks, G. C., Gooty, J., Ross, R. L., Williams, C. E., & Harrington, N. T. (2018). Construct redundancy in leader behaviors: A review and agenda for the future. *The Leadership Quarterly, 29*, 236–251.

Barbuto, J. E., & Gifford, G. T. (2010). Examining gender differences of servant leadership: An analysis of agentic and communal properties of the servant leadership questionnaire. *Journal of Leadership Education, 9*, 5–22.

Barbuto, J. E., & Wheeler, D. W. (2006). Scale development and construct clarification of servant leadership. *Group & Organizational Management, 31*, 300–326.

Barbuto, J. E., Gottfredson, R. K., & Searle, T. P. (2014). An examination of emotional intelligence as an antecedent of servant leadership. *Journal of Leadership & Organizational Studies, 21*, 315–323.

Barnes, C. M., Lucianetti, L., Bhave, D. P., & Christian, M. S. (2015). "You wouldn't like me when I'm sleepy": Leaders' sleep, daily abusive supervision, and work unit engagement. *Academy of Management Journal, 58*, 1419–1437.

Bavik, A., Bavik, Y. L., & Tang, P. M. (2017). Servant leadership, employee job crafting, and citizenship behaviors: A cross-level investigation. *Cornell Hospitality Quarterly, 58*, 364–373.

Beck, C. D. (2014). Antecedents of servant leadership: A mixed method study. *Journal of Leadership & Organizational Studies, 21*, 299–314.

Bettencourt, L. A., & Brown, S. W. (1997). Contact employees: Relationships among workplace fairness, job satisfaction and prosocial service behaviors. *Journal of Retailing, 73*, 39–61.

Blau, P. M. (1964). *Exchange and power in social life.* New York: John Wiley & Sons.

Bobbio, A., van Dierendonck, D., & Manganelli, A. M. (2012). Servant leadership in Italy and its relation to organizational variables. *Leadership, 8*, 229–243.

Chan, C. H., S., & Mak, W. M. (2014). The impact of servant leadership and subordinates' organizational tenure on trust in leader and attitudes. *Personnel Review, 43*, 272–287.

Chen, C. Y., Chen, C. H. V., & Li, C. I. (2013). The influence of leader's spiritual values of servant leadership on employee motivational autonomy and eudaemonic well-being. *Journal of Religion and Health, 52*(2), 418–438.

Chen, Z., Zhu, J., & Zhou, M. (2015). How does a servant-leader fuel the service fire? A multilevel model of servant leadership, individual self-identity, group competition climate, and customer service performance. *Journal of Applied Psychology, 100*, 511–521.

Chiniara, M., & Bentein, K. (2016). Linking servant leadership to individual performance: Differentiating the mediating role of autonomy, competence and relatedness need satisfaction. *The Leadership Quarterly, 27*, 124–141.

Chiniara, M., & Bentein, K. (2018). The servant leadership advantage: When perceiving low differentiation in leader-member relationship quality influences team cohesion, team task performance and service OCB. *The Leadership Quarterly, 29*, 333–345.

Chughtai, A. A. (2016). Servant leadership and follower outcomes: Mediating effects of organizational identification and psychological safety. *The Journal of Psychology, 150*, 866–880.

Courtright, S. H., Gardner, R. G., Smith, T. A., McCormick, B. W., & Colbert, A. E. (2016). My family made me do it: A cross-domain, self-regulatory perspective on antecedents to abusive supervision. *Academy of Management Journal, 59,* 1630–1652.

De Clercq, D., Bouckenooghe, D., Raja, U., & Matsyborska, G. (2014). Servant leadership and work engagement: The contingency effects of leader–follower social capital. *Human Resource Development Quarterly, 25,* 183–212.

De Sousa, M. J. C., & van Dierendonck, D. (2014). Servant leadership and engagement in a merge process under high uncertainty. *Journal of Organizational Change Management, 27,* 877–899.

Dennis, R. S., & Bocarnea, M. (2005). Development of the servant leadership assessment instrument. *Leadership & Organization Development Journal, 26,* 600–615.

Dennis, R., & Winston, B. E. (2003). A factor analysis of Page and Wong's servant leadership instrument. *Leadership and Organizational Development Journal, 24,* 455–459.

Dinh, J. E., Lord, R.G., Gardner, W., Meuser, J. D., Liden, R. C., & Hu, J. (2014). Leadership theory and research in the new millennium: Current theoretical trends and changing perspectives. *The Leadership Quarterly, 25,* 36–62.

Donaldson, L. (1996). The normal science of structural contingency theory. In S. R. Clegg, C. Hardy, & W. R. Nord (Eds.), *Handbook of organization studies* (pp. 57–76). Thousand Oaks, CA: Sage.

Donia, M., Raja, U., Panaccio, A., & Wang, Z. (2016). Servant leadership and employee outcomes: the moderating role of subordinate motives. *European Journal of Work and Organizational Psychology, 25,* 722–734.

Duan, J., Kwan, H. K., & Ling, B. (2014). The role of voice efficacy in the formation of voice behaviour: A cross-level examination. *Journal of Management & Organization, 20*(4), 526–543.

Ehrhart, M. G. (1998). *Servant leadership: An overview and directions for future research.* Working paper. University of Maryland.

Ehrhart, M. G. (2004). Leadership and procedural justice climate as antecedents of unit-level organizational citizenship behavior. *Personnel Psychology, 57*, 61–94.

Eisenberger, R., Karagonlar, G., Stinglhamber, F., Neves, P., Becker, T. E., Gonzalez-Morales, M., & Steiger-Mueller, M. (2010). Leader–member exchange and affective organizational commitment: The contribution of supervisor's organizational embodiment. *Journal of Applied Psychology, 95*, 1085–1103.

Epitropaki, O., Sy, T., Martin, R., Tram-Quon, S., & Topakas, A. (2013). Implicit leadership and followership theories "in the wild": Taking stock of information-processing approaches to leadership and followership in organizational settings. *The Leadership Quarterly, 24*, 858–881.

Eva, N., Robin, M., Sendjaya, S., van Dierendonck, D., & Liden, R. C. (2019). Servant leadership: A systematic review and call for future research. *The Leadership Quarterly, 30*, 111–132.

Flynn, C. B., Smither, J. W., & Walker, A. G. (2016). Exploring the relationship between leaders' core self-evaluations and subordinates' perceptions of servant leadership: A field study. *Journal of Leadership & Organizational Studies, 23*, 260–271.

Fridell, M., Belcher, R. N., & Messner, P. E. (2009). Discriminate analysis gender public school principal servant leadership differences. *Leadership & Organization Development Journal, 30*, 722–736.

Graham, J. W. (1991). Servant-leadership in organizations: Inspirational and moral. *The Leadership Quarterly, 2*, 105–119.

Grant, A. M. (2008). Does intrinsic motivation fuel the prosocial fire? Motivational synergy in predicting persistence, performance, and productivity. *Journal of Applied Psychology, 93*, 48–58.

Grant, A. M., & Parker, S. K. (2009). Redesigning work design theories: The rise of relational and proactive perspectives. *Academy of Management Annals, 3*, 317–375.

Grant, A. M., Dutton, J. E., & Rosso, B. D. (2008). Giving commitment: Employee support programs and the prosocial sensemaking process. *Academy of Management Journal, 51*, 898–918.

Greenleaf, R. K. (1970). *The servant as leader.* Newton Centre, MA: The Robert K. Greenleaf Center.

Greenleaf, R. K. (1977). *Servant leadership: A journey into the nature of legitimate power and greatness.* New York: Paulist Press.

Grisaffe, D. B., VanMeter, R., & Chonko, L. B. (2016). Serving first for the benefit of others: Preliminary evidence for a hierarchical conceptualization of servant leadership. *Journal of Personal Selling & Sales Management, 36,* 40–58.

Hale, J. R., & Fields, D. L. (2007). Exploring servant leadership across cultures: A study of followers in Ghana and the USA. *Leadership, 3,* 397–417.

Han, Y., Kakabadse, N. K., & Kakabadse, A. (2010). Servant leadership in the People's Republic of China: A case study of the public sector. *Journal of Management Development, 29*(3), 265–281.

Harvey, P., & Dasborough, M. T. (2015). Entitled to solutions: The need for research on workplace entitlement. *Journal of Organizational Behavior, 36,* 460–465.

Heider, F. (1958). *The psychology of interpersonal relations.* New York: John Wiley.

Higgins, E. T. (1997). Beyond pleasure and pain. *American Psychologist, 52,* 1280–1300.

Hobfoll, S. E. (1989). Conservation of resources: A new attempt at conceptualizing stress. *American Psychologist, 44,* 513–524.

Hobfoll, S. E., Halbesleben, J., Neveu, J., & Westman, M. (2018). Conservation of resources in the organization context: The reliability of resources and their consequences. *Annual Review of Organizational Psychology and Organizational Behavior, 5,* 103–128.

Hoch, J. E., Bommer, W. H., Dulebohn, J. H., & Wu, D. (2018). Do ethical, authentic, and servant leadership explain variance above and beyond transformational leadership? A meta-analysis. *Journal of Management, 44,* 501–529.

Hu, J., & Liden, R. C. (2011). Antecedents of team potency and team effectiveness: An examination of goal and process clarity and servant leadership. *Journal of Applied Psychology, 96,* 851–862.

Huang, J., Li, W., Qiu, C., Yim, F. H. K., & Wan, J. (2016). The impact of CEO servant leadership on firm performance in the hospitality industry. *International Journal of Contemporary Hospitality Management, 28,* 945–968.

Hunter, E. M., Neubert, M. J., Perry, S. J., Witt, L. A., Penney, L. M., & Weinberger, E. (2013). Servant-leaders inspire servant followers: Antecedents and outcomes for employees and organization. *The Leadership Quarterly, 24,* 316–331.

Jaramillo, F., Bande, B., & Varela, J. (2015). Servant leadership and ethics: A dyadic examination of supervisor behaviors and salesperson perceptions. *Journal of Personal Selling & Sales Management, 35*(2), 108–124.

Jaramillo, F., Grisaffe, D. B., Chonko, L. B., & Roberts, J. A. (2009a). Examining the impact of servant leadership on salesperson's turnover intention. *Journal of Personal Selling & Sales Management, 29,* 351–365.

Jaramillo, F., Grisaffe, D. B., Chonko, L. B., & Roberts, J. A. (2009b). Examining the impact of servant leadership on sales force performance. *Journal of Personal Selling & Sales Management, 29,* 257–275.

Johnson, R. E., Lin, S. H., & Lee, H. W. (2018). Self-Control as the Fuel for Effective Self-Regulation at Work: Antecedents, Consequences, and Boundary Conditions of Employee Self-Control. In *Advances in Motivation Science* Vol. 5 (pp. 87–128). Elsevier.

Johnson, R. E., Venus, M., Lanaj, K., Mao, C., & Chang, C. (2012). Leader identity as an antecedent of the frequency and consistency transformational, consideration, and abusive supervision. *Journal of Applied Psychology, 97,* 1262–1272.

Kahn, R. L., Wolfe, D. M., Quinn, R. P., Snoek, J. D., & Rosenthal, R. A. (1964). Adjustment to role conflict and ambiguity in organizations. *Role theory: Concepts and research,* 277–282.

Kelley, H. H. (1967). Attribution theory in social psychology. In Nebraska Symposium on Motivation, Vol. 15 (pp. 192–238). University of Nebraska Press.

Kelley, H. H. (1973). The processes of causal attribution. American Psychologist, 28, 107–128.

Kerr, S., & Jermier, J. M. (1978). Substitutes for leadership: Their meaning and measurement. *Organizational Behavior and Human Performance, 22*(3), 375–403.

Kuenzi, M., & Schminke, M. (2009). Assembling fragments into a lens: A review, critique, and proposed research agenda for the organizational work climate literature. *Journal of Management, 35*, 634–717.

Lacroix, M., & Verdorfer, A. P. (2017). Can servant-leaders fuel the leadership fire? The relationship between servant leadership and followers' leadership avoidance. *Administrative Sciences, 7*(1), 6.

LaPointe, É., & Vandenberghe, C. (2018). Examining the relationship between servant leadership, organizational commitment, and voice and antisocial behaviors. *Journal of Business Ethics, 148*, 99–115.

Laub, J. A. (1999). *Assessing the servant organization: Development of the servant organizational leadership (SOLA) instrument*. Boca Raton, FL: Florida Atlantic University (Unpublished Doctoral Dissertation).

Lemoine, G. J., Hartnell, C. A., & Leroy, H. (2019). Taking stock of moral approaches to leadership: An integrative review of ethical, authentic, and servant leadership. *Academy of Management Annals, 13*, 148–187.

Lee, A., Lyubovnikova, J., Tian, A. W., & Knight, C. (in press). Servant leadership: A meta-analytic examination of incremental contribution, moderation, and mediation. *Journal of Occupational and Organizational Psychology*.

Liao, C., Lee, H. W., Johnson, R. E., & Lin, S.-H. (2017). *Serving today, laissez-faire tomorrow? An actor-centric examination of daily servant-leader behaviors and the moderating role of perspective taking*. Michigan State University. Unpublished manuscript.

Liden, R. C., Erdogan, B., Wayne, S. J., & Sparrowe, R. T. (2006). Leader-member exchange, differentiation, and task interdependence: implications for individual and group perfor-mance. *Journal of Organizational Behavior, 27*, 723–746.

Liden, R. C., Panaccio, A., Meuser, J. D., Hu, J., & Wayne, S. J. (2014a). Servant leadership: Antecedents, processes, and out-comes. In: Day D (Eds.), *Oxford Handbook of Leadership and Organizations* (pp. 357– 379). New York: Oxford University Press.

Liden, R. C., Wayne, S. J., Liao, C., & Meuser, J. D. (2014b). Servant leadership and serving culture: Influence on individual and unit performance. *Academy of Management Journal, 57*, 1434–1452.

Liden, R. C., Wayne, S. J., Meuser, J. D., Hu, J., Wu, J. F., & Liao, C. W. (2015). Servant leadership: Validation of a short form of the SL-28. *The Leadership Quarterly, 26*, 254–269.

Liden, R. C., Wayne, S. J., Zhao, H., & Henderson, D. (2008). Servant leadership: Development of a multidimensional mea-sure and multi-level assessment. *The Leadership Quarterly, 19*, 161–177.

Lin, S-H., Scott, B. A., & Matta, F. K. (2019). The dark side of transformational leadership behaviors for leaders themselves: A conservative of resources perspective. *Academy of Management Journal, 62*(5), 1556–1582.

Ling, Q., Lin, M., & Wu, X. (2016). The trickle-down effect of servant leadership on frontline employee service behaviors and performance: A multilevel study of Chinese hotels. *Tourism Management, 52*, 341–368.

Ling, Q., Liu, F., & Wu, X. (2017). Servant versus authentic lead-ership: Assessing effectiveness in China's hospitality industry. *Cornell Hospitality Quarterly, 58*, 53–68.

Linuesa-Langreo, J., Ruiz-Palomino, P., & Elche-Hortelano, D. (2018). Integrating servant leadership into managerial strategy to build group social capital: The mediating role of group citizen-ship behavior. *Journal of Business Ethics, 152*, 899–916.

Lord, R. G., Foti, R. J., & De Vader, C. L. (1984). A test of lead-ership categorization theory: Internal structure, information processing, and leadership perceptions. *Organizational Behavior and Human Performance, 34*, 343–378.

Mayer, D. M., Bardes, M., & Piccolo, R. F. (2008). Do ser-vant-leaders help satisfy follower needs? An organizational justice perspective. *European Journal of Work and Organizational Psychology, 17,* 180–197.

Meuser, J. D., Liden, R. C., Wayne, S. J., & Henderson, D. (2011). *Is servant leadership always a good thing? The moderating influence of servant leadership prototype.* Paper presented at the annual meeting of the Academy of Management, San Antonio, TX.

Mittal, R., & Dorfman, P. W. (2012). Servant leadership across cultures. *Journal of World Business, 47,* 555–570.

Neubert, M. J., Hunter, E. M., & Tolentino, R. C. (2016). A servant-leader and their stakeholders: When does organizational structure enhance a leader's influence? *The Leadership Quarterly, 27,* 896–910.

Neubert, M. J., Kacmar, K. M., Carlson, D. S., Chonko, L. B., & Roberts, J. A. (2008). Regulatory focus as a mediator of the influence of initiating structure and servant leadership on employee behavior. *Journal of Applied Psychology, 93,* 1220–1233.

Newman, A., Schwarz, G., Cooper, B., & Sendjaya, S. (2017). How servant leadership influences organizational citizenship behavior: The roles of LMX, empowerment, and proactive personality. *Journal of Business Ethics, 145,* 49–62.

Offermann, L. R., Kennedy Jr, J. K., & Wirtz, P. W. (1994). Implicit leadership theories: Content, structure, and generalizability. *The Leadership Quarterly, 5,* 43–58.

Oh, H., Labianca, G., & Chung, M. H. (2006). A multilevel model of group social capital. *Academy of Management Review, 31,* 569–582.

Organ, D. W. (1988). A restatement of the satisfaction-performance hypothesis. *Journal of Management, 14,* 547–557.

Page, D., & Wong, T. P. (2000). A conceptual framework for measuring servant leadership. *The human factor in shaping the course of history and development.* Lanham MD: University Press of America.

Panaccio, A., Donia, M., Saint-Michel, S., & Liden, R. C. (2015a). Servant leadership and well-being. In Burke, R. J., Cooper, C. L., & Page, K. M. (Eds.), *Flourishing in life, work, and careers:*

New horizons in management (pp. 334–358). Cheltenham, UK: Edward Elgar Publishing.

Panaccio, A., Henderson, D. J., Liden, R. C., Wayne, S. J., & Cao, X. (2015b). Toward an understanding of when and why servant leadership accounts for employee extra behaviors. *Journal of Business Psychology, 30*, 657–675.

Parolini, J., Patterson, K., & Winston, B. (2009). Distinguishing between transformational and servant leadership. *Leadership & Organization Development Journal, 30*, 274–291.

Peterson, S. J., Galvin, B. M., & Lange, D. (2012). CEO servant leadership: Exploring executive characteristics and firm performance. *Personnel Psychology, 65*, 565–596.

Politis, J. D., & Politis, D. J. (2018). Examination of the relationship between servant leadership and agency problems: Gender matters. *Leadership and Organization Development Journal, 39*, 170–185.

Reed, L. L., Vidaver-Cohen, D., & Colwell, S. R. (2011). A new scale to measure executive servant leadership: Development, analysis, and implications for research. *Journal of Business Ethics, 101*, 415–434.

Roark, C. S. (2013). *A mixed methods study exploring the relationship between servant leadership and emotional intelligence* (Unpublished doctoral dissertation). Indiana Wesleyan University.

Rodell, J. B. (2013). Finding meaning through volunteering: Why do employees volunteer and what does it mean for their jobs? *Academy of Management Journal, 56*, 1274–1294.

Rodell, J. B., Breitsohl, H., Schröder, M., & Keating, D. J. (2016). Employee volunteering: A review and framework for future research. *Journal of Management, 42*, 55–84.

Rodríguez-Carvajal, R., Herrero, M., van Dierendonck, D., de Rivas, S., & Moreno-Jiménez, B. (2018), Servant Leadership and Goal Attainment Through Meaningful Life and Vitality: A Diary Study. *Journal of Happiness Studies,* 1–23.

Ryan, R. M., & Deci, E. L. (2000). Self-determination theory and the facilitation of intrinsic motivation, social development, and well-being. *American Psychologist, 55*, 68–78.

Schaubroeck, J., Lam, S. S. K., & Peng, A. C. (2011). Cognition-based and affect-based trust as mediators of leader behavior influences on team performance. *Journal of Applied Psychology, 96*, 863–871.

Schwepker, C. H., & Schultz, R. J. (2015). Influence of the ethical servant-leader and ethical climate on customer value enhancing sales performance. *Journal of Personal Selling & Sales Management, 35*, 93–107.

Sendjaya, S., & Cooper, B. (2011). Servant leadership behaviour scale: A hierarchical model and test of construct validity. *European Journal of Work and Organizational Psychology, 20*, 416–436.

Sendjaya, S., Eva, N., Butar-Butar, I., Robin, M., & Castles, S. (2019). SLBS-6: Validation of a short form of the servant leadership behavior scale. *Journal of Business Ethics, 156*, 941–956.

Sendjaya, S., Sarros, J. C., & Santora, J. C. (2008). Defining and measuring servant leadership behavior in organizations. *Journal of Management Studies, 45*, 402–424.

Smith, B. N., Montagno, R. V., & Kuzmenko, T. N. (2004). Transformational and servant leadership: Content and contextual comparisons. *Journal of Leadership & Organizational Studies, 10*, 80–91.

Stone, G. A., Russell, R. F., & Patterson, K. (2004). Transformational versus servant leadership: A difference in leader focus. *Leadership & Organization Development Journal, 25*(4), 349–361.

Sun, J., Liden, R.C., & Ouyang, L. (2019). Are servant-leaders always appreciated? An investigation of how relational attributions influence employee feelings of gratitude and prosocial behaviors. *Journal of Organizational Behavior, 40*, 528–540.

Tajfel, H. (1978). Social categorization, social identity and social comparison. In H. Tajfel (Ed.). *Differentiation between social groups: Studies in the social psychology of intergroup relations* (pp. 61–76). London: Academic Press.

Van Dierendonck, D. (2011). Servant leadership: A review and synthesis. *Journal of Management, 37*, 1228–1261.

Van Dierendonck, D., & Nuijten, I. (2011). The servant leadership survey: Development and validation of a multidimensional measure. *Journal of Business and Psychology, 26*, 249–267.

Van Dierendonck, D., Sousa, M., Gunnarsdóttir, S., Bobbio, A., Hakanen, J., Pircher Verdorfer, A., ... Rodriguez-Carvajal, R. (2017). The cross-cultural invariance of the servant leadership survey: A comparative study across eight countries. *Administrative Sciences, 7*, 8.

Van Dierendonck, D., Stam, D., Boersma, P., de Windt, N., & Alkema, J. (2014). Same difference? Exploring the differential mechanisms linking servant leadership and transformational leadership to follower outcomes. *The Leadership Quarterly, 24*, 544–562.

Van Knippenberg, B., & van Knippenberg, D. (2005). Leader Self-Sacrifice and Leadership Effectiveness: The Moderating Role of Leader Prototypicality. *Journal of Applied Psychology, 90*, 25–37.

Van Knippenberg, D. (2011). Embodying who we are: Leader group prototypicality and leadership effectiveness. *The Leadership Quarterly, 22*, 1078–1091.

Verdorfer, A. P. (2016). Examining mindfulness and its relations to humility, motivation to lead, and actual servant leadership behaviors. *Mindfulness, 7*, 950–961.

Verdorfer, A. P., Steinheider, B., & Burkus, D. (2015). Exploring the socio-moral climate in organizations: An empirical examination of determinants, consequences, and mediating mechanisms. *Journal of Business Ethics, 132*, 233–248.

Walumbwa, F. O., Hartnell, C. A., & Oke, A. (2010). Servant leadership, procedural justice climate, service climate, employee attitudes, and organizational citizenship behavior: A cross-level investigation. *Journal of Applied Psychology, 95*, 517–529.

Walumbwa, F. O., Muchiri, M. K., Misati, E., Wu, C., & Meiliani, M. (2018). Inspired to perform: A multilevel investigation of antecedents and consequences of thriving at work. *Journal of Organizational Behavior, 39*, 249–261.

Wang, M., Kwan, H. K., & Zhou, A. (2017). Effects of servant leadership on work–family balance in China. *Asia Pacific Journal of Human Resources, 55,* 387–407.

Wang, Z., Xu, H., & Liu, Y. (2018). Servant leadership as a driver of employee service performance: Test of a trickle-down model and its boundary conditions. *Human Relations, 71,* 1179–1203.

Weiner, B. (1985). An attributional theory of achievement motivation and emotion. *Psychological Review, 92,* 548–573.

Williams, W. A., Randolph-Seng, B., Hayek, M., Haden, S. P., & Atinc, G. (2017). Servant leadership and followership creativity: The influence of workplace spirituality and political skill. *Leadership & Organization Development Journal, 38,* 178–193.

Wu, L. Z., Tse, E. C. Y., Fu, P. P., Kwan, H. K., & Liu, J. (2013). The impact of Servant leadership on hotel employees' servant behavior. *Cornell Hospitality Quarterly, 54,* 383–395.

Xu, H., & Wang, Z. (2018). *Implications of Servant Leadership for Leaders.* Paper presented at the annual meeting of the Academy of Management, Chicago, IL.

Yang, J., Liu, H., & Gu, J. (2017). A multi-level study of servant leadership on creativity: The roles of self-efficacy and power distance. *Leadership and Organization Development Journal, 38,* 610–629.

Yang, J., Mossholder, K. W., & Peng, T. K. (2007). Procedural justice climate and group power distance: An examination of cross-level interaction effects. *Journal of Applied Psychology, 92,* 681–692.

Yang, Z., Zhang, H., Kwan, H. K., & Chen, S. (2018). Crossover effects of servant leadership and job social support on employee spouses: The mediating role of employee organizational-based self-esteem. *Journal of Business Ethics, 147,* 595–604.

Yoshida, D. T., Sendjaya, S., Hirst, G., & Cooper, B. (2014). Does servant leadership foster creativity and innovation? A multi-level mediation study of identification and prototypicality. *Journal of Business Research, 67,* 1395–1404.

Zhang, H. N., Kwan, H. K., Everett, A. M., & Jian, Z. Q. (2012). Servant leadership, organizational identification and work-to-family enrichment: The moderating role of work climate for sharing family concerns. *Human Resource Management, 51,* 747–768.

Zhang, Y., Zheng, Y, Zhang, L., Xu, S., Liu, X., & Chen, W. (in press). A meta-analytic review of the consequences of servant leadership: The moderating roles of cultural factors. *Asia Pacific Journal of Management.*

Zhao, C., Liu, Y., & Gao, Z. (2016). An identification perspective of servant leadership's effects. *Journal of Managerial Psychology, 31,* 898–913.

Zou, W. C., Tian, Q., & Liu, J. (2015). Servant leadership, social exchange relationships, and follower's helping behavior: Positive reciprocity belief matters. *International Journal of Hospitality Management, 51,* 147–156.

Chapter 3

The Qualitative Essence of Servant Leadership

Jiying Song & Shann Ray Ferch

ROBERT K. GREENLEAF (2002) EFFECTIVELY EMBODIED lesser-known servant leadership aspects such as prophecy, foresight, and the will to better society, often through personal and collective sacrifice. In his telling essay on Robert Frost's poem "Directive," Greenleaf showed not only his strengths in linear thinking, but his uncommon and profound gifts with regard to nonlinear, mystery-based, and more circular aspects of wisdom. This type of wisdom is more readily associated with poets and painters than business practitioners or social scientists.

Greenleaf's essay titled "The Inward Journey," from Greenleaf's (2002) *Servant Leadership: A Journey into the Nature of Legitimate Power and Greatness,* contains an elegant, artistic, and in many respects, qualitative, look at the nature of the servant leader. In the essay, Greenleaf relates how his reading Robert Frost's poem, "Directive," deepened his understanding of the courageous and wise presence of the servant as leader. In this chapter, we want to present qualitative research studies that reflect Greenleaf's profound understanding of humanity in more enriched, more mystery based, and more collectivist (vs. individualistic) ways than are often found in normative quantitative research studies.

Notably, the burgeoning quantitative research in servant leadership conducted by Liden (Hu & Liden, 2011; Liden et al., 2015; Liden, Fu, Liu, & Song, 2016; Liden, Wayne, Liao,

& Meuser, 2014; Liden, Wayne, Zhao, & Henderson, 2008; Panaccio, Henderson, Liden, Wayne, & Cao, 2015), van Dierendonck (Sousa & van Dierendonck, 2016, 2017a, 2017b; van Dierendonck et al., 2017; van Dierendonck & Nuijten, 2011; van Dierendonck, Stam, Boersma, de Windt, & Alkema, 2014), and many others, has revealed weighty implications for servant leadership across many dimensions of human experience. This body of research significantly fortifies and brings to the fore the new quantitative frontier of servant leadership understandings, leading the field in unforeseen directions while contributing invaluable new knowledge.

That said, qualitative studies in servant leadership perform a different function—again, a function less aligned with linear or super-rational knowledge, and more aligned with poetic or symbolic knowledge. Quantitative research, in its emphasis on numerical reliability, validity, and generalizability, and at the expense of more intimate individual and collective expressions of human capacity, cannot, by definition, draw on the empirical grounding in lived experience found in qualitative research (Crotty, 1998; Denzin & Lincoln, 2011; van Manen, 1990, 2016). Quantitative research typically disallows, or rather occludes the researcher from acknowledging and challenging personal biases, a research practice that is a common requirement for qualitative studies. This refusal to acknowledge and detail personal bias can often prevent the servant-leader from true self-knowledge, and thus it can be a shadow force or unknown frailty in much quantitative research. At times this results in calcification, brittleness, and eventual fracture of the knowledge base. Certainly, research using qualitative, quantitative, and mixed methodologies is necessary for more complete and robust understanding of servant leadership. The gift of in-depth, well-designed, and deeply informed qualitative studies in servant leadership offers the opportunity to expose our blind spots as people and leaders, and bring us to a more intimate understanding of ourselves, others, and the world.

Though the extent of Greenleaf's personal connection with Pulitzer Prize-winning poet Robert Frost is unknown, they did know each other, and spent time in one another's presence. The possibility that they directly influenced one another's thought is apparent and is a compelling thread in the history of leadership studies. Consider this moment, relayed by Greenleaf (2002):

> In a group conversation with him [Frost] one evening, he digressed on the subject of loyalty. At one point I interjected with: "Robert, that is not the way you have defined loyalty before." He turned to me with a broad friendly grin and asked softly, "How did I define it?" I replied, "In your talk on Emerson a few years ago, you said, 'Loyalty is that for the lack of which your gang will shoot you without benefit of trial by jury.'" To this man who had struggled without recognition until he was forty, and then had to move to England to get it, nothing could have pleased him more in his old age than to have an obscure passage like this quoted to him in a shared give-and-take with non-literary people. (p. 326)

In Greenleaf's (2002) "engagement" with Frost's poem, he affirmed the necessity of a prophetic, circular orientation in going further into the depths of human awareness: "Our problem is circular: we must understand in order to be able to understand. It has something to do with awareness and symbols" (p. 329). Symbolic understanding is formless, it cannot be linearized, and it cannot be understood by simple 1-2-3 progressions. Rather, it is absorbed, it is an element of life and leadership in which the servant-leader chooses to become willingly submerged.

> Awareness, letting something significant and disturbing develop between oneself and a symbol, comes more by being waited upon rather than by being asked. One of the most baffling of life's experiences is to stand beside one who is aware, one who is looking at a symbol and is deeply moved by it, and, confronting the same symbol, to be unmoved. Oh, that we could just be open in the presence of symbols that cry

out to speak to us, let our guards down, and take the risks of being moved!

The power of a symbol is measured by its capacity to sustain a flow of significant new meaning. The substance of the symbol may be a painting, a poem or story, allegory, myth, scripture, a piece of music, a person, a crack in the sidewalk, or a blade of grass. Whatever or whoever, it produces a confrontation in which much that makes the symbol meaningful comes from the beholder.

The potentiality is both in the symbol and in the beholder. (Greenleaf, 2002, p. 329)

From the foundations of qualitative research, philosophers of human nature such as Husserl (1970), Heidegger (1962), Gadamer (2004, 1976), and Ricoeur (1981), have spoken to the impossibility of knowing humanity without knowing one-self. Qualitative research helps us find a more accessible avenue toward increased self-awareness: through symbol, depth, and meaning. The need to name, articulate, and bracket one's own biases in the attempt to show the lived human experience more clearly, is inherent to qualitative research, even as it generally remains obscured in quantitative research. By extension, the person with a leader-first mentality—often mired in self-aggran-dizement without foreknowledge, ambition at the expense of love and service, and an inappropriate power drive obscuring or negating authentic intimacy—generally lacks healthy self-aware-ness. The leader-first leader has limited or no capacity to name his or her own faults, let alone invite others to influence, chal-lenge, and help change his or her faults. In this light Greenleaf's (2002) prophetic truths—warning individuals, communities, and nations against the leader-first mentality—take on pivotal and in fact crucial meaning.

The core of this chapter is a review of six qualitative studies to express how qualitative servant leadership research and inquiry can benefit our understanding of the world, ourselves, and servant leadership theory and practice. Servant leaders—aligned with the ancient history of servant-first leading, rather than leader-first leading—seek greater self-awareness and greater awareness of others. Servant-leaders seek the essence of what it means not only to lead and follow, but to live. In so doing, they embody great will, considerable modesty, and active engagement with a circular world. The following six articles by Ramsey (2006), Reynolds (2013, 2014), Matesi (2013a, 2013b), Kincaid (2017), Campbell (2017), and McCollum and Moses (2009), two based in the qualitative hermeneutic phenomenological tradition, one based in mixed-methods content analysis, one based in ethnographic content analysis, one based directly in prophetic foresight, and the final one based on Greenleaf's original longitudinal research at AT&T, reveal the richness of human understanding associated with in depth studies of human nature in light of servant leadership. In this chapter, we discuss servant leadership essence in six major themes: (a) servant leadership, empathy, and healing; (b) servant leadership and gender balance; (c) servant leadership and foresight; (d) servant leadership and corporate responsibility; (e) servant leadership, forgiveness, and reconciliation; and (f) servant leadership and Greenleaf's modeling. The chapter ends with a section that covers essential understandings.

Servant Leadership Essence

At the outset of my research I was unsure, even questioning the heart of humanity. I can now say a life for others, a servant-led life, exists, heals the world, restores us to one another, and gracefully makes us whole. (Ramsey, 2006, p. 134)

Servant leadership, empathy, and healing

In 2002, Marleen Ramsey set out to interview six political perpetrators from the Apartheid era in South Africa who were found guilty of murder and other gross human rights abuses. Going through political turmoil and being tormented by violence, South Africa had its first democratic elections in 1994. Nelson Mandela became the president and initiated the process of investigating human-rights abuses and negotiating national reconciliation through the Truth and Reconciliation Commission (TRC), which was chaired by Desmond Tutu. Mandela and Tutu modeled servant leadership through the process of the TRC. The TRC employed public truth-telling hearings to give voice to the victims who had been silent about the suffering they had been through and to let political perpetrators be honest about their violent deeds. Through this process, truth was revealed, suffering was heard, forgiveness was given and received, and lives were transformed. Ramsey's (2006) hermeneutic phenomenological study depicted a particular and fine-grained picture of this movement a decade after the fall of Apartheid. Among Ramsey's six participants, two were responsible for the death of Amy Biehl in 1993, one was tried for the Heidelberg Tavern attack in 1994, one was responsible for the St. James Church massacre in 1993, one commanded the attacks on the Heidelberg Tavern and the St. James Church in Cape Town, and one ordered the attack on a house in the village of Trust Feed in 1988. In each case, lives were taken and innocent blood was shed.

Amy Biehl, an American Fulbright scholar, had been helping black South Africans complete registration forms so that they could vote in the forthcoming democratic elections, which were to be held in 1994. Her work was a powerful example of servant leadership. Increasing black-on-white violence took place in South Africa in the years of 1993 and 1994, under the influence of the slogan, "One settler, one bullet, we want our country right now, liberate" (Ramsey, 2003, p. 124). What happened to Biehl in the black township of Gugulethu on July 25, 1993 was the result of one of these uprisings. The crowd spotted a government truck and behind it was Biehl driving a yellow car. Someone saw Biehl's white face and shouted that there was a settler and the crowd began throwing stones at Biehl's car. They caught her, stabbed her multiple times, and stoned her to death. Two of Ramsey's participants were found guilty for the death of Amy Biehl.

In another set of interviews, focusing on a different and also traumatic set of events, Ramsey interviewed a white commander of the State security forces. This commander was in charge of controlling the region and thwarting the activities against whites in a remote corner of the Kwa-Zulu Natal Midlands. The commander's forces, all white, oversaw a village—Trust Feed—with 7,000 black people. On December 3, 1988, the commander ordered an attack on a house in Trust Feed. He thought he was destroying an ammunition holding house and a location where petrol bombs were being manufactured. When he walked into the house the morning after the attack, blood covered the room and eleven bodies lay still, mostly women and children. He realized that the wrong house had been targeted and innocent people had been killed. In order to protect the image of the South African State Security Forces, he and his superiors planned a cover-up of the atrocity by blaming the attack on the black United Democratic Front forces.

Ramsey's data did not come from a questionnaire distributed to hundreds of people, but from in-depth interviews on the lived experiences of six participants. Her questions sought the heart of the matter:

- Please describe what it was like to face your victim or victim's family and to receive empathy and forgiveness from them.

- If it came as a surprise to you to receive empathy and forgiveness from the victim's family, please describe what response…

- Please describe the thoughts, feelings, and perceptions you experienced…

- Have your thoughts, goals, or behaviors changed in any way due to your experience of receiving empathy and forgiveness, and if so, please describe them for me.

- Would you please describe the most transforming moment you experienced throughout the ordeal? (Ramsey, 2003, p. 261)

By using a phenomenological approach, Ramsey (2003, 2006) gave space to the participants and let them share what they had experienced. This formed the starting point for inquiry, reflection, and interpretation. Hermeneutic phenomenology goes beyond merely describing the foundations of lived experience and looks for meanings embedded in the essences of the life-world (Lopez & Willis, 2004; van Manen, 2016). Reflecting on her work, Ramsey (2006) said:

> Time and again, during the interviews and during the inter-pretation of these men's stories, I was struck by the enormity of the psychological pain that we often cause others and our-selves. I was also struck by the realization of how healing the experience of forgiveness can be to both victims and perpe-trators. It is through the stories of these six men that greater understanding may be gained regarding the transforming powers of empathy and forgiveness. It is also through their stories that we can see how the practices of servant leadership can restore community to people deeply separated by vio-lence and brutality. (p. 120)

Ramsey (2006) found five themes through her study: (a) violence harms both victim and perpetrator, (b) denial and arrogance are self-protections used to shield the perpetrator from shame, (c) empathy creates an environment whereby the perpetrator can ask for and receive forgiveness, (d) the gift of forgiveness increases the ability to forgive oneself, and (e) for-giveness is a bridge to the future. Facing violence and tragedy, we learn some of the details of damage through news reports and numbers of deaths, but in order to know the impact on victims' and perpetrators' hearts and souls, we have to listen to their stories. Ramsey pointed out that labeling perpetrators as "evil" or "inhuman" does not help us understand them. All of her participants revealed intense pain such as "I felt a pain in my heart," "I felt pressed with a huge weight," "I felt as if I was being suffocated," and "There was a poison that needed to be released" (p. 124). However, many amnesty seekers appeared unbroken, unrepentant, arrogant, and with no sign of remorse as they were testifying before the TRC. Ramsey developed deeper understanding of human blame-shifting through her interviews. One participant said, "I was not prepared to make myself appear weak because it would create more shame than I could bear" (p. 125). Five of the six participants mentioned their needs to maintain dignity and self-respect in an environment they felt was extremely hostile. After capturing the human side of the perpetrators, Ramsey found that perpetrators' feelings of empathy for their victims and receiving empathy from victims' families were emotional bridges that perpetrators could use to ask for and receive forgiveness. She showed the long and torturous journey toward self-forgiveness each of these participants faced. In the attack on Trust Feed, one participant's action resulted in the death of eleven innocent people. Years later, in response to Mandela and Tutu's servant leadership, the people of Trust Feed brought him back for reconciliation and forgiveness and invited him to live with them. He said, "I was dead until that day … And after that day I lived" (pp. 135-136). Today he has succeeded in helping raise the funds to build a community center, hand in hand with people whose family members he killed.

All six participants received empathy and forgiveness from victims' family members or loved ones, but only four developed close relationships with the people they had harmed. These four participants expressed a greater feeling of self-forgiveness and hope for the future than the other two who did not have such relationships with their victims' families. Today, after years of profound relationship, the men who killed Amy Biehl call Biehl's mother their mother, and she calls them her sons. They all see this as a miracle, and the world echoes their sentiment. Together these men, along with Amy Biehl's parents, have worked to improve quality of life for families and children of South Africa. The conclusions of Ramsey's (2006) study contribute to understanding the role of empathy and forgiveness in the healing of interpersonal wounded relationships. Even with the most hardened and unrepentant perpetrators, the practice of the principles of servant leadership—empathy and healing— have the generative power to bring hope for redemption and the restoration of community. Servant-leaders help those who have been lost in the wilderness find their way home.

Servant leadership and gender balance

Through a feminist perspective, Reynolds (2013) used a mixed-methods content analysis to study commencement messages delivered by 50 of the top female and male American business leaders based on the ranking of their organizations on Fortune lists from 2005 to 2012. Her purpose was to understand gender differences between expressions of leadership in the constructs of servant leadership and expressions of decision making in the constructs of the ethic of care. She also explored whether gender differences among prominent American business leaders support the conceptualization that servant leadership is a gender-integrative mode of leadership. She found this to be intuitively and qualitatively true. In other words, no overall gender distinction was found on the main servant leadership characteristics, but some gender differences were observed. For instance, women spoke more about humility and standing back in leadership, whereas men highlighted accountability; female speakers considered the motivation to lead as an ethical drive and a choice, whereas male speakers articulated it as an obligation (Reynolds, 2013). She stated that gender differences found in the qualitative analysis could serve to reify gender congruency expectations if read without critical gender understanding. To counteract such reification, her study presented evidence of female leaders combining care orientation and relationality (typically feminine aspects of leadership) with courage and contrarian thinking (typically masculine aspects) and evidence of male leaders combining accountability and risk taking (typically masculine aspects) with forgiveness and being attuned to others' needs (typically feminine aspects). Reynolds (2013) concluded that servant leadership combines both feminine and masculine aspects of leadership.

Furthermore, Eicher-Catt (2005) proposed that the serving aspect of servant leadership is associated with submissive femininity, and the leading aspect with oppressive masculinity. Reynolds (2014) challenged Eicher-Catt's framework, revealing Eicher-Catt's conclusions with regard to servant leadership to be largely based on her perception of the two words "servant" and "leader" and not on Greenleaf's own interpretations of these words. Greenleaf's interpretations serve to deconstruct the words and return them to their original meanings, affirming their value across gender, culture, time, and context. Reynolds analyzed Spears' (2002) 10 characteristics to examine servant leadership constructs in terms of gender. She argued that six of the 10 characteristics distinguish servant leadership from other forms of leadership whereas the other four are more in line with traditional notions of leadership (Reynolds, 2014). These six distinguishing characteristics are: stewardship, listening, empathizing, healing, commitment to the growth of people, and building community; the other four are comprised of foresight, conceptualization, awareness, and persuasion. Reynolds (2014) asserted that foresight, conceptualization, awareness, and persuasion can be characterized as leader behaviors, which are often associated with the more traditionally masculine aspect of leadership. The six distinguishing characteristics of servant leadership, on the other hand, are predominantly needs focused and other oriented, and thus, for Reynolds (2014), comprise the feminine-attributed aspects of leadership.

Eicher-Catt (2005) claimed, from her particular feminist perspective, that the apposition of servant with leader associated with subjugation and domination respectively, instantiates a paradoxical discourse game that perpetuates male-centric patriarchal norms rather than neutralizes gender bias. Reynolds (2014) agreed that Eicher-Catt's (2005) critique reveals otherwise-obscure discursive and behavioral meanings and hidden cultural assumptions in servant leadership. However, Reynolds (2014) exposed how Eicher-Catt lacked the will to go deeply into Greenleaf's original texts in order to find a more central discursive and deconstructive essence that can be ascribed to Greenleaf's sense of "making things whole" across gender, culture, and context. Reynolds (2014) argued that the combination of servant facets and leader facets of servant leadership do not automatically confirm the negatives Eicher-Catt associated with gendered notions, but on the contrary, provides a model of ethical and gender-equity-enhancing leadership. "Servant-leadership espouses a nonhierarchical, participative approach to defining organizational objectives and ethics that recognizes and values the subjectivity and situatedness of organizational members" (Reynolds, 2014, p. 57). It can serve as "a driving force for generating discourse on gender-integrative approaches to organizational leadership" (p. 51).

Reynolds proposed the paradoxical linguistic term "servant-leader" is not a disguise for male-centric norms as Eicher-Catt (2005) claimed, but a complementary and harmonious dualism. This dualism resonates with the concepts of *yin* and *yang*, which represent female and male, respectively, in ancient Chinese literature:

> As for yin and yang, they are the Way of heaven and earth, the fundamental principles [governing] the myriad beings, father and mother to all changes and transformations, the basis and

beginning of generating life and killing, the palace of spirit brilliance. (Unschuld, Tessenow, & Zheng, 2011, p. 95)

Lao Tzu (2005) said, "All the myriad things carry the Yin on their backs and hold the Yang in their embrace, deriving their vital harmony from the proper blending of the two vital Breaths" (p. 49). *Yin* and *yang* cannot exist without each other. They are a contradictory, yet complementary unit. Women were degraded in ancient China based on the ascendancy of patriarchy, the focus on the contradictory aspect of *yin* and *yang*, and the elevation of *yang* (Bao, 1987). The same kind of degradation still exists in the leadership field today. Having stressed the equally and mutually complementary character of *yin-yang*, some scholars paved the way for the women's egalitarian movement in 19th-century China (Bao, 1987). Likewise, this is what Reynolds (2013, 2014) and many other servant leadership scholars are doing—elevating complementary without neglecting contradictory aspects of gender.

Through a discussion of the complementary character of *yin-yang* and servant-leader elements, without ignoring the contradictory aspect, leaders may establish harmony and gender-integrative models wherever they serve. Although the results of Reynolds' (2013) study indicated that gender stereotyping continues to affect conceptualizations of leadership, her study also provided evidence of servant-leaders crossing gender boundaries and integrating gendered traits and behaviors. As Reynolds (2014) noted, by integrating the female perspective with a male perspective, a paradigm shift in leadership theory (through avenues inherent to servant leadership) could move organizations from hierarchy-driven, rules-based, and authoritative models to value-driven, follower-oriented, and participative models with gender balance.

Servant leadership and foresight

Foresight has been recognized as the most important virtue for leaders in China since ancient times. Chinese historian Sima (1993) wrote from approximately 145 BCE to 86 BCE: "An enlightened [person] sees the end of things while they are still in bud, and a wise [person] knows how to avoid danger before it has taken shape" (p. 294). For Greenleaf (2002), "Foresight is the 'lead' that the leader has" (p. 40).

> One goes in prepared with strategies, with knowledge, and with as much as can be anticipated by foresight in the way of preparation. Belief that the needed insight will come, in the situation, is then the supporting faith that relieves one of stress in a way that permits the creative process to operate, that makes dynamic visionary leadership possible. (Greenleaf, 1996a, p. 324)

Matesi (2013a) outlined Greenleaf's (1996a) understanding of foresight in three creative and cognitive capacities: intellection—the capacity to strategically prepare and analyze; imagination—the capacity to visualize scenarios or symbols that complement or expand intellection; and insight—the capacity to be open to what lies beyond intellect and image. Matesi (2013a) claimed that intellection, imagination, and insight constitute foresight, which fuels vision and is deployed through narrative forms of servant leadership. Based on Sashkin's (2004) articulation of vision—constructed mentally and behaviorally—Matesi (2013a) argued that the mental construction of vision is achieved through foresight and the behavioral construction of vision is achieved through narrative leadership. Foresight requires a leader to live at two levels of consciousness: the real world and the detached one (Greenleaf, 2002). Vision is fueled by foresight and exercising foresight employs intellection to see underlying structures and consequences, imagination to embrace and wrestle with paradoxes and visualize the whole, and insight to open awareness and perception through purposeful disorientation (Matesi, 2013a).

Vision is meant not only to be mentally constructed, but also behaviorally, emotionally, and spiritually conveyed and carried out. Through a literature review on the relationship between vision and narrative, Matesi (2013a) concluded that narrative leadership is the mechanism by which foresight-informed visions are communicated: "Narrative leadership draws out the cognitive, creative, and moral power of the leader through mentally and behaviorally constructing a narrated vision that intends to move, raise, and invigorate" (p. 83). Matesi supported her statement through the words of Wangari Maathai (2004) of Kenya:

> In the course of history, there comes a time when humanity is called to shift to a new level of consciousness, to reach a higher moral ground. A time when we have to shed our fear and give hope to each other. That time is now…there can be no peace without equitable development; and there can be no development without sustainable management of the environment in a democratic and peaceful space. This shift is an idea whose time has come. (para. 28-30)

Maathai was awarded the Nobel Peace Prize in 2004 and the above words were from her Nobel lecture. Her whole lecture was intellection driven, imaginative, and insightful (Matesi, 2013a). Maathai (2004) conveyed her vision through narrative and called on people to examine their own environmental values. A vision, constructed through foresight, cannot mediate social movements without narratives.

Matesi (2013b) examined the relationships among foresight, vision, and narrative leadership through an ethnographic content analysis of the text of 17 lectures delivered by Nobel Peace Prize laureates who won the prize for their leadership in human rights. She discerned each laureate's vision and then the textual traces of foresight used by the laureate to fuel that vision. In all lectures, a clearly articulated vision was identified. Foresight enables servant-leaders to understand the lessons from the past, see and rise above the events in the present, and foresee the consequences of a decision for the indefinite future (Greenleaf, 2002; Spears, 2010). A leader is "at once, in every moment of time, historian, contemporary analyst, and prophet—not three separate roles" (Greenleaf, 1996a, p. 319). In her study, Matesi (2013b) found these three roles in the narratives of laureates who incorporated past, present, and future time orientations in their visions. Concerning the three creative and cognitive capacities of leader foresight, Matesi found the capacities of intellection and imagination existed explicitly in the lectures whereas the capacity of insight was present but not as extensive as the other two. Furthermore, in her study, the Nobel Peace laureates employed narrative leadership to share their visions of peace and to inspire and mobilize people through directly addressing the audience, referencing allies, naming opponents, capturing metanarratives and visions, and participating in a form of peace leadership attribution chain. Through her study, we can see that mental construction of vision through foresight, and behavioral construction of vision through narrative leadership, tie social knowing and acting together. To fuel narrative leadership, leaders may consider cultivating foresight by strengthening their intellection, imagination, and insight (Matesi, 2013a).

Servant leadership and corporate responsibility

Although today's industrialized society in the context of servant leadership is ethically meant to satisfy the needs of people— especially the least privileged, many organizational leaders still put profits ahead of people, instead of building a profitable community that helps people flourish. Paradoxically, in the midst of the profit-first culture, servant leadership research reveals how some people lead by putting others' needs first even if great sacrifice is required in order to do so. Kincaid (2017) described his study as sitting at servant leaders' feet and learning from their stories. Sitting at a master's feet is the sign of becoming his or her disciple in ancient Greco-Roman culture. The nature of this gesture in terms of qualitative studies is to join into a shared dialogue with participants, achieving a deeper level of engagement, and gaining a richer understanding of the topic under study. Kincaid employed a hermeneutic phenomenological approach to explore the essence of corporate social responsibility from a servant leadership perspective. He interviewed three male and three female corporate leaders from different industries and variously sized organizations, which are preliminarily considered servant led and socially responsible organizations.

Kincaid (2017) built his study on the literature surrounding corporate social responsibility and servant leadership. No single definition for corporate responsibility is sufficient; therefore, Blowfield and Murray (2008) suggest using it as an umbrella term to capture the various ways to define, manage, and act upon business' relationship with society. They offered prominent areas or key pillars of corporate responsibility: business ethics, legal compliance, philanthropy and community investment, environmental management, sustainability, animal rights, human rights, worker rights and welfare, market relations, corruption, and corporate governance. Kincaid (2017) used these key pillars as a framework for organizations practicing servant leadership in socially responsible ways.

Greenleaf (2002) asserted that the quick shift of our society from one of individuals to one dominated by large institutions and the failure of trusteeship in these institutions causes societal problems. He contended that for a better society to be built, we have to "raise both the capacity to serve and the very performance as servant of existing major institutions by new regenerative forces operating within them" (p. 62). Kincaid (2017) selected leaders who understood the imperative role of the institution as servant. In his study, all participants shared rich stories about successful business practice in financially, environmentally, and socially responsible ways. In other words, their organizational leadership teams had acted as a servant to their workers and their surrounding communities.

Comparing his participants' notions of social responsibility in servant-led organizations with the key pillars of corporate social responsibility in the literature, Kincaid (2017) found three themes. The most prevalent one was that "the language surrounding corporate social responsibility is uninspiring and therefore not embraced" (pp. 262-263). In his study, Kincaid's participants, despite being leading practitioners in the field of corporate responsibility, were neither aware of, nor able to make a meaningful connection with, the key pillars of corporate responsibility provided by Blowfield and Murray (2008). These leaders also did not consider corporate social responsibility as a goal with specific checklists. Kincaid (2017) pointed out that the most effective leadership goes beyond objective definition and prescribed behavior, reaching people at the level of heart, thought, and insight. Kincaid's participants shared the value of forming a mission statement and holding themselves and their fellow workers accountable to the mission. This finding reinforced the role of vision as an intrinsic motivator and the inspiring power of the servant leader:

> The leader does this [inspiring people] by engaging the entire team or organization in a process that creates a shared vision that inspires each to stretch and reach deeper within themselves and to use their unique talents in whatever way is necessary to independently and interdependently achieve that shared vision. (Covey, 1998, p. xii)

In his study, Kincaid (2017) discerned a vital difference between the uninteresting language of corporate social responsibility and the robust, inspiring, and even illumined language of servant leadership. He suggested that the reason for the disengagement of organizational leaders from the literature of corporate social responsibility is that it is imposing and autocratic and fails to motivate people. The disengagement produced by more autocratic terms did not mean that these leaders failed to care deeply about social responsibility; they were, in fact, making great efforts in shaping their organizations in a socially responsible way. They did it through cultivating visions, empowering fellow workers, and fostering intrinsic meanings (Kincaid, 2017). As Ferch (2005) said, "A common experience of being led from the traditional model is one of dominance or control, while the experience of being servant-led is one of freedom" (p. 99). Kincaid (2017) suggested that in the corporate social responsibility movement, a shift—from dominance and control to empowerment and freedom—needs to take place. This is not just a challenge to the field of corporate responsibility, but also a challenge to all leaders—encouraging leaders and followers to move from leadership that *works* to leadership that *inspires* and *endures* (Covey, 2002).

Servant leadership, forgiveness, and reconciliation

Campbell (2017) deepened the field of servant leadership through building a theoretical foundation upon which leaders can integrate forgiveness and reconciliation as an organizational leadership competency to resolve conflicts and sustain peace and harmony in the face of local and global challenges. First, the author introduced definitions and conceptualizations of forgiveness and reconciliation within transitional-justice and organizational-leadership disciplines. Second, the author compared religious themes of forgiveness in Hinduism, Islam, Judaism, and Christianity. Third, the author discussed the necessities of integrating forgiveness and reconciliation as an organizational-leadership competency. Finally, Campbell suggested that servant leadership can serve as a theoretical framework to facilitate forgiveness and reconciliation within organizations.

Enright, Freedman, and Rique (1998) defined forgiveness as "a willingness to abandon one's right to resentment, negative judgment, and indifferent behavior toward one who unjustly injured us, while fostering the undeserved qualities of compassion, generosity, and even love toward him or her" (pp. 46-47).

Forgiveness is a process of replacing complex negative emotions with positive other-oriented emotions; and it requires empathy, sympathy, compassion, and love along with clear understanding in the face of social tensions and injustice (Worthington, 2006).

A study, conducted in Uganda by the Refugee Law Project and the Center for Civil and Human Rights from 2014 to 2015, found that the practice of forgiveness, combined with transitional-justice measures—such as judicial accountability, truth telling, governance, and reparations—can be a strong asset for peace building (Shaffic, 2015). Campbell (2017) claimed that transitional-justice practitioners, who may be called to lead victims through the emotional and intellectual process of forgiveness, need to develop their leadership capacities, such as empathy, emotional intelligence, accountability, humility, and compassion. Within an unforgiving organization, Campbell stated, leaders may employ dishonesty, power politics, and manipulative measures; employees may be afraid to speak out and may be hiding their feelings; and such organizational climates are definably toxic. He asserted that forgiveness plays a principal role in restoring relationships, rebuilding trust, nurturing healthy work climates, improving organizational performance, and transforming organizations. Campbell discerned that forgiveness in the context of servant leadership is "a social interaction among individuals designed to resolve intrapersonal and interpersonal conflicts toward organizational and national peaceful coexistence" (p. 151). Furthermore, he pointed out that forgiveness not only frees victims and perpetrators from guilt and pain, but also fosters personal, organizational, and global reconciliation.

Campbell (2017) claimed that the process of forgiveness focuses on individual healing while the process of reconciliation fosters social healing. Brouneus (2007) defined reconciliation as "a societal process that involves mutual acknowledgment of past suffering and the changing of destructive attitudes and behavior into constructive relationships toward sustainable peace" (p. 6). Reconciliation involves changes in emotion, attitude, and behavior; social healing among victims and perpetrators; and an ongoing process in which relations are rebuilt for sustainable and peaceful coexistence (Brouneus, 2007). Campbell (2017) proposed two levels of the conceptualization of reconciliation: the microlevel, where reconciliation is both a leadership competency and an interpersonal endeavor; and the macrolevel, where reconciliation redresses the physical, emotional, and spiritual wounds generated by abusers at organizational, communal, national, and global levels. For Campbell, the best example of this two-level reconciliation is found in the process of the TRC in South Africa. Tutu (1999), the leader of the TRC, said: "Forgiveness will follow confession and healing will happen, and so contribute to national unity and reconciliation" (p. 120). Furthermore, Tutu claimed that South Africa had to move "beyond retributive justice to restorative justice, to move on to forgiveness, because without it there was no future" (p. 260). Campbell (2017) proposed that restorative justice through servant leadership builds a narrative toward reconciliation, facilitates forgiveness and societal reconciliation, and creates a therapeutic impact on the society.

Campbell (2017) compared religious themes of forgiveness in Hinduism, Islam, Judaism, and Christianity and found that forgiveness is accompanied by moral virtues, benevolence, and reliance on leaders' spirituality. Perpetrator accountability and psycho-social healing is impossible without a spiritual component, Campbell concluded. Thus, he confirmed that "forgiveness is an integral ingredient of individual psycho-social healing, facilitates restoration of individual and community healing, and necessitates spiritual strength as societies heal from human rights atrocities in a post conflict environment" (p. 164).

Campbell (2017) pointed out that organizational conflicts may come from the misperceptions generated from a lack of dialogue, listening, empathy, and understanding between leaders and the fellow workers. Leaders' decisions and actions based on misperceptions may produce an environment that lacks forgiveness and hinders peace building. In order to avoid misperceptions,

Campbell proposed that communications at individual and organizational levels take place by building an atmosphere of trust, collaboration, and dialogue. Integrating forgiveness within an organization can not only free victims and perpetrators from their wounds, but can also nurture and sustain such an atmosphere, further increasing retention and productivity. Thus, by fostering forgiveness and reconciliation, servant-leaders "create a supportive environment where individual growth toward emotional, relational, and spiritual maturity strengthens" and organizational performance increases (Campbell, 2017, p. 174).

Yergler (2005) asserted that "a servant-leader must incorporate forgiveness as a leadership competency if the benefactors of that leadership are to experience true transformation into servant-leaders themselves" (para. 3). When Mandela laid down his vengeance after 27 years in jail, a spirit of forgiveness was kindled in the whole nation. Campbell (2017) argued that servant leadership has essential ingredients that end up fostering an organizational climate of forgiveness and reconciliation. He compared the characteristics of unforgiving leaders with forgiving leaders at different levels—individually, dyadic, in teams, and organizationally—and listed servant leadership competencies needed to nurture forgiveness and reconciliation within organizations. To form the formless and to chart the uncharted, servant leadership scholars like Campbell (2017), strive to shift the stereotypical paradigms in leadership.

Servant leadership and Greenleaf's modeling

The above servant leadership studies we have analyzed find some of their roots in Greenleaf's original research shown in McCollum and Moses' (2009) article. In this article, McCollum and Moses presented Greenleaf's legacy at AT&T—the shaping of the contemporary development of assessment centers that were naturally qualitative, personal, and communal in nature and paired with certain quantitative understandings. After college, Greenleaf was hired by AT&T Ohio Bell subsidiary in

1926. Three years later he was moved to the headquarters of AT&T in New York. In the 1920s, Bell initiated a comprehensive study to evaluate the success of college recruits. Through the study of 3,800 college hires, it concluded that college grades and class standing can predict salary and job success (McCollum & Moses, 2009). A thriving program had been developed to attract and retain these talented graduates within AT&T when Greenleaf came to New York.

In the 1950s, Greenleaf spearheaded the Bell Humanities Program—developing executives through exposure to the humanities. The Program provided opportunities of a year-long liberal-arts curriculum from 1953 to 1958 and later a series of shorter programs until 1970 (Frick, 2004). Greenleaf incorporated these programs into the Initial Management Development Program (IMDP) for the development of potential managers in their early career (McCollum & Moses, 2009). In order to better understand how these programs had been developed, we have to look at Greenleaf's Management Progress Study (MPS), which explored the factors in the shaping of managers' development. MPS' roots began during World War II. The Office of Strategic Services (OSS) was responsible for selecting spies who could work in Europe in resistance to Nazi Germany. In 1943, Dr. Henry Murray, given his groundbreaking research in the field of personality development in the 1920s, was assigned the task to develop a special school to select and train spies (Frick, 2004). After the war, the results of Murray and his colleagues' efforts were published in a 1946 *Fortune* article called "A Good Man is Hard to Find" and a book entitled *The Assessment of Men* in 1948. Greenleaf saw the relevance of formal assessment in the OSS and in a business like AT&T. He brought this article and the book to the attention of executives at AT&T, and eventually launched a highly visionary project—MPS—a twenty-five-year longitudinal study.

In 1956, Greenleaf hired Douglas Bray to design and deliver the first AT&T assessment program. During the first four years,

the program assessed 422 high-potential new recruits or beginning managers. The initial assessment was conducted in a one-
week assessment center, where psychologists and managers
observed the participants and rated them according to 26 specific
assessment dimensions (Bray, 1982).[1] A second assessment was
conducted eight years later and a third assessment 20 years later.
The same set of dimensions was used for years zero and eight
while 21 new dimensions were added at year 20 to reflect the
challenges of middle age (Bray, 1982). Yearly follow-up interviews were used to learn about participants' work and life activities. Two hundred and sixty-six out of 422 participants went
through all three assessments; the rest left AT&T at some point
(Bray, 1982). This landmark study has had a great impact on
the identification and development of leaders. Its success kindles
thousands of corporate-assessment centers all over the world.

Keeping this longitudinal qualitative and quantitative study
viable in the long term did not hinder Greenleaf from transfer-
ring the results from the research into operational programs and
sharing with others as early as possible. McCollum and Moses
(2009) pointed out that a key finding of MPS is that more
challenging job assignments in one's early career could make
a manager progress faster and further regardless of his or her
assessed potential. Thus, we see the seeds of Greenleaf's deep-
seeded affinity for developing the autonomy of others. Based on
this finding, rotational assignments and formal training were
provided to the participants. Paralleling with MPS, Greenleaf
developed IMDP to provide a framework for manager development during their early years in the company. IMDP integrated
classroom learning with job experiences and contributed to the
development of thousands of managers in AT&T. It continued

---

1   These 26 dimensions were described as 25 attributes in Bray,
Campbell, and Grant (1974) because oral communication skill and
written communication skill were combined as one attribute in Bray
et al. (1974).

for many years after Greenleaf's retirement in 1964 and spawned a new industry in adult learning and development.

Another key finding of MPS, as mentioned by McCollum and Moses (2009), is the strong correlation between assessment-center predictions on participants' managerial potential and the actual progress of the participants. Assessment centers were used to select and develop leaders. By Greenleaf and Bray's idea, the research model of MPS was modified into an operational program in 1958, which soon spread throughout various AT&T subsidiaries (Frick, 2004). IBM, Standard Oil, and Sears were among the first companies that adopted the process of operational-assessment centers after AT&T (McCollum & Moses, 2009). Alverno College, a Catholic liberal-arts women's college, was the first educational institution to integrate assessment centers into an educational curriculum (McCollum & Moses, 2009). Today, assessment centers are widely studied and used in various settings all over the world for identifying and developing potential leaders. As McCollum and Moses pointed out, this is mainly due to Greenleaf's pioneering, prophetic, and foresight-oriented vision regarding human development.

Greenleaf's innovations in human development were radical and remain radical. Bartlett and Ghoshal (2002) described a strategic shift from financial resources to human and intellectual capital in the late 1980s and early 1990s. Without Greenleaf's mental construction through foresight and behavioral, emotional, and spiritual construction through narrative servant leadership, a paradigm shift in the field of management development may not have happened, and certainly would have been dampened. McCollum and Moses (2009) said of Greenleaf's MPS: "among behavioral research conducted over the last 100 years, the Management Progress Study stands out as one of the luminary events in the development of managers" (pp. 104-105). The authors stated that not only through his leadership roles and impact in management development, but also through his embodiment of the concept of empowerment, "Greenleaf left a major mark on contemporary business practices" (p. 108). Greenleaf's modeling of servant leadership not only nurtured this twenty-five-year longitudinal qualitative and quantitative study, but also contributed to its paradigm-shifting fruit.

According to Bray (1982), "the most significant single finding from the Management Progress Study is that success as a manager is highly predictable" (p. 183). Thus the 26 assessment dimensions used by MPS offer a tool to assess abilities, motives, traits, and attitudes and predict potential managers' success. These assessment dimensions include: administrative skills—organizing and planning, decision making, and creativity; interpersonal skills—leadership skills, oral communication skill, behavior flexibility, personal impact, social objectivity, and perceptions of threshold social cues; cognitive skills—general mental ability, range of interest, and written communication skill; stability of performance—tolerance of uncertainty and resistance to stress; work motivation—primacy of work, inner work standards, energy, and self-objectivity; career orientation—need for advancement, need for security, ability to delay gratification, realism of expectations, and Bell System value orientation; dependency—need for superior approval, need for peer approval, and goal flexibility (p. 184).

Two interesting discernments emerge after comparing these 26 dimensions with the 10 characteristics of servant leadership. First, three of the initial four areas of these dimensions—administrative skills, cognitive skills, and stability of performance—resonate with Reynolds' (2014) notion of traditionally masculine aspect of leadership—conceptualization, persuasion, awareness, and foresight. For example, organizing and planning, decision making, and general mental ability relate to conceptualization; leadership skills, oral and written communication skills, and personal impact are necessary for persuasion; while creativity, general mental ability, and tolerance of uncertainty may help generate foresight (Bray, 1982; Reynolds, 2014). Meanwhile, interpersonal skills, including social objectivity (the degree of being free from prejudices) and perceptions of threshold social cues are associated with more circular or feminine attributes such as awareness listening, healing, empathy, commitment to the growth of others, and community building (Bray, 1982; Reynolds, 2014).

Second, the next three areas of the MPS' assessment dimensions—work motivation, career orientation, and dependency—relate to personal motivation and needs, rather than the needs of others as embodied in servant leadership's characteristics of stewardship, commitment to others' growth, and building community (Bray, 1982). Throughout MPS' 26 dimensions, listening, empathy, and healing are less noticeable, but were likely subtle yet present in successful mentoring of future servant-leaders (Bray, 1982). For instance, in the case of oral and written communication skills in MPS, the goal was to convey information and thus persuade others, rather than articulating the element of listening with openness as a key element (Bray, 1982). After AT&T, Greenleaf further developed his understanding of the servant leader. Therefore, we found it likely that the notions of listening, empathy, and healing were present to him, but not yet fully articulated. For example, being that the six distinguishing characteristics of servant leadership—the more feminine aspect of leadership (Reynolds, 2014)—are present, but not specifically named in the MPS' assessment dimensions, we see Greenleaf's personal growth in later life lending to the growth of others in more unified and far-reaching ways. Greenleaf's later developments in servant leadership, after he left the corporate environment, appear to have bloomed in the direction of the greater gender balance found in the 10 characteristics of servant leadership.

As Bray (1982) pointed out, MPS has its own historical and social limitations, such as women and members of minority groups not being included. Bray questioned whether the characteristics underlying their successful performance would be different from the ones for white males. Yes, Greenleaf's vision of servant leadership was far ahead of his time; and yes, it was also bound by blind spots associated with the dominant white and male corporate culture of his day. The 10 characteristics that eventually showed the symbolic wholeness of servant leadership as a more rounded and holistic female-honoring and male-honoring form of leadership are abstract principles, hard to measure, and even more difficult to embody. Greenleaf (2003) himself offered a practical example of a fictional character in his writing "Teacher as Servant." Through the story of Mr. Billings, Greenleaf portrayed a true servant leader, who cares deeply about his students, nurtures the servant motive in them, and lives out his beliefs. Therefore, the quest to be a servant leader, like the quest to be an authentic and whole person, sustains itself in commitment to seek to understand life in all its mystery, abundance, and grace—tested in the furnace of human relations.

Essential Understandings

In this chapter, we reviewed six qualitative studies and discussed servant leadership essence around six themes: (a) servant leadership, empathy, and healing; (b) servant leadership and gender balance; (c) servant leadership and foresight; (d) servant leadership and corporate responsibility; (e) servant leadership, forgiveness, and reconciliation; and (f) servant leadership and Greenleaf's modeling. These essential themes of servant leadership, interwoven with one another, give us a more in depth and more enriched understanding of qualitative research of servant leadership.

Greenleaf, in leading others to transcend the human furnace through listening and grace, through gentle strength and unique wisdom, was imperfect, a man with feet of clay, a devoted husband, father, and friend. He was not unlike the rest of us: imbued with gifts and faults. That said, he was, in the truest sense, a believer: one who believes. In his explication of the Frost

(1947) poem "Directive," one of the very latest writings of his life, he again warns against the too rational mind:

> Those of us who undertake the journey must accept that, simply by living in the contemporary world and making our peace with it as it is, we may be involved in a way that blocks our growth. Primitive people may have suffered much from their environment, but they were not alienated; the Lascaux cave paintings attest to this. They probably did not articulate a theology, but they may have been religious in the basic sense of "bound to the cosmos." With us, sophistication, rationality, greater mastery of the immediate environment have taken their toll in terms of a tragic separation from the opportunity for religious experience, that is, growth in the feeling of being bound to the cosmos. (Greenleaf, 2002, p. 330)

Greenleaf calls servant-leaders to follow wise people, guides who have in mind the opportunity to be lost, to lose oneself, in order to be found, in order to find oneself. Qualitative studies take us into the powerful gravity of human experience, laced as it is with losses beyond our comprehension, in order to gain greater compassion, greater fullness, and greater wholeness with others. Greenleaf (2002) speaks beautifully of our need to be humble and to be willingly lost:

> We already feel lost. Why then would we want a guide who only has at heart our getting lost?
>
> This is the ground on which the great religious traditions of the world have always stood. The tradition built around the ministry of Jesus of Nazareth, the one in which I grew up and which has the greatest symbolic meaning to me now, seems especially emphatic on this point. Jesus seemed only to have at heart our getting lost; he was mostly concerned with what must be taken away rather than with what would be gained. We find clues to what must be lost in such sayings as "Unless you turn and become like children you will never enter the kingdom of heaven," "It is easier for a camel to go through

the eye of a needle than for a rich man to enter the kingdom," "Cleanse the inside of the cup, that the outside also may be clean," and "Unless one is born anew, he cannot see the kingdom of God."

A few general terms describe what will be received: heaven, eternal life, salvation, the kingdom of God. The believers of the literal word know what these terms mean; they have to. But seekers who are responding to symbols don't know, don't have to know, wouldn't be helped by knowing. They are not too interested in meaning as bounded by the vagaries of language. Rather they seek a guide who only has at heart their getting lost. (p. 331)

Those who lead us into a blessed sense of being lost—lost in love, lost in service to others—lead us to the kind of servant leadership Greenleaf envisioned. Having escaped the ever-indulgent desires of ego, need, power, and ambition, we are free to be lost in the best sense of being lost.

Lost, we are found.

Greenleaf (2002) reminds us the journey is beautiful, and fraught with suffering. Servant-leaders are required to help guide us into the most ultimate sense of what it means to be a person who lives with and for others.

To be on with the journey one must have an attitude toward loss and being lost, a view of oneself in which powerful symbols like *burned, dissolved, broken off*—however painful their impact is seen to be—do not appear as senseless or destructive. Rather the losses they suggest are seen as opening the way for new creative acts, for the receiving of priceless gifts. Loss, *every loss one's mind can conceive of,* creates a vacuum into which will come (if allowed) something new and fresh and beautiful, something unforeseen—and the greatest of these is *love.* (pp. 339-340, emphasis in original)

Chapter 3 References

Bao, J. (1987). Yin yang xue shuo yu fu nv di wei [The idea of *yin-yang* and women's status in China]. *Han Xue Yan Jiu,* *5*(2), 501-512. Retrieved from http://ccsdb.ncl.edu.tw/ccs/ image/01_005_002_01_07.pdf

Bartlett, C. A., & Ghoshal, S. (2002). Building competitive advantage through people. *MIT Sloan Management Review, 43*(2), 34-41.

Blowfield, M., & Murray, A. (2008). *Corporate responsibility: A critical introduction.* New York, NY: Oxford University Press.

Bray, D. W. (1982). The assessment center and the study of lives. *American Psychologist, 37*(2), 180-189.

Bray, D. W., Campbell, R. J., & Grant, D. L. (1974). *Formative years in business: A long-term AT&T study of managerial lives.* New York, NY: John Wiley & Sons.

Brouneus, K. (2007). Reconciliation and development. *Dialogue on Globalization,* (Occasional paper N° 36), 3-19. Retrieved from http://library.fes.de/pdf-files/iez/04999.pdf

Campbell, A. (2017). Forgiveness and reconciliation as an organizational leadership competency within transitional justice instruments. *The International Journal of Servant-Leadership, 11*(1), 139-186.

Covey, S. R. (1998). Foreword: Servant-leadership from the inside out. In L. C. Spears (Ed.), *Insights on leadership: Service, stewardship, spirit, and servant-leadership* (pp. xi-xviii). New York, NY: John Wiley & Sons.

Covey, S. R. (2002). Foreword. In L. C. Spears (Ed.), *Servant leadership: A journey into the nature of legitimate power and greatness* (25th anniversary ed., pp. 1-13). New York, NY: Paulist Press.

Crotty, M. (1998). *The foundations of social research: Meaning and perspective in the research process.* London, England: Sage.

Denzin, N. K., & Lincoln, Y. S. (2011). Introduction: The discipline and practice of qualitative research. In N. K. Denzin & Y. S.

Lincoln (Eds.), *The Sage handbook of qualitative research* (4th ed., pp. 1-20). Los Angeles, CA: Sage.

Eicher-Catt, D. (2005). The myth of servant-leadership: A feminist perspective. *Women and Language, 28*(1), 17-25.

Enright, R. D., Freedman, S., & Rique, J. (1998). The psychology of interpersonal forgiveness. In R. D. Enright & J. North (Eds.), *Exploring forgiveness* (pp. 46-62). Madison, WI: The University of Wisconsin Press.

Ferch, S. R. (2005). Servant-leadership, forgiveness, and social justice. *The International Journal of Servant-Leadership, 1*(1), 97-113.

Frick, D. M. (2004). *Robert K. Greenleaf: A life of servant leadership.* San Francisco, CA: Berrett-Koehler.

Frost, R. (1947). *Steeple bush.* New York, NY: Henry Holt and Company.

Gadamer, H. (1976). *Philosophical hermeneutics* (D. E. Linge Trans. & Ed.). Berkeley, CA: University of California Press.

Gadamer, H. (2004). *Truth and method* (J. Weinsheimer & D. G. Marshall Trans.). (2nd, rev. ed.). London, England: Continuum. (Original work published 1975)

Greenleaf, R. K. (1996a). *On becoming a servant-leader.* D. M. Frick & L. C. Spears (Eds.). San Francisco, CA: Jossey-Bass.

Greenleaf, R. K. (1996b). *Seeker and servant: Reflections on religious leadership.* A. T. Fraker & L. C. Spears (Eds.). San Francisco, CA: Jossey-Bass.

Greenleaf, R. K. (1998). *The power of servant-leadership: Essays.* L. C. Spears (Ed.). San Francisco, CA: Berrett-Koehler.

Greenleaf, R. K. (2002). *Servant leadership: A journey into the nature of legitimate power and greatness* (25th anniversary ed.). L. C. Spears (Ed.). New York, NY: Paulist Press. (Original work published 1977)

Greenleaf, R. K. (2003). *The servant-leader within: A transformative path.* H. Beazley, J. Beggs, & L. C. Spears (Eds.). New York, NY: Paulist Press.

Heidegger, M. (1962). *Being and time* (J. Macquarrie & E. Robinson Trans.). Malden, MA: Blackwell.

Hu, J., & Liden, R. C. (2011). Antecedents of team potency and team effectiveness: An examination of goal and process clarity and servant leadership. *Journal of Applied Psychology, 96*(4), 851-862. doi:10.1037/a0022465

Husserl, E. (1970). *The crisis of European sciences and transcendental phenomenology: An introduction to phenomenological philosophy* (D. Carr Trans.). Evanston, IL: Northwestern University Press.

Kincaid, M. (2017). Sticky like butter: The language surrounding corporate social responsibility is uninspiring and therefore not embraced. *The International Journal of Servant-Leadership, 11*(1), 257-276.

Lao Tzu. (2005). *Tao teh ching.* J. C. H. Wu (Ed. & Trans.). Boston, MA: Shambhala.

Liden, R. C., Fu, P., Liu, J., & Song, L. (2016). The influence of CEO values and leadership on middle manager exchange behaviors: A longitudinal multilevel examination. *Nankai Business Review International, 7*(1), 2-20. doi:10.1108/NBRI-12-2015-0031

Liden, R. C., Wayne, S. J., Liao, C., & Meuser, J. D. (2014). Servant leadership and serving culture: Influence on individual and unit performance. *Academy of Management Journal, 57*(5), 1434-1452. doi:10.5465/amj.2013.0034

Liden, R. C., Wayne, S. J., Meuser, J. D., Hu, J., Wu, J., & Liao, C. (2015). Servant leadership: Validation of a short form of the SL-28. *The Leadership Quarterly, 26*(2), 254-269. doi:10.1016/j.leaqua.2014.12.002

Liden, R. C., Wayne, S. J., Zhao, H., & Henderson, D. (2008). Servant leadership: Development of a multidimensional measure and multi-level assessment. *The Leadership Quarterly, 19*(2), 161-177. doi:10.1016/j.leaqua.2008.01.006

Lopez, K. A., & Willis, D. G. (2004). Descriptive versus interpretive phenomenology: Their contributions to nursing knowledge. *Qualitative Health Research, 14*(5), 726-735. doi:10.1177/1049732304263638

Maathai, W. (2004). Nobel lecture. Retrieved from https://www.nobelprize.org/nobel_prizes/peace/laureates/2004/maathai-lecture-text.html

Matesi, L. M. (2013a). The significance of foresight in vision and narrative leadership. *The International Journal of Servant-Leadership, 8/9*(1), 71-86.

Matesi, L. M. (2013b). *Vision and foresight as narrated by Nobel Peace laureates* (Doctoral dissertation). Retrieved from http://foley.gonzaga.edu/

McCollum, J., & Moses, J. (2009). The management development legacy of Robert Greenleaf. *The International Journal of Servant-Leadership, 5*(1), 97-110.

Panaccio, A., Henderson, D. J., Liden, R. C., Wayne, S. J., & Cao, X. (2015). Toward an understanding of when and why servant leadership accounts for employee extra-role behaviors. *Journal of Business and Psychology, 30*(4), 657-675. doi:10.1007/s10869-014-9388-z

Ramsey, I. M. (2003). *The role of empathy in facilitating forgiveness: The lived experience of six political perpetrators in South Africa* (Doctoral dissertation). Retrieved from http://foley.gonzaga.edu/

Ramsey, I. M. (2006). Servant-leadership and unconditional forgiveness: The lives of six South African perpetrators. *The International Journal of Servant-Leadership, 2*(1), 113-139.

Reynolds, K. (2013). *Gender differences in messages of commencement addresses delivered by Fortune 1000 business leaders: A content analysis informed by servant-leadership and the feminist ethic of care* (Doctoral dissertation). Retrieved from http://foley.gonzaga.edu/

Reynolds, K. (2014). Servant-leadership: A feminist perspective. *The International Journal of Servant-Leadership, 10*(1), 35-63.

Ricoeur, P. (1981). *Hermeneutics and the human sciences: Essays on language, action, and interpretation* (J. B. Thompson Trans. & Ed.). Cambridge, England: Cambridge University Press.

Sashkin, M. (2004). Transformational leadership approaches: A review and synthesis. In J. Antonakis, A. T. Cianciolo, & R.

J. Sternberg (Eds.), *The nature of leadership* (pp. 171-196). Thousand Oaks, CA: Sage.

Shaffic, O. (Ed.). (2015). Forgiveness: Unveiling an asset for peace-building. Retrieved from http://refugeelawproject.org/files/others/Forgiveness_research_report.pdf

Sima, Q. (1993). *Records of the grand historian: Han dynasty II* (B. Watson Trans.). (Revised ed.). Hong Kong, China: Columbia University Press.

Sousa, M., & van Dierendonck, D. (2016). Introducing a short measure of shared servant leadership impacting team performance through team behavioral integration. *Frontiers in Psychology, 6,* 1-12. doi:10.3389/fpsyg.2015.02002

Sousa, M., & van Dierendonck, D. (2017a). Servant-leaders as underestimators: Theoretical and practical implications. *Leadership & Organization Development Journal, 38*(2), 270-283. doi:10.1108/LODJ-10-2015-0236

Sousa, M., & van Dierendonck, D. (2017b). Servant leadership and the effect of the interaction between humility, action, and hierarchical power on follower engagement. *Journal of Business Ethics, 141*(1), 13-25. doi:10.1007/s10551-015-2725-y

Spears, L. C. (2002). Introduction: Tracing the past, present, and future of servant-leadership. In L. C. Spears & M. Lawrence (Eds.), *Focus on leadership: Servant-leadership for the twenty-first century* (pp. 1-16). New York, NY: Wiley.

Spears, L. C. (2010). Character and servant leadership: Ten characteristics of effective, caring leaders. *The Journal of Virtues & Leadership, 1*(1), 25-30.

Tutu, D. (1999). *No future without forgiveness.* New York, NY: Doubleday.

Unschuld, P. U., Tessenow, H., & Zheng, J. (Eds. & Trans.). (2011). *Huang Di nei jing su wen: An annotated translation of Huang Di's inner classic—basic questions* (Vol. 1). Berkeley, CA: University of California Press.

van Dierendonck, D., & Nuijten, I. (2011). The servant leadership survey: Development and validation of a multidimensional measure. *Journal of Business and Psychology, 26*(3), 249-267. doi:10.1007/s10869-010-9194-1

van Dierendonck, D., Sousa, M., Gunnarsdóttir, S., Bobbio, A., Hakanen, J., Pircher Verdorfer, A., ... Rodriguez-Carvajal, R. (2017). The cross-cultural invariance of the servant leadership survey: A comparative study across eight countries. *Administrative Sciences, 7*(2), 1-11. doi:10.3390/admsci7020008

van Dierendonck, D., Stam, D., Boersma, P., de Windt, N., & Alkema, J. (2014). Same difference? Exploring the differential mechanisms linking servant leadership and transformational leadership to follower outcomes. *The Leadership Quarterly, 25*(3), 544–562. doi:10.1016/j.leaqua.2013.11.014

van Manen, M. (1990). *Researching lived experience: Human science for an action sensitive pedagogy.* Albany, NY: SUNY.

van Manen, M. (2016). *Phenomenology of practice.* London, England: Routledge.

Worthington, E. L. (2006). *Forgiveness and reconciliation: Theory and application.* New York, NY: Routledge.

Yergler, J. D. (2005). Servant leadership, justice and forgiveness. Retrieved from http://www.refresher.com/Archives/!jdyservant.html

Chapter 4

Servant Leadership Translated Across Cultures: Emerging Scholarship and Practice

Betty J. Overton & Alan J. Carter, Sr.

SCHOLARS HAVE LONG RECOGNIZED THAT LEADERSHIP THE-
ories and practices grow out of particular cultural contexts and,
to become meaningful cross culturally, these theories must transcend their cultural moorings to gain acceptance and usefulness
in diverse settings. Schein (2004) notes that the connections
between leadership and culture are the most debated subjects
in management literature. Indeed, these debates focused on culture and leadership, both hard to pin down concepts, are often
framed in relation to helping scholars and practitioners think
about how different cultures give meaning to work relationships
across various leadership environments. But there is no debate
that leadership is contextual, and as the world becomes increasingly connected, the interest in examining the commonalities
and sometimes the differences in leadership practices is a necessary means to learn from them, use them, mitigate issues, con-
solidate practice, and even eliminate those practices that are not
helpful in serving a world marketplace of more interconnected
global relations. Some scholars (Chin, Tremble, & Garcia, 2018;
Day & Antonakis, 2012) suggest that this connection between
leadership and culture gets inadequate attention, at least in the
widely used leadership textbooks and other publications, and
the interplay between leadership and culture gets relegated to
special-topics considerations on the periphery of the discipline.

They advocate for greater inclusion of social and cultural context as focal points for leadership study.

Servant leadership, we suggest in this chapter, as both theory and practice, has actually been fairly successful in spanning cultural borders. The reason for this success may be found in what researchers (Laub, 1999; Liden, 2008; Reed, 2011; Barbuto and Wheeler, 2006) identify as the essential components of the theory—egalitarianism, moral integrity, empowering and developing of others, empathy, humility, and creating value for community. They see these elements as being the precise elements that serve as touchstones to other cultural realities and position servant leadership for global adoption. Mittal and Dorfman (2012) suggest that current models of servant leadership are anchored in "the human drive to bond with others and contribute to the betterment of the society" (p. 555). In an increasingly interconnected world, this focus seems to transcend cultural idiosyncrasies and give rise to adaptations of those theoretical essentials embedded in the theory, linking them to universal principles and beliefs that undergird culture around the globe. At the same time that servant leadership researchers and practitioners have been touting its transcendent, universal features, another social change has also been occurring. Growing attention has also been given to the recognition and respect for cultural differences in leadership, and a substantial body of work is emerging examining this diversity of perspectives produced by cultures and the benefits of this diversity (Hofstede, 2001). We are discovering that difference can be good, and that not all leaders need to act like models of Western-leadership-development schools. These two streams—finding commonalities and honoring difference—produce a complex picture of the ways in which culture and leadership comingle in modern society.

This chapter is intended to focus on servant leadership as it gets manifested in various cultural settings. It is an attempt to interrogate the literature emerging about these different cultural manifestations and to ask what does the scholarship tell us

about servant leadership's reception, adoption, and use in different cultural settings, and how does applying a cultural lens to
servant leadership modify or amplify our understanding of the
theory and its practice? If the world is flat as Thomas Friedman
(2005) suggests and the new globalization is having an impact
on organizations throughout the world, certainly attention must
turn to how these evolving organizational cultures are having an
influence on what we are learning about leadership and leading. Modern organizational leaders across all sectors will need to
understand the work in culturally diverse environments where
concepts of leadership will be significantly determinant to organizational outcomes and effectiveness.

As we begin this discussion, it is important that we share
how are we defining culture. As with leadership, culture has a
number of definitions. A central theme of these definitions is
a focus on the attitudes and knowledge that a group of people
come to know or absorb through living within a particular historic, geographic, social, and political environment. Culture, as
we understand it, is all of those things we often unknowingly or
unconsciously take on and act out of based on the social environments we are born into or adopt. Our religious beliefs, language, and food preferences are products of our cultural milieus,
but also our attitudes about work, time, gendered roles, and
views about leaders are linked to what we absorb most often
unconsciously as lived experiences within cultural (and subcultural) environments. Hofstede (2001), well known for his work
in classifying work-related cultural frameworks, defines culture
as a term that encompasses all of a society's norming attitudes,
behaviors, and traditions. He suggests:

> Culture could be defined as the interactive aggregate of com-
> mon characteristics that influence a human group's response
> to its environment. Culture determines the uniqueness of a
> human group in the same way personality determines the
> uniqueness of an individual. (Hofstede, 2001, pp. 550-551)

This notion that individuals learn a way of thinking and behavior and these attitudes influence how they see and function in the world grounds the importance of our cultural perspectives, not just about leadership, but in all aspects of our existence. Culture is an important shaping tool for societies and provides them their identities and cohesion. While cultural perspectives can change or alter, their role in influencing our beliefs and actions is significant in shaping our actions as either leaders or followers. While culture has a norming role, we acknowledge that within major cultural groups there may exist many subcultures as variants or extensions of dominant cultural messages. These too have to be taken into consideration in any discussion of culture. With this definitional framing, we can understand why the role of culture would be important to organizations and important to those who lead within or across various cultural settings. Organizations and leaders are created in and often for a particular culture and are part of the fabric of that cultural environment.

In this paper, we also use the term cross cultural. As with culture, there are multiple definitions of cross cultural, and especially cross-cultural leadership. Smith and Peterson (2001) remind us that the term is sometimes used interchangeably with "international leadership." In their work entitled "Cross Cultural Leadership," they acknowledge that most leadership studies over the last 50 years have come out of the United States and therefore, studies that examine leadership outside the context of this venue are seen as "cross cultural" or spanning the normative American frame for leadership. This highly hegemonic view is reason enough for looking at this topic. The other use of the term cross cultural is assigned to the study of organizational teams whose make up is multicultural. In this chapter, our use of cross cultural leadership means that leadership that involves the examination of leadership practices that operates outside a U.S.-dominated contextual framing. For the most part, that points to consideration of leadership outside the North American continent, but there is also room within our framing for considering contexts within the U.S. that may be countercultural to traditional models and emerge from subcultural reconstructions of traditional leadership models.

Leadership itself emerges in a context of culture. A consideration of culture, therefore, is important as scholars' study how leadership theories and practices operate in and translate across cultural borders. Trompenaars and Voerman (2010) tell us that "the question of what makes someone a leader is answered differently by different cultures" (p. 46), and this influence should not be underestimated. Hofstede's research, as one example, provides important foundational work used by the leadership community in exploring how we understand the impact of cultural values on both individuals and organizations. From his longitudinal studies have come substantial cross-cultural findings which serve as benchmarks for the instructive cultural studies that are a growing part of leadership research. As noted earlier, with the expansion of globalization, the amount of attention to issues of culture and leadership has spread. Although the scholarship in this area is still sparse, it is becoming more central to the interests in the field because of the need to learn from the varied experiences accumulating in different cultural settings, and to mine these experiences so we all benefit.

Servant leadership and culture

Servant leadership, like other leadership theories and models, evolved out of a particular cultural context. Despite attempts by some to emphasize its origins in the images of the Eastern philosophies and Christian teachings, Greenleaf, its originator, was most strongly influenced by his longstanding research and observations within traditional Western culture, and more specifically American culture. While it is clear that his own cultural beliefs helped shape the theory, its roots in Western culture is clear. The uniqueness of servant leadership is about how Greenleaf chose to focus, not on the power of the leader, but on the leader's choice to serve those being led. The service motivation of servant leadership is the major framework for this popular theory and stands as a counter voice to traditional leadership options which offer a more hierarchical model (Spears, 2004). Servant leadership and its establishment of the "leader as servant" is the only leadership theory with the specific focus on the leader in an identified role in service to the followers. The "servant" approach, heavily reliant on human relations and what may be seen as a de-emphasis on the leader's power and influence in preference for a more nuanced role that some cultures could dismiss as "leading." Servant leadership's unique focus may be a partial reason why the theory has gained attention and is being applied in many cross-cultural settings. The popularity of servant leadership within the business community in a number of countries may have also benefited because servant leadership seems less focused on self-centered outcomes. Liden, Waynes, Zhao, and Henderson (2008) note, "With confidence shaken in business leadership, interest has been increasing in the development of leaders (globally) who set aside self-interest for the betterment of their followers and organizations" (p161). But this "servant approach" may also offer the theory's most serious challenge as it spans global communities. Can cultures in which a "great man" model of leadership still dominates embrace servant leadership's service motif? Is the "service" model demeaning to the cultural picture of leading in some environments, and can the essential components of servant leadership mentioned earlier—egalitarianism, empowerment and development of others, and creating value for community, and others—sufficiently "sell" this model as a viable alternative to culturally inspired models? In fact, the challenges to the theory's cross-culture attraction came early and on its home ground. Many in the African American community were slow to embrace the idea of servant leadership. The major launch of servant leadership coincided with the Civil Rights

Movement, and the conceptualization of "servant" and "service" was too closely associated with the servant status of this cultural subgroup who were actively trying at the time to demand access to the power seats of the society. The language and construct of servant leadership seemed as if it were asking this group to give up a relationship to power in leadership for a "weaker" leadership model than that held by those who the group still identified as the oppressor. While this initial conceptualization has evolved for most, it is a recognition that the cultural histories of some people may not always have them eager to embrace servant leadership for many reasons. Scholars studying this area must ask whether there are other features of the model that cause cultural groups to question the theory's applicability to their unique historical context. The role of the servant leadership scholar is to understand how servant leadership is received, interpreted, and used across different cultural expressions.

The scholarship of servant leadership

An examination of the scholarly works on the topic of servant leadership requires a set of cross-culturally accepted components grounded in both the historic and evolving understandings of the theory. In the United States, the early work of Robert Greenleaf (1904-1990) in the early sixties and the continued intellectual developmental work of The Greenleaf Center set servant leadership apart from the nebulous generalized definition Sen Sendjaya (2015) once provided to an undergraduate leadership class: "Leadership is ubiquitous and elusive" (p. 15)! Greenleaf (2017) distinguished servant leadership from other leadership theories by extricating the conceptual framework of servant leadership from organizational performance and refocusing on the picture of the servant-leader as an agent of holistic moral and ethical development of followers, what we identified as the empowerment and development of others (Sendjaya, 2015).

Subsequent to the establishment of the moral and ethical underpinnings of servant leadership (and somewhat paradoxically), scholarly activity and pursuit of publication of research on servant leadership was somewhat hampered "as critics debate[d] whether this new leadership theory is significant, distinct, viable, and valuable for organizational success" (Parris & Peachey, 2012, abs.), which should not be surprising given Greenleaf (1977) himself conceded the unorthodox nature of servant leadership would contribute to difficulty regarding its operationalization as "it is meant to be neither a scholarly treatise nor a how-to-do-it manual" (p. 49). Nevertheless, proponents encouraging the academic acceptance of servant leadership and its adoption within organization theory clearly recognized the need for substantial empirical research, which Russell & Stone (2002) hoped to facilitate through a literature study that identified both functional behaviors and accompanying attributes of servant leadership in order to "provide the basis for a model of servant leadership, which in turn provides the structural foundation for research regarding the theory, as well as direction for practical implementation" (p. 153).

Parris and Peachey (2012) conducted a systematic literature review of servant leadership theory which, in addition to identifying the work of Russel and Stone (2002) and Barbuto and Wheeler (2006), was (according to the authors) the "first review to provide a synthesis, based upon evidence in peer-reviewed journals, of empirical studies on servant leadership theory in organizations" (p. 380). Their review identified a first-level sample of 255 articles, of which 39 empirical studies (published in 27 separate peer-reviewed journals) met their inclusion criteria.

Consistent with Greenleaf's (1977) prediction, their review of 39 studies concluded: "Leadership theory remains under-defined with no consensus in its definition or theoretical framework. Scholars are still seeking to articulate Greenleaf's conceptualization of servant leadership by using a variety of definitions sourced from multiple works" (p. 384-385). While the above conclusion might appear to work at odds with the purposes of this chapter regarding servant leadership research in cross-cultural contexts, the authors noted that:

> Our sample illustrates servant leadership theory is being studied across cultures, contexts, and across a diversity of research foci. Overall, the sample consisted of studies in 11 countries, which included four cross-cultures studies. These findings demonstrate that servant leadership is being practiced in various cultures, specifically: U.S. (n = 23), Canada (n = 4), China (n = 2), Turkey (n = 2), Indonesia (n = 1), New Zealand (n = 1), Kenya (n = 1), and the Republic of Trinidad (n = 1), with five cross-culture studies comparing U.S. and Ghana, U.S. and UK, U.S. and China (n = 2), and Indonesia and Australia (p. 385).

It is important to note before going further that Greenleaf (1977) introduced the concept of servant leadership, which he claimed was not in a scholarly form or defined in terms of recommended application. Servant leadership, nonetheless, continued to gain strength as a potential academically accepted theory of leadership. Greenleaf's (1977) reluctance to establish research parameters or operationalizing recommendations opened the door for subsequent researchers to develop multiple definitions and study considerations comprising characteristic servant leadership behaviors and supporting attributes. Nevertheless, although perhaps not strictly adhering to Larry Spears' (1998), CEO of the Greenleaf Center, list of ten major attributes of servant leadership, research continued to the point that Parris and Peachey (2012) were able to identify the application of servant leadership in numerous cultures outside of the United States.

Additional progress regarding research on servant leadership has been the development of several servant leadership measurement instruments, including: Page & Wong, (2000); the Servant Leadership Assessment Instrument, "SLAI" (Dennis, & Bocarnea, 2005); the Servant Leadership Behavior Scale, "SLBS"

(Sendjaya, Sarros, & Santora 2007); the Servant Leadership 28, "SL28" (Linden, et.al. 2008); and the Servant Leadership Survey, (SLS) (van Dierendonck & Nuijten, 2010), of which the SLS has been validated within multiple cross-cultural contexts, (Rodriguez-Carvajal, et.al., 2014), (Van Dierendonck, et. al., 2017).

There is an old adage that what is not measured cannot be managed. If this is correct, then the development of servant leadership measurement instruments is a profound step forward in operationalizing the characteristics of servant leadership in a manner that they might be tested in real-world organizational environments. The purpose of this chapter is to focus on the operationalization of servant leadership in cross-cultural contexts. This heightens the importance of validating the reliability of a measurement instrument (such as the SLS) in languages other than English. Doing so permits researchers to study the applicability (and perhaps non-applicability) of individual or collective characteristics of servant leadership in countries other than the United States, U.K., Canada, Australia, and other native English-speaking cultures, leading to greater diversification of reporting on the model and understandings its effectiveness in organizations who can benefit from it.

Of further interest is scholarship regarding the acceptance and/or preference of servant leadership as a culturally appropriate management style such that it rises to the level of cultural expectation of cross-cultural and cross-national leadership effectiveness and organizational success (Van Dierendonck, et. al., 2017).

As noted earlier, there is an increasing number of leadership researchers beginning to examine the relationship between leadership and culture. However, the most significant cross-cultural study of leadership has been the Globe Leadership and Organizational Behavior Effectiveness Project, begun in 1991 by Robert House. GLOBE represents a twenty-year, multi-phase, multi-method, multi-sample research effort, the objectives and findings of which were released in three separate publications:

Culture, Leadership, and Organizations: The GLOBE Study of 62 Societies (House, et.al., 2004); *Culture and Leadership Across the World: The GLOBE Book of In-Depth Studies of 25 Societies* (Chhokar, Brodbeck & House, 2007); and *Strategic Leadership Across Cultures: The GLOBE Study of CEO Leadership Behavior and Effectiveness in 24 Countries* (House, et al., 2014). While a number of cross-cultural studies have been pursued since GLOBE many of them use data derived from the GLOBE outcomes. "The central proposition in GLOBE's research is that the attributes and characteristics that differentiate societal cultures from each other may also suggest organizational practices and leader attributes/behaviors that will be frequently enacted and effective in that culture" (House, 2014, p. 5).

For purposes of their work, GLOBE defined culture as: "Shared motives, values, beliefs, identities, and interpretations or meanings of significant events that result from common experiences of members of collectives that are transmitted across generations" (GLOBE, 2004). The 2004 project report comprised the culmination of an initial ten-year quantitative survey-based study of data received from 17,300 middle managers in 951 organizations across 62 countries, which yielded nine cultural dimensions reflecting cultural values and practices within each of the countries: Performance Orientation; Assertiveness; Future Orientation; Humane Orientation; Institutional Collectivism; In-Group Collectivism; Gender Egalitarianism; Power Distance; and Uncertainty Avoidance.

Defining leadership "as the ability of an individual to influence, motivate, and enable others to contribute toward the effectiveness and success of the organizations of which they are members" (House et al, 2004), the researchers applied implicit leadership theory (Lord & Maher, 1991) to national culture to test whether different societies have different leader expectations affected by cultural values. Data analysis from a questionnaire comprising 112 leader attributes and behaviors resulted in 21 primary dimensions of leadership, from which a second-order factor analysis yielded 6 global leadership dimensions: Charismatic/Value Based Leadership; Team-Oriented Leadership; Participative Leadership; Humane Oriented Leadership; Autonomous Leadership; and Self-Protective Leadership. One further important feature of the GLOBE project was their division of the 62 countries into cross-cultural clusters for purposes of examining differences between cultures regarding leadership dimensions.

GLOBE sparked a number of other studies, some focused more generically, and some began to pin down specific models on leadership as they found cross-cultural adoption. Winston and Ryan (2008) looked specifically at servant leadership as an organizational model. They reported anecdotal evidence that their initial attempts to engage non-U.S. audiences regarding servant leadership was met with rejection because it was viewed as a Western construct of value only to Western organizations. However, they took issue with these out-of-hand rejections and reframed their work on servant leadership in the context of the GLOBE Humane Oriented Leadership Global Dimension. In doing so, they provided additional support for their contention that servant leadership and Humane Orientation were similar constructs and they sought to examine a number of cross-cultural ideals which mirror those of the servant leader. Included in their paper were *Ubuntu and Harambee* from Africa; *Taoism and Confucianism* from East Asia; *Jewish Tradition* in the Mediterranean; and *Hindu* teachings about compassion and generosity from India. The authors conclude the following:

> This article used the GLOBE study construct of humane orientation […] Specific attention was given to the leader characteristics of humility, care, concern, benevolence, altruism, service, fairness, and friendship related definitions of love. All of these characteristics are part of the servant leadership concept, and the overlap between servant leadership and the global acceptance of the humane orientation is evidence that servant leadership can be presented as a global rather than a

Western concept. (p. 221)The continuing difficulty in defining the characteristics of servant leadership and the GLOBE project yielded no straightforward classification of servant leadership on any of the GLOBE dimensions. That said, researchers have observed that both the Humane Cultural Orientation and Humane Oriented Leadership dimension favorably relate to specific characteristics of servant leadership. GLOBE defines the Humane Cultural Orientation as: "The degree to which a collective encourages and rewards (and should encourage and reward) individuals for being fair, altruistic, generous, caring, and kind to others" (House, 2004); and Humane-Oriented Leadership as reflecting "supportive and considerate leadership and includes compassion and generosity. This leadership dimension includes two primary leadership dimensions labeled (a) modesty and (b) humane orientation" (House, 2004). These dimensions track well with Spears' characteristics of servant leadership and have been found to map consistently with correlations among the cultural values and aspects of servant leadership found in more recent studies (Mittal & Dorfman, 2012).

Although the 21 primary dimensions of leadership from GLOBE Phase 1 and Phase 2 are not exact matches to the 10 characteristics of servant leadership outlined by Larry Spears (2004), a comparison between the two lists reflects an association between 9 (positively related dimensions) of the 21 Leadership Dimensions and Spears' (2004) 10 servant leadership characteristics:

GLOBE Phase 1 and Phase 2 Primary Leadership Dimensions (Phase 2 – 5/27/2004)	Characteristics of the Servant-leader (Spears, 2004, p. 2-4)
Visionary*, Inspirational*, Self-Sacrificial*, Integrity*, Decisive*, Performance Oriented*, Collaborative-Team Orientated*, Team Integrator, Diplomatic*, Malevolent, Administratively Competent*, Participative*, Autocratic, Modesty*, Humane Orientation*, Autonomous, Self-Centered, Status Conscious, Internally Competitive, Face-Saver, Bureaucratic	Listening, EmpathyHealing, Awareness, Persuasion, Conceptualization, Foresight, Stewardship, Commitment to Growth of People, Building Community, Collaborative-Team Orientated, Humane Orientation Inspirational, Integrity, Diplomatic, Visionary, Visionary, Self-Sacrificial, Participative, Team Integrator
indicates GLOBE assessment to be positive	

In 2004, GLOBE reported results from Phase 3, which comprised in-depth qualitative and quantitative research in 25 societal cultures regarding these societies enactment of highly effective leadership, dedicating an individual chapter of the report for each country (Chhokar, Brodbeck, & House, 2004). In 2014, House, et.al. published *Strategic Leadership Across Cultures,* which focused on the relationship of national culture to CEO leadership in 24 specific countries measuring CEO behavior against six global dimensions: Charismatic, Team Oriented, Participative, Humane Oriented, Autonomous, and Self-Protective. The study examined CEO effectiveness against internal and external measures of effectiveness comprising Top Management Team (TMT) Dedication and Firm Competitiveness. The researchers discovered the following:

> The global CEO Charismatic leadership behavior is consistently the most impactful leadership behavior on TMT

Dedication. CEO Team-Oriented behavior is the next most important and then followed by Humane-Oriented leadership behaviors. Participative leadership is moderately important. [...] Humane-Oriented leadership was particularly important for TMT Commitment. (House, 2014, p. 260)

Regarding Firm Competitive Performance, Charismatic Leadership ranked highest, followed by Team Oriented, with Humane-Oriented still ranked in the top three predictors of this measure of CEO success.

Of interest, among the dimensions of Charismatic Leadership are *Visionary, Inspirational, Self-Sacrificial, and Integrity*; among the dimensions of second place Team Oriented are *Collaborative Team Orientation, Team Integrator, and Diplomatic*. When combined with Humane Orientation, eight of the 21 dimensions have an impact on both TMT Dedication and Firm Competitive Performance. As might be predicted, since servant leadership is focused on organizational followers, the above characteristics of servant leadership are strong contributors to cross-cultural TMT Dedication. Further, although servant leadership effectiveness is not normally measured in terms of organization performance, its characteristics are nonetheless solid factors in cross-cultural Firm Competitive Performance.

Mittal & Dorfman (2012), noting "an almost complete absence of country comparison on servant leadership" (p. 555), used data from GLOBE to evaluate the level to which five aspects of servant leadership (Egalitarianism, Moral Integrity, Empowering, Empathy and Humility) were considered to be valid components of cross-cultural effective leadership. The authors claim that the above five characteristics were not tied directly to either Greenleaf (1970) or Spears (1995) because Greenleaf's (1970) definitions "were not based on research or logic but on a keen intuitive sense of people and their relationships within institutions [and] the resulting fuzziness in the interpretation and conceptualization of servant leadership was to be expected" (p. 556). The authors chose instead to work from studies conducted by Page and Wong (2000), Dennis and Bocarnea (2005), Barbuto and Wheeler (2006), Liden, Wayne, Zhao, and Henderson (2008), van Dierendonck (2011), Van Dierendonck and Nuijten (2011) and Reed, Vidaver-Cohen, and Colwell (2011) (p. 556) to develop their core characteristics of servant leadership: Egalitarianism, Moral Integrity, Empowering, Empathy, and Humility, followed by research focused on cross-cultural differences regarding the acceptance and value of these characteristics.

The results of their study indicated that their defined characteristics of servant leadership were viewed as important components of effective leadership across all cultures. "Each of our five dimensions was rated above mid-point of the scale and three dimensions were rated towards the high end of the scale, indicating strong support for servant leadership" (p. 562). However, with the exception of Moral Integrity (which was highly accepted across all cultures), significant differences existed across the GLOBE cultural clusters regarding the endorsement of individual dimensions of servant leadership:

> More specifically, we found that the dimensions of Egalitarianism and Empowering were endorsed more strongly in Nordic/European cultures but not so strongly in Asian and similar cultures. On the other hand, servant leadership dimensions of Empathy and Humility were more strongly endorsed in Asian cultures than European cultures. (p. 562)

Of particular interest to this chapter was their Hypothesis 6 which was based upon a predicted correlation between servant leadership (as they define the same) and humane orientation:

> There is an instinctive affinity between the cultural value of humane orientation and the behavioral profile of a servant

leader. [...] We expect this cultural value to be positively related to servant leadership dimensions. *Hypothesis 6. Humane orientation would be positively related to servant leadership.* (p. 558).

In contrast to the expected correlation, they reported they found no correlation between humane orientation and any of the five servant leadership dimensions. "Though this may appear perplexing, we would suggest that one of the reasons could be that a major part of this construct [...] is being captured by other dimensions, e.g. gender egalitarianism and performance orientation" (p. 568).

Differing from Mittal & Dorfman (2012), for whom Humane Orientation was not considered as a constitutive dimension of servant leadership, Elizabeth Hunt (2017) focused specifically on Humane Orientation as a moral construct and its relationship to transformational, servant, and authentic leadership in the U.S., Mexico, and China. Relying upon House's (2004) descriptions of cultural humane orientation as the manner in which culture incentivizes individuals for kindness, caring, and altruism, Hunt also adopts House's (2004) evidence of humane leadership behavior as a willingness to be supportive and exercise compassion toward followers in the form of resources and assistance. Observing that House *et al.* (2004) also recognized the pursuit of self-transcendence, universalism, and benevolence to reside within humane orientation she concludes,

> Universalism includes understanding, tolerance, and protectiveness. Benevolence includes social and financial support. Both practices encourage a more humane orientation to others [...] Humane orientation's concern with right and wrong conduct, its concern with ethical behaviour, and its practice of altruistic behaviours make it a moral construct. (Hunt, 2017, p. 3).

Hunt acknowledges than developing servant leadership models and testing directly on Greenleaf's conception of the servant paradigm, researchers have advanced multiple definitions and constituent components of the same. Adopting the work of Patterson (2003), Winston (2003), and Winston and Fields (2015), Hunt positioned the compatibility of the GLOBE study's human orientation with servant leadership by applying Winston and Field's (2015) ten specific behaviors to servant leadership:

> 1) practicing what you preach; 2) serving people regardless of differences; 3) serving as a mission and responsibility to others; 4) showing interest in followers as people; 5) serving others as most important; 6) making sacrifices for others; 7) seeking to instill trust over fear; 8) honesty; 9) being driven by a higher calling; and 10) promoting values that transcend self-interest and material success. (p. 5)

> Hunt's (2017) comparison of humane orientation within the culture of the U.S., China, and Mexico reveals several paradoxical results:

United States:
Cultural leadership *preference* in the U.S. places humane orientation third, behind charismatic and participative. This *preference* however, is offset by the lack of humane orientation in leadership *behavior*, primarily due to strong cultural preferences for individualism and masculinity, which encourage followers to be responsible for themselves, pursue individual accomplishment over organizational objectives. The paradox rises from the low level of humane oriented leadership behavior in a society that highly values humane orientation from a cultural perspective.

China:

Similar to the U.S., cultural leadership *preferences* in China ranks third, behind charismatic and team orientation. China is culturally collectivist, highly valuing collaboration, association, and subordination in the context of high-power distance and risk/uncertainty avoidance. Chinese cultural morality is based upon the Confucianist practice of jen, which a number of humane oriented features but also encourages followership and loyalty. Much like the U.S., China's *preference* for humane leadership does not appear in leadership *practice*.

Mexico:

Mexico reflects a patriarchal culture with a strong emphasis on masculinity and deference to authority. In-group collectivism within family groups is strong although collectivism gives way to individualism outside of the family. Unlike the U.S. and China, humane orientation does not rank in the top three leadership cultural *preferences*. That said, "The cultural ideal of *simpatico* or the 'acute sensitivity to the dignity and worth of the individual' expressed through empathy and respect exemplifies humane orientation leadership behaviour practiced in Mexican culture" (p. 9). Cultural expectations regarding humane orientation within Mexico are tied more closely to the paternalistic practice, which views leaders as benevolent patrons to followers.

While Hunt's study did not include an Africa grouping, the Globe study provides a comparable profile for Sub-Saharan Africa, which we thought important to include as it creates another cultural model in which servant leadership relations may be useful.

Sub-Saharan Africa: *(Namibia, Nigeria, South Africa, Zambia, Zimbabwe)*

Sub-Saharan Africa reflects a mixture of patriarchal and matrilineal cultures. Despite the presence of strong roles for females, there is still predisposition for male leadership and a deference for inherited and lineage-based leadership. Tribal and family-oriented allegiances often determined the power and leadership structure. Ubuntu (I am because you are) and similar collectivist philosophies present in many African countries tend to be buried within more Western-style conceptions of power adapted from a long history of colonial rule and patronage. Cultural expectations regarding humane orientation are linked to the tribal and family connections rather than more universal conceptions of followers as persons to be served. Leadership dimensions viewed as contributing the most to outstanding leadership include charismatic, value-based, team-oriented, and participatory leadership. The Humane–Orientation leadership score is the second highest for all the Globe clusters.

Hunt's (2017) comparative analysis provides a valuable linkage between servant leadership and the work of the GLOBE project. Although the defined characteristics of servant leadership differ from Greenleaf (2017), this linkage provides researchers with access to the GLOBE data as an important source of leadership paradigms across cultures.

We remember that Greenleaf (2017) chose to not develop a scholarly research basis for his construct of servant leadership, essentially leaving that task to those who followed. This choice obviously provides a wide doorway for those who desire to include servant leadership as either a primary target of cross-cultural research. It also opened the door to multiple interpretations regarding model development and research paradigms. The existence of numerous approaches, including multiple instruments for measuring servant leadership, creates a number of obstacles to direct research linkage to Greenleaf's original work. Attempting to apply this research cross culturally is further hampered by language usage and customary leadership practices on a widely diverse international stage.

However, the GLOBE project has provided a tangential pathway to cross-cultural research through its extensive leadership preferences, prevailing leadership practices, and in-depth country-based research on the cultural influences of CEO leadership practice and success. The tangential pathway is GLOBE's designation of humane orientation, which, although not specifically developed with servant leadership as a model, includes a number of servant leadership related components. Further scholarly research will be required, such as that of Hunt (2017), to provide stronger ties between servant leadership, alternative leadership behaviors, and servant leadership theory. The existing scholarly work to date is unlikely to merge into a single academically accepted servant leadership paradigm. That said, the more researchers are willing to join forces in an effort to reduce the number of accepted servant leadership components, the greater the likelihood of increased reliable cross-cultural scholarship.

Before we leave this part of the discussion, it is important to be clear that the research on the cross cultural use of servant leadership has yielded directional findings that point to significant positive usefulness of the theory and practice. For example, the Mittal & Dorfman research, built on the GLOBE Model, found in almost every one of the seven characteristics (drawn from the original list by Spears) some cultural connects to the components of servant leadership in such diverse countries as China, Egypt, Kuwait, Argentina, El Salvador, Japan, Austria, New Zealand, or Germany. The study did not probe deeply to extract reasons for strong correlational findings between cultural values and servant leadership dimensions, and continued research is needed to discover the cross-cultural areas that most align with the servant leadership models. Further, the GLOBE bases research, which is most useful, is still limited as the questionnaires and were not developed to directly assess servant leadership. Nonetheless, the outcome of these studies has produced strong evidence to use as pathways to new research.

As we conclude this chapter, we return to the questions that initiated its development. What does scholarship tell us about servant leadership's reception, adoption, and use in different cultural settings, and how does applying a cultural lens to servant leadership modify or amplify our understanding of the theory and its practice?

First, after we examined the scholarship available to us, we returned to our earlier statement that servant leadership, as both theory and practice has actually been fairly successful in spanning cultural boundaries. Important to our first question is the noted growing familiarity of servant leadership theory and its practice on every continent as found in leadership literature (research and non-research), other scholarship, textbooks, and in the popular press (Mittal & Dorfman, 2012). We base this on not only the findings from studies such as Hunt, Mittal and Dorfma, and GLOBE, but from the proliferation of studies now being found in the leadership journals and other publications. Servant leadership is increasingly accepted and adopted as a working model in many countries and across a variety of industries and organizations. The existing scholarship gives evidence of a robust interest in how servant leadership is impacting organizational leadership within a variety of non-U.S. settings in Europe, Asia, the Middle East, and Africa. Encouraging also is the fact that much of the new scholarship in the area is being offered by non-American scholars and writers. Mittal and Dorfman (2012) conclude their study on servant leadership across cultures noting "the importance and endorsement of servant leadership and its components across cultures" is recognized (p. 565). While they admit the need for further study, they and others (Trompenaars & Voerman, 2010; Johnson, 2009) posit a positive sense that servant leadership is playing a significant role when international cultures discover and adopt the model as a construct from which to reimage leadership within various organizational settings. Johnson (2009) offers four compelling reasons/strengths for servant leadership's adoption in other cultures. The first is altruism. Servant leadership is after all about a concern for others. The need for greater productivity and innovation calls for a deeper

working relationship within organizations, institutions, govern-
ments, and other entities. He sees the cross-cultural adoption of
servant leadership as cultural groups having identified within the
theory a mindset about working with others, and in that conceptualization identifying uncoercively ways to bring people into
stronger working relations. The second strength he identifies as
simplicity, arguing that the many ethical abuses and corruptions
of leadership power emerge from organizational leaders putting
their personal interests first. The effective implementation of servant leadership perhaps mitigates against these types of abuse and
simplifies the focus of the leader to one thing—caring for those
being led. The third reason offered is identified as self-awareness.
Johnson images that to function well, the organization operating under servant leadership principles must attract leaders and
followers who are more self-aware and reflective, understanding
the needs of individuals within the organization and ultimately
the needs of the organization itself. The fourth and final reason is
moral sensitivity. Related closely to awareness, moral sensitivity
is a prevailing push to pursue ethical purposes in an organization's internal and external interactions, allowing for a greater
sense of trustworthiness and support. He identifies these as reasons cross-cultural organizations adopt servant leadership. There
may be many other reasons that have yet to be uncovered, but
these are sufficiently compelling for proponents of the theory to
be elated.

The second question we surfaced was whether we learn
anything from applying this cultural lens that allows us to, in
essence, do servant leadership better. How does it further our
knowledge or ability to apply servant leadership principles
whether cross culturally or in its culture of origin? The Global
Studies point to a number of conclusions that help us respond to
this question, and we can add to this information from work by
Mittal and Dorfman (2012), House, Wright, and Aditya (1997),
and Dorfman (2004). The Globe research tells us that culture
has less of an impact on certain industries than others, but that

overall, culture does matter. More specifically, in looking at studies of servant leadership in cross-cultural settings, scholars are beginning to see, for example, that while "cultural values differentially correlated with various dimensions of servant leadership, overall societies high in performance orientation would welcome servant leadership more than societies with high power distance" (Mittal & Dorfman, 2010). The emerging research also demonstrates that servant leadership in cross-cultural settings may be more tempered by concepts such as power distance, collectivism, and uncertainty avoidance, and therefore our measuring instruments for servant leadership may not as accurately capture nuances of cultural difference (Hale & Field, 2007). But our studies do allow us to know more about servant leadership and its power to organize human resources of organizations around more egalitarian models that seem consistent with modern organizational trends proven to yield higher productivity and effective, cohesive work relations.

Finally, while servant leadership is no panacea for leadership ills in the U.S. or beyond, it is beginning to find resonance in many cross-cultural contexts. Scholars are finding that its tenets present a strong and compelling counter narrative to the power models of leadership. What appeals to many cross-cultural leaders is servant leadership's "capability to reconcile opposites and optimize diversity" (Tropmpenaars & Voerman, p. 9). If it does only this, it will make an impact.

Chapter 4 References

Barbuto, J., & Wheeler, D. (2006). Scale development and construct clarification of servant leadership. *Group & Organization Management, 31*, 300–326.

Chin, J. C., Trimble, J.E., & Garcia, J.E. (2018). *Global and culturally diverse leaders and leadership: New dimensions and challenges for business, education, and society.* UK: Emerald Publishing Limited.

Chhokar, J., Brodbeck, F., & House, R. (2007). *Culture and leadership across the world: The GLOBE book of in-depth studies of 25 societies* (Organization and Management Series). Taylor and Francis. Kindle Edition.

Dennis, R. & Bocarnea, M. (2005). Development of the servant leadership assessment instrument. *Leadership & Organization Development Journal, 26*(8), 600–615. https://doi.org/10.1108/01437730510633692

Dennis, R., & Winston, B. E. (2003). A factor analysis of Page and Wong's servant leadership instrument. *Leadership & Organization Development Journal, 24*(7), 455-459. Retrieved from http://proxy.myunion.edu/login/?url=https://search-proquest-com.proxy.myunion.edu/docview/226925980?accountid=14436

Dierendonck D, Nuijten I. (2010). The servant leadership survey: Development and validation of a multidimensional measure. *J Bus Psychol. 26*(3), 249-267.

Dierendonck, D., et al. (2017). The cross-cultural invariance of the servant leadership survey: A comparative study across eight countries. *Administrative Sciences (2076-3387), 7*(2), 1–11. https://doi-org.proxy.myunion.edu/10.3390/admsci7020008

Friedman, T. (2005). *The world is flat: A brief history of the twenty-first century.* New York: Farrar, Straus, and Gircoux.

Greenleaf, R. K. (1977). *Servant leadership: A journey into the nature of legitimate power and greatness.* New York: Paulist Press.

Greenleaf, Robert K. (2017). *The servant-leader within: A transformative path.* Paulist Press. Kindle Edition.

Hale, J. & Fields, D.L. (2007). Exploring servant leadership across cultures: A study of followers in Ghana and the USA. *Leadership, 3*(4) November 2007, 397-417.

Hofstede, G. (2001). *Culture's consequences: Comparing values, behaviors, institutions, and organizations across nations* (2nd ed.). Newbury Park, CA: Sage.

House, R. *et al.* (2004). *Culture, leadership and organizations: The GLOBE study of 62 cultures.* Thousand Oaks, CA: Sage.

House, R. et.al. (2014). *Strategic leadership across cultures: GLOBE study of CEO leadership behavior and effectiveness in 24 countries.* SAGE Publications. Kindle Edition

House, R. J., Wright, N.S., & Aditya, R.N. (1997). Cross-cultural research on organizational leadership: A critical analysis and a proposed theory. In P.C. Early& M. Erez (Eds.), *New perspectives on international industrial organizational psychology* (pp. 535-625). San Francisco: New Lexington Press.

Hunt, E. (2017). Humane orientation as a moral construct in ethical leadership Theories: A comparative analysis of transformational, servant, and authentic leadership in the United States, Mexico, and China. *International Journal on Leadership, 5*(2).

Johnson, C. E. (2009). *Meeting the ethical challenges of leadership: Casting Light or Shadow.* (3ʳᵈ ed.). Newbury Park, CA: Sage.

Laub, J. (1999). Assessing the servant organization: Development of the organizational leadership assessment (OLS) Model. *Dissertation Abstracts International, 60*(2), 308A.

Liden, R., Wayne, S., Zhao, H., & Henderson, D. (2008). Servant leadership: Development of a multidimensional measure and multi-level assessment. *The Leadership Quarterly, 19*(2), 161–177.

Liden RC, Wayne S. J., Meuser JD, Hu J, Wu J. (2015). Servant leadership: validation of a short form of the SL-28O. *The leadership quarterly: LQ; an international journal of political, social and behavioral science. 26*(2),287-269. http://proxy.myunion.edu/login?url=https://search.ebscohost.com/login.aspx?direct=true&db=edszbw&AN=EDSZBW828834482&site=eds-live&scope=site. Accessed November 13, 2018.

Lord, R., & Maher, K. (1991). Cognitive theory in industrial and organizational psychology. In Dunnette, M. & Hough, L. *Handbook of Industrial Organizational Psychology (2nd Ed.)* Vol 2 (pp. 1-62). Palo Alto, CA: Consulting Psychological Press.

Mittal, R. & Dorfman, P. (2012). Servant leadership across cultures. *Journal of World Business 47*, 555–570.

Page, D., & Wong, T. (2000). A conceptual framework for measuring servant leadership. In Adjibolosoo, S. (Ed.). *The Human Factor in Shaping the Course of History and Development.* Lanham, MD: University Press of America.

Parris, D. & Peachey, J. (2012). A systematic review of servant leadership theory in organizational contexts. *Journal of Business Ethics,* 113:377. https://doi.org/10.1007/s10551-012-1322-6

Patterson, K. (2003). *Servant leadership: A theoretical model.* [Dissertation]. Regent University. Retrieved from http://0-search.proquest.com.library.regent.edu/docview/305234239?accountid=13479

Rodriguez-Carvajal, R., de Rivas, S., Herrero, M., Moreno-Jimenez, B., & Dierendonck, D. (2014). Leading people positively: cross-cultural validation of the Servant Leadership Survey (SLS). *Spanish Journal of Psychology, 17.* Retrieved from http://link.galegroup.com.proxy.myunion.edu/apps/doc/A419413299/AONE?u=vol_m761j&sid=AONE&xid=e0c7c777

Russell, R., & Stone, A. (2002). A review of servant leadership attributes: Developing a practical model. *Leadership and Organizational Development Journal, 23*(3), 145–157.

Schein, E. (2004). *Organizational culture and leadership.* (3rd ed.). New York: Jossey-Bass.

Sendjaya, S. (2015). Servant leadership research. In *Personal and organizational excellence through servant leadership: Learning to serve, serving to leading to transform.* Management for Professionals Series. Switzerland: Springer International Publishing. DOI 10.1007/978-3-319-16196-9_2

Sendjaya, S., Sarros, J., & Santora, J. (2008). Defining and measuring servant leadership behaviour in organizations. *Journal of Management Studies*, Wiley Blackwell, *45*(2), 402–424.

Sendjaya, S. (2015). Servant leadership research. In *Personal and orga-nizational excellence through servant leadership: Learning to serve, serving to leading to transform.* Management for Professionals Series. Switzerland: Springer International Publishing. DOI 10.1007/978-3-319-16196-9_2

Spears, L. (2004). Practicing servant-leadership. *Leader to Leader, 34,* 7–11. Retrieved from https://apscomunicacioenpublic.files.word-press.com/2012/12/larry-spears-practicing-servant-leadership.pdf

Trompenaars, F. &Voerman, E. (2010). *Servant leadership across cul-tures.* New York: McGraw Hill.

Winston, B. (2003). *Extending Patterson's servant leadership model: Coming full circle.* Paper presented at the University School of Leadership Studies Servant Leadership Research Roundtable, Virginia Beach, VA. Retrieved from http://www.regent.edu/acad/cls/2003ServantLeadershipRoundtable

Winston, B, & Ryan, B. (2008). Servant leadership as a humane orientation: Using the GLOBE study construct of humane orien-tation to show that servant leadership is more global than west-ern. *International Journal of Leadership Studies, 3*(2), 212–222. Retrieved from https://www.regent.edu/acad/global/publications/ijls/new/vol3iss2/IJLS_V3Is2_Winston_Ryan.pdf

Winston, B., & Fields, D. (2015). Seeking and measuring the essen-tial behaviors of servant leadership. *Leadership & Organization Development Journal, 36*(4), 413–434. Retrieved from http://proxy.myunion.edu/login/?url=https://search-proqst.com.proxy.myunion.edu/docview/1681237884?accountid=14436

Chapter 5

Servant leadership within organizational contexts: Identifying core beliefs underlying servant leadership and infusing servant leadership into organizations

Chad A. Hartnell, G. James Lemoine, Hamed Ghahremani, & Derek J. Stolter

PREVIOUS CHAPTERS IN THIS VOLUME PRESENTED SERVANT leadership's historical background and its emergence as a unique leadership style. In the present chapter, we take a more detailed look at servant leadership and how it applies to modern organizations. Four main questions guide our inquiry: 1) What are relational forms of leadership and how is servant leadership distinct from other relational leadership styles?; 2) What do themes among relational forms of leadership reveal about servant leadership's core beliefs and how do the core beliefs manifest in organizations?; 3) What are common misconceptions about servant leadership when applied within organizational contexts?; and 4) How can servant leadership be better infused into today's organizations?

What are relational forms of leadership and how is servant leadership distinct from other relational styles?

Servant leadership is one of several different approaches to leadership which might be described as "relational," or those that focus on interpersonal relationships between leaders and followers and joint pursuit of mutual goals (Uhl-Bien, 2006). Relational leadership is different from instrumental forms of leadership that rely upon transactional exchanges to influence followers. Instrumental forms of leadership treat followers as resources, but relational forms of leadership treat followers as partners. At their worst, instrumental forms of leadership manipulate, coerce, and abuse followers to attain compliance. In contrast, relational forms of leadership build positive, mutually enriching relationships with followers. They engage followers' hearts and minds and equip them with social and emotional resources to improve their own leadership capacity. As a result, several relational forms of leadership are expected to arouse the motivation and lift the ethical aspirations of followers.

Relational leadership encompasses a number of leadership styles beyond the servant approach, including authentic, ethical, empowering, charismatic, Level 5, multiplicative, and humble leadership (see Table 1). Given the increasing number of leadership approaches that exist in the relational leadership domain, it is important to clarify servant leadership's similarities and differences with other forms of relational leadership. Table 1 provides a summary of conceptual definitions, leadership emphases, and underlying core beliefs. We offer here a brief description of these approaches for the purposes of comparison with the concepts embodied in servant leadership. The key elements of each leadership style's definition are accentuated by boldfaced text.

Leadership Style	Conceptual Definition	Leadership Emphasis	Core Beliefs
Authentic Leadership	"A process that draws from both positive psychological capacities and a highly developed organizational context, which results in both greater self-awareness and self-regulated positive behaviors on the part of leaders and associates, fostering positive self-development" (Luthans & Avolio, 2003, p. 243).	Self-awareness and self-consistency	Morality
Ethical Leadership	"The demonstration of normatively appropriate conduct through personal actions and interpersonal relationships, and the promotion of such conduct to followers through two-way communication, reinforcement, and decision-making" (Brown, Treviño, & Harrison, 2005, p. 120).	Conformity to social norms	Morality
Empowering Leadership	"The process of implementing conditions that enable sharing power with an employee by delineating the significance of the employee's job, providing greater decision-making autonomy, expressing confidence in the employee's capabilities, and removing hindrances to performance" (Zhang & Bartol, 2010, p. 109).	Delegating authority	Empowerment

Leadership Style	Conceptual Definition	Leadership Emphasis	Core Beliefs
Charismatic Leadership	"[Charismatic leadership] is based on behavioral tendencies and personal characteristics of the leader, including the articulation of a clear vision derived from firmly held values or moral justifications, role modeling of those values, communication of high performance expectations and confidence in followers' abilities to meet those expectations, references to the greater collective and its identity, symbolic behaviors, and the assumption of personal risks and sacrifices" (Waldman & Yammarino, 1999, p. 268).	Communicating an inspiring vision to accomplish collective goals	Self-transcendence
Level 5 Leadership	Level 5 leaders are highly capable individuals who work effectively with others, organize people and resources to achieve objectives, catalyze commitment to a clear vision, and demonstrate personal humility and professional will (Collins, 2001, p. 20).	Humble determination to achieve a collective purpose	Self-transcendence

Leadership Style	Conceptual Definition	Leadership Emphasis	Core Beliefs
Multiplicative Leadership	Multiplicative leadership can be conceptualized as one who builds on subordinates strengths and provides opportunities for subordinates to become leaders themselves who will, in turn, develop the following generation of leaders (Maxwell, 2011, pp. 233-237).	Growing other leaders	Regeneration
Humble Leadership	Humble leadership is characterized as "an interpersonal characteristic that emerges in social contexts that connotes (a) a manifested willingness to view oneself accurately, (b) a displayed appreciation of others' strengths and contributions, and (c) teachability" (Owens, Johnson, & Mitchell, 2013, p. 1218).	Mutual influence via coaching and teachability	Regeneration
Servant Leadership	"Servant leadership is composed of influence behaviors, manifested humbly and morally within relationships, oriented towards continuous and meaningful improvement for all stakeholders" (Lemoine & Blum, 2018).	A servant first who aspires to lead and who aims to benefit all stakeholders	Morality, Empowerment, Self-transcendence, and Regeneration

Authentic leaders are self-aware and behave in a manner that is consistent with their personal values (Luthans & Avolio, 2003). Ethical leaders adhere and promote others' adherence to socially appropriate norms and standards (Brown, Treviño, & Harrison, 2005). Empowering leaders delegate authority to followers through providing decision-making discretion, expressing confidence in their abilities, highlighting the significance of their work, and removing barriers to successful performance (Zhang & Bartol, 2010). Charismatic leaders encourage employees to transcend their personal interests in favor of achieving collective goals by communicating a clear and inspiring vision for the organization (Waldman & Yammarino, 1999). Similarly, Level 5 leaders combine personal humility with enduring willpower to organize people to commit to a collective purpose that transcends one's personal interests (Collins, 2001). Multiplicative leaders emphasize the importance of identifying and developing the next generation of leaders as a means to satisfy the leadership demands of an expanding organization (Maxwell, 2011). Humble leaders emphasize the interpersonal and intrapersonal growth that occurs through trusting relationships, openness to personal feedback, and receptiveness to leader-follower mutual coaching (Schein & Schein, 2018; Owens, Johnson, & Mitchell, 2013).

As discussed earlier in this volume (Lemoine & Blum, 2020), servant leadership's major point of distinction from other relational forms of leadership is its attention to multiple stakeholders (Greenleaf, 1977). Greenleaf himself referred to these stakeholders as "constituents" or "all interested parties" (1977: p. 172) and argued that effective leaders must consider the impact of their actions on all of them. The emphasis on multiple stakeholders, including but not limited to business owners and profit imperatives, has challenged the traditional assumption that businesses should be solely focused on building shareholder value, a concept advanced by Milton Friedman (among others) in the 1970's and 1980's (Friedman, 1982). Empirical research provides support for the positive financial effects associated with a multiple stakeholder focus. Research indicates that organizations with a broader stakeholder focus yield superior financial returns compared to organizations that limit their priorities to profits alone (e.g. de Luque et al., 2008). Servant leadership's multi-stakeholder focus has led it to become the preeminent stakeholder-focused model of leadership within organizations (Eva et al., 2019; Lemoine et al., 2019).

In addition to servant leadership's multi-stakeholder focus, it is further distinguished from other relational forms of leadership by Greenleaf's (1977) contention that servant leaders' behaviors emanate from their serving values and beliefs. According to Greenleaf (1977, p. 27), "the servant-leader *is* servant first...It begins with the natural feeling that one wants to serve, to serve *first*. Then conscious choice brings one to aspire to lead." This quote reveals that servant leadership is defined by two factors: (1) who a servant-leader *is*, and (2) what a servant-leader *does*. Both elements are essential; however, we know much more about what servant-leaders do than who they are (i.e., what constitutes a servant). This gap is problematic because servant leaders' core principles, values, and beliefs help us explain why they engage in seven specific behaviors: behaving ethically, putting subordinates first, empowering, conceptual skills, creating value for the community, helping subordinates grow and succeed, and emotional healing (Ehrhart, 2004; Liden, Wayne, Zhao, & Henderson, 2008). What compels servant-leaders to engage in these seven specific behaviors? It is difficult to explain how they work, or how managers can become servant leaders, without greater clarity regarding who servant-leaders are.

Servant leaders' core principles, values, and beliefs help us explain why they engage in these seven specific behaviors. Research suggests that core values and beliefs influence people's motivation and intentions, and, ultimately, their behaviors (Ajzen, 1991). In other words, we do what we do because of who we are. But how clear is our understanding of what modern servant-leaders value and believe? How can servant-leaders "[go] out ahead and show the way" (Greenleaf, 2002, p. 28) if we lack clarity about their core beliefs and internal motivations? Identifying themes among relational forms of leadership can help to answer these questions.

What do themes among relational forms of leadership reveal about servant leadership's core beliefs and how do the core beliefs manifest in organizations?

Underlying themes among relational forms of leadership reveal four core beliefs that compose a servant leader's heart: morality, empowerment, self-transcendence, and regeneration. Although other relational forms of leadership feature some of these four core beliefs (see Table 1), all of them are central to servant leadership's ethos and provide multifaceted insight into a servant leader's heart. Servant-leaders believe that their influence should benefit multiple stakeholders (i.e., morality), free others to experience higher levels of personal autonomy and responsibility (i.e., empowerment), inspire others to collectively pursue a cause greater than themselves that builds a good and better society (i.e., self-transcendence), and grow others through building their leadership capacity and strengthening their socioemotional resources (i.e., regeneration). These four core beliefs compose a servant leader's heart. They represent the servant leader's fundamental convictions about what others need in order to flourish and how others should be treated. Taken together, they are guiding principles that shape servant leaders' thoughts, internal motivations, intentions, and behaviors.

Figure 1 identifies the four core beliefs and illustrates how they link to specific servant leadership behaviors. The innermost ring encapsulates the four beliefs. The middle ring depicts servant leadership's internal motivations. The outermost ring shows servant leadership's seven competencies that have been the predominant focus of servant leadership theory and research (Ehrhart, 2004; Liden et al., 2008). Moving from the innermost to the outermost ring, Figure 1 illustrates a linkage between beliefs, motivations, and behaviors. This model helps to explain why a servant-leader must be a servant first. Their core beliefs influence their internal motivations, which are then naturally expressed as behaviors. Although servant leadership shares core beliefs with other relational forms of leadership, servant-leaders express the beliefs differently based on the distinctions in their underlying motivations. The heart of the servant-leader might best be understood by examining relational leadership's four core beliefs in more detail.

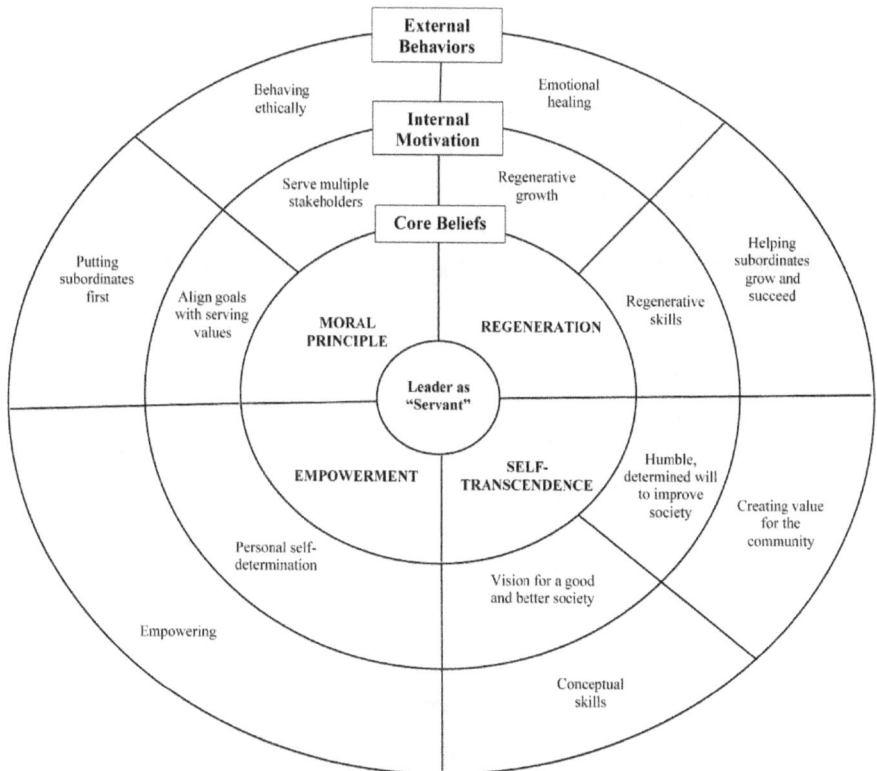

Relational Leadership Core Belief #1 – Moral Principle

The first core belief underlying relational leadership is moral principle. Servant, ethical, and authentic leadership share a common belief that morality is an important component of leadership, beneficial for employees and the organization. Different moral principles undergird the three leadership styles, however, resulting in different perspectives about what is moral; considering how these perspectives differ can help us understand the nature of the servant-leader (Lemoine, Hartnell, & Leroy, 2019).

Ethical leadership emphasizes conformance to organizational or professional standards and norms. It surged to the forefront of leadership research in response to a series of corporate accounting scandals (e.g., Enron, WorldCom, Tyco, and Freddie Mac) at the turn of the 21st century. Ethical leadership is defined as "the demonstration of normatively appropriate conduct through personal actions and interpersonal relationships, and the promotion of such conduct to followers through two-way communication, reinforcement, and decision-making" (Brown et al., 2005, p. 120). In other words, the ethical leader acts as a moral person and a moral manager, holding herself and her followers accountable for compliance with organizational and cultural standards (Brown et al., 2005). Ethical leadership's standard for appropriate conduct is thus understood as adherence to a set of guiding principles such as formal rules or informal social norms.

In contrast to ethical leadership's emphasis on behavioral conformance, authentic leadership adopts an introspective focus on the self. It emphasizes self-awareness and alignment between leaders' beliefs and behaviors. Authentic leaders are "deeply aware of how they think and behave and are perceived by others as being aware of their own and others' values/moral perspectives, knowledge, and strengths" (Avolio, Gardner, Walumbwa, Luthans, & May, 2004, p. 802). They make decisions based on their own deeply held values rather than placating others' expectations (George, 2010). In sum, Shamir and Eilam-Shamir

(2018) describe authentic leaders as having a strong leader identity, self-concept clarity (i.e., a deep understanding of one's beliefs), self-concordant goals (i.e., goals are consistent with personal passions, values, and beliefs), and self-expression (i.e., transparent expression of one's values, thoughts, and feelings).

Servant leadership's moral foundation is different from that of ethical leadership and authentic leadership. It stems from a concern for multiple stakeholders and producing the greatest good for the greatest number of people. Greenleaf (2002) carefully prescribes that servant-leaders invest in followers' personal growth and well-being, but not at the expense of other stakeholders, particularly the underprivileged and underrepresented in society: "And, what is the effect on the least privileged in society? Will they benefit or at least not be further deprived?" (p. 27). He also suggests that servant-leaders do not focus on follower growth *to the exclusion of* organizational goals. They balance concern for followers and concern for the organization's productivity such that they serve followers while getting everything else done to ensure organizational survival (Greenleaf, 1970). Servant-leaders attend to the higher-order needs of all stakeholders. Hence, servant leadership's standard for determining whether behavior is right or wrong is based upon its effect on all constituents who may be affected by it.

The Expression of Servant Leadership's Guiding Moral Principle

Within complex organizational contexts, servant leaders' guiding moral principle—concern for multiple stakeholders—compels them to serve multiple stakeholders and thus behave ethically—in a manner that benefits multiple stakeholders (see Figure 1). Let us consider how servant leaders' concern for multiple stakeholders drives servant leadership behavior in organizational practice.

EA Engineering, Science, and Technology (referred to hereafter as EA), which provides national environmental consulting services, offers a cogent example of a multiple stakeholder focus via its organizational design and business practices. According to the company's historical account ("History", n.d.), EA became an employee-owned firm and implemented an Employee Stock Ownership Plan (ESOP) that provided employees an owner-ship interest in company stock in 2005. In 2014, the company became 100% employee-owned by the ESOP. In the same year, Ian MacFarlane, President and CEO of EA, led the company's transition to become a public benefit corporation (PBC) under Delaware law. A PBC is a corporate classification that codifies corporate social responsibility and environmental stewardship as a central part of the organization's purpose. These organiza-tional design elements illustrate the company's commitment to its primary stakeholders: employees, clients, and the natural environment.

EA's business practices also offer evidence of its commitment to multiple stakeholders. According to MacFarlane, servant leadership is about stakeholder management. Stakeholder management refers to "making sure that you are balancing the appropriation and allocation of value fairly between all of your stakeholders" (I. MacFarlane, personal communication, February 28, 2019). To achieve the equitable distribution of value across all stakeholders, the company needs to identify and empower "individuals…within the company who are the champions for these various stakeholders… [and] who are tagged with making sure we are doing right by them" (I. MacFarlane, personal communication, February 28, 2019). These actions underscore the servant leader's commitment to attend to and benefit all of its stakeholders. Taken together, EA's 100% employee-owned organizational design and stakeholder-focused business practices reflect a moral commitment to the multiple stakeholders the company serves.

A multiple stakeholder focus does not just yield economic or environmental benefits for its stakeholders. It also provides social and societal benefits. These benefits accrue from servant leaders' genuine love for people. Greenleaf (1977, p. 38) contends, "*Love* is an undefinable term, and its manifestations are both subtle and infinite. But it begins, I believe, with one absolute condition: unlimited liability! As soon as one's liability for another is qualified *to any degree,* love is diminished by that much." Servant-leaders subordinate self-interest to benefit others *regardless of personal cost.* This selfless expression is love in action. Blanchard and Broadwell (2018) cogently note that servant-leaders demonstrate the power of love, not the love of power. Servant leaders' love for others thus prompts them to invest in their stakeholders' social and societal growth.

Starbucks Corporation (hereafter Starbucks), a large multi-national coffee retail chain, provides a cogent example of how an organization invests in the social and societal welfare of the employees and communities it serves. Starbucks Corporation's 2018 Global Social Impact Report (Starbucks Corporation, 2019) outlines a consistent pattern of investment in education, sustainability, and community involvement. As evidence of its investment in education, Starbucks provides the opportunity for employees to earn a bachelor's degree from Arizona State University with full tuition coverage and has set a goal to graduate 25,000 employees by 2025. As evidence of its commitment to sustainability, Starbucks has set ambitious goals, including eliminating single-use straws by 2020, developing 100% compostable and recyclable cups by 2022, and donating 100 million trees to coffee farmers by 2025. As evidence of its commitment to strengthening communities, Starbucks opened a "signing store" (where employees are proficient in American Sign Language) in a location where there is a high density of individuals with hearing impairments. Starbucks demonstrates support for people in need by donating over 10 million meals to community food banks and homeless shelters. In 2018, Starbucks employees contributed more than 66 thousand hours of community service in ways that were most relevant and impactful to the local community (Starbucks Corporation, 2019).

Starbucks' multifaceted philanthropic approach to invest in multiple stakeholders' social and societal well-being demonstrates love for its employees and communities as a unidirectional flow of resources without a corresponding expectation of reciprocity. These munificent behaviors suggest that the company's primary drive to succeed is so they can serve those within their sphere of influence, both internal and external to the organization. This motivation illustrates the important distinction between doing well by doing good (i.e., profiting from benevolence) and doing good by doing well (i.e., profit to be benevolent). In sum, EA and Starbucks provide cogent and unique depictions of a leader's moral commitment to benefit others both internal and external to the organization.

Relational Leadership Core Belief #2 – Empowerment

Empowerment is relational leadership's second core belief. Empowerment is an active orientation toward tasks in which employees believe they are capable of doing meaningful work, with a degree of autonomy and the potential to impact their organization (Spreitzer, 1995). Empowerment is a powerful tool for relational leaders because it meets two of employees' highest order innate psychological needs: competence and autonomy. In other words, it effectively fulfills desires that employees may not even know they had. These needs, along with employees' need for relatedness, "are essential for ongoing psychological growth, integrity, and well-being" (Deci & Ryan, 2000, p. 229).

Empowering leaders "share power with their employees by delegating authority to employees, hold employees accountable, involve employees in decision making, encourage self-manage-ment of work, and convey confidence in employees' capabilities to handle challenging work" (Chen, Sharma, Edinger, Shapiro, & Farh, 2011, p. 543). Empowering leaders' underlying motivation is for followers to take a proactive orientation toward their work, and to succeed. Servant-leaders are happy to see followers suc-ceed at work, but this is secondary to their goal of helping others achieve personal autonomy. Personal autonomy from the servant leadership perspective means helping others become independent evaluators of information and efficacious contributors to society. It is a building block in equipping others to contribute toward serving others and building a good and better society.

Servant-leaders empower followers by giving them responsibility and discretion to make decisions using their best judgment. These empowering behaviors give followers opportunities to develop their ability to think and advocate for themselves by evaluating information and making independent decisions. As followers become more self-sufficient, they reduce their unnecessary dependence on others to make decisions that affect their well-being. Servant-leaders also liberate followers to choose whom they should follow—to reject the coercive influence of manipulative, self-serving leaders, for instance. As a result, servant leadership helps followers grow freer and more autonomous (Greenleaf, 1977), unshackled from overdependence on others and coercive influence that diminishes them. Servant leaders' core belief in empowerment cultivates an underlying motivation to help followers achieve self-determination. This motivation results in servant-leaders empowering followers through encouraging them to take responsibility and make autonomous decisions.

Nordstrom is a renowned retail service provider that is famous for empowering employees to independently evaluate information and make autonomous decisions. Nordstrom's employee handbook is a single card that reads as follows:

> Our number one goal is to provide outstanding customer service. Set both your personal and professional goals high. We have great confidence in your ability to achieve them, so our employee handbook is very simple. We have only one rule…
>
> OUR ONE RULE: Use good judgment in all situations.
>
> Please feel free to ask your department manager, store manager or Human Resources any questions at any time. (Lutz, 2014)

Ritz-Carlton, a hotel company that is famous for its world-class hospitality and customer service, encourages employee ownership, responsibility, and proactive, independent problem-solving and decision-making. These behaviors equip employees to provide "anticipatory service" to their guests ("Gold Standards", n.d.). Ritz-Carlton outlines 12 service values that define the gold standard of service ("Gold Standards", n.d.). Consider the following five service values that exemplify empowerment:

- I am always responsive to the expressed and unexpressed wishes and needs of our guests.

- I continuously seek opportunities to innovate and improve The Ritz-Carlton experience.

- I own and immediately resolve guest problems.

- I am involved in the planning of the work that affects me.

- I am responsible for uncompromising levels of cleanliness and creating a safe and accident-free environment. ("Gold Standards", n.d.)

Responsiveness, proactivity, ownership, involvement, and responsibility illustrate the power of empowerment. Laborious policies, practices, and procedures discourage autonomous decision-making. They also deter employees from taking responsibility and undermine their efficacy to improve their own as well as others' well-being. Overbearing rules tend to change employees' focus from proactive (i.e., value creating) to protective (i.e., compliance). Servant-leaders counter these constraints by celebrating followers' proactivity, encouraging innovation, and inviting employee involvement.

Servant-leaders also create space for employees to model organizational values through their own special qualities and unique characteristics. Interstate Batteries, a company that offers automotive and specialty batteries, outlines eight core values—seven of which are love, servant's heart, excellence, courage, fun, team, and integrity ("Our Culture", n.d.). The eighth core value reflects the unique character that each team member brings to the organization. Among members of the top leadership team, the eighth value embodies personal growth, relationships (with God, family, and others), care, growth, transparency, and humility. This eighth value affirms employees' individual worth and celebrates the unique strengths that equip them to be efficacious contributors to the organization and society.

Nordstrom, Ritz-Carlton, and Interstate Batteries exemplify values that build others' self-sufficiency, enhance their self-worth, and increase their confidence in their ability to make a difference in the lives of others. Whereas some leaders delegate sufficient authority as a motivational tool to increase employees' work output, servant-leaders lead others in a liberating process of self-discovery that equips them with opportunities and confidence to proactively make a prosocial difference. Taking ownership and responsibility thus become autonomous acts of self-expression. Rather than being empowered to perform, followers are empowered for a larger purpose.

Relational Leadership Core Belief #3 – Self-Transcendence

The third core belief undergirding relational leadership is self-transcendence. A person experiences self-transcendence when he/she is devoted, or committed, to a cause greater than him/herself. Charismatic leadership, Level 5 leadership, and servant leadership all highlight this foundational principle. Charismatic leadership is a visionary, inspirational form of leadership that motivates followers' self-transcendence via a 3-step process (Conger & Kanungo, 1998). First, charismatic leaders assess the current situation and identify problems, or gaps, between where the organization is and where it should be. Second, they articulate a clear and compelling vision that inspires followers to action. That is, they communicate a picture of an ideal, desirable future that evokes dissatisfaction with the present situation and an emotional attachment to the future (Shamir, House, & Arthur, 1993). Third, charismatic leaders express confidence in followers' ability to achieve the mission. Throughout the 3-step process, charismatic leaders use persuasion to arouse and inspire their followers (House, 1977). As a result, charismatic leadership motivates followers to transcend individual self-interest and work toward the benefit of the collective; charismatic leaders themselves, however, may not necessarily transcend their own self-interests.

History is replete with examples of charismatic leaders who manipulatively cultivate followers' emotional attachment and compel them to self-transcendence to serve the leader's own nefarious purposes (e.g., Adolf Hitler and Benito Mussolini). In the book *Good to Great*, Jim Collins (2001) distinguishes between charismatic leadership (which he calls "Level 4 leadership") and Level 5 leadership. Charismatic leaders foster others' commitment to a cause, whereas Level 5 leaders exhibit personal commitment to the cause—the organization's mission. Level 5 leaders combine personal humility with professional will to serve that cause. They recognize that their organization's mission is so big and audacious that their ability alone is insufficient. They must engage and inspire others' complementary talents to pursue the cause together. Both charismatic and Level 5 leadership thus highlight the role of self-transcendence (either followers' self-transcendence or leaders' self-transcendence) to achieve the organization's mission.

Servant leadership similarly accentuates self-transcendence as a core belief but with a different motivational impetus. A servant leader's cause is arguably grander than the organization's mission. It is an idealistic and inspirational vision to build a good and better *society*. Servant-leaders articulate an impassioned vision of the future in which individuals express love, compassion, acceptance, and empathy out of a genuine desire to create a world where sacrificing self-interest and serving others is the norm rather than the exception. This vision moves us toward a future state of societal well-being in which its members experience and exercise freedom to do for others what is best for them without expecting (or needing) something from them in return.

Servant leaders' vision of, or ability to see, a good and better society is dependent upon two elements of sight: foresight and insight. Foresight combines an understanding of past events, present moments, and future possibilities into one cohesive view that informs one's decisions. According to Greenleaf (2002, pp. 38-39), "One is at once, in every moment of time, historian, contemporary analyst, and prophet—not three separate roles. This is what the practicing leader is, every day of his or her life." A leader's attentiveness to the past, present, and future gives them a rich context to gain an accurate and deep understanding (i.e., insight) about how to move forward and successfully achieve the vision of the future. These two elements equip servant-leaders with pragmatic conceptual skills to achieve their vision.

Leadership at M&T Bank, a regional bank in the Northeast and the mid-Atlantic U.S., provides an example of self-transcendence as a guiding core belief within an organization. M&T Bank is a community bank that strives to facilitate economic growth, prosperity, and well-being for the communities it serves. Robert Wilmers, who served as the bank's Chairman and CEO from 1983 until he passed away in 2017, saw the mission of M&T as "carefully taking deposits and making loans that better the cities and towns they [the bank] serve by supporting investments in new homes, new cars, and new businesses, by contributing resources and expertise to community-based nonprofits, and by promoting overall economic development and job creation" ("DardenMBA", 2015). For Wilmers, this was a calling and a source of great pride. Serving as the Chariman and CEO for over three decades gave him a unique opportunity to create a culture and supporting infrastructure at M&T that would support this approach. M&T is involved in the communities they serve in several ways, including but not limited to community reinvestment initiatives, sponsorship, and charitable contributions. Robert Wilmers believed and emphasized that "when our communities succeed, we all succeed...[all employees at M&T] believe that a rising tide lifts all boats" (DardenMBA, 2015). As such, under his leadership, M&T was, and still is, so involved in the Northeast and the mid-Atlantic, especially the Western New York region, that Wilmers was "widely viewed as the dean of the local business community" (Glynn & Epstein, 2017).

Several examples of M&T's initiatives represent a commitment beyond financial benefits that might accrue to a bank. For example, a committee including top regional M&T managers in New Jersey have monthly meetings to evaluate organizations, especially charitable organizations, to decide how to deploy funds that will assist their efforts to help the community (Adubato, 2017). One example was providing funds to Garden State Episcopal Community Development Corporation to help rehabilitate a church and build units around the church to revitalize the neighborhood. Another example is Buffalo Promise Neighborhood, an initiative that involves a partnership between M&T and its community in Buffalo to empower schools, students, and families. Buffalo Promise Neighborhood currently manages four schools, from early childhood education to elementary school, serving more than a thousand students in areas that have been impoverished with a nearly 90% risk of students dropping out of high school before graduation. M&T has 15 employees solely dedicated to this initiative. Partnered with the community, Buffalo Promise Neighborhood provides financial and educational support to these schools and students as well as parents and families through skill development programs.

EA also models self-transcendence through community engagement and environmental conservation efforts. EA offers full-time employees eight hours of paid time annually to volunteer at an organization of their choice that is aligned with the company's core purpose: "Improving the quality of the environment in which we live, one project at a time'" (EA Engineering,

2017). Such activities have included stream cleanups, raising community awareness about reducing pollution in local water sources, and leading educational initiatives to teach elementary-aged children about water and environmental conservation (Hennick, 2019). Employee involvement in the program has increased impressively from 24% in 2016 to 60% in 2018. The company also partners with mission-aligned nonprofits such as Water For People by raising money to provide access to clean drinking water and sanitation services in developing countries (Allen & Williams, 2019).

EA drives employees' engagement in a self-transcendent effort to improve society through connecting organizational and employee goals to corporate social responsibility. The company's "Purpose Realization Pyramid" starts with a foundation of improving the organization's viability (i.e., financial strength and service to clients and each other). The organization's viability creates opportunities to invest in and identify new frontiers for employee career and organizational revenue growth. Employee and organizational growth then position the company to expand its corporate social responsibility efforts such as "professional involvement, community support, and charitable giving" (EA Engineering, 2017). The purpose realization pyramid reflects MacFarlane's conviction that the organization he leads is a mechanism to do good. In his view, EA's employee ownership structure, environmental improvement initiatives, and prosocial purpose offer opportunities to envision a more compassionate capitalism that narrows socioeconomic disparities and includes more people in the pursuit of creating a better and brighter society. Although the specific steps to achieve this future possibility remain unclear, MacFarlane's foresight is consonant with a servant leader's self-transcendent determination to envision and work toward a better society.

The examples above reify Greenleaf's (1977) contention that the sustaining force behind servant leaders' vision is their humble and determined will to improve society. They lead by example.

As such, servant-leaders inspire followers' self-transcendence and experience it themselves. Altogether, servant leaders' core belief in a self-transcendent cause develops their internal motivation to communicate a clear and compelling vision for a good and better society, and to pursue it with a humble and determined will.

Relational Leadership Core Belief #4 – Regeneration

Regeneration is the fourth core belief of relational leadership. Regeneration refers to growing others through building their leadership capacity and strengthening their socioemotional resources. Multiplicative leadership (Maxwell, 2011), humble leadership (Schein & Schein, 2018), and servant leadership touch upon this relational leadership principle through developing leadership skills and personal growth. Similar to Collins (2001), Maxwell (2011) identified five levels of leadership, but defined the 5th level as multiplied influence, or developing others' leadership capacity. The focus of multiplicative leadership is to regenerate leadership such that leaders develop others to *exceed* their own skills and abilities so they can eventually *succeed* them. Multiplicative leaders thus leave a legacy by developing a succession plan and cultivating other leaders' skills to carry on the organization's mission.

The key to sustaining multiplicative leadership is to be humble (Maxwell, 2011). Humble leadership focuses on the internal and interpersonal processes that foster regenerative growth. Humble leaders develop personal and cooperative relationships with their followers by nurturing trust, openness, supportiveness, and respect. They also help followers' meet their need for relatedness. According to Schein and Schein (2018), "The humble leader needs to be aware of members' needs to develop their identity in the group, to learn how they can contribute, and, most important, to develop understanding and acceptance of the others in the group." These behaviors help followers flourish through gaining confidence in who they are and how they can contribute to the group. When followers feel that they belong, they are then well equipped to nurture a similar sense of belonging to others. In combination, multiplicative leadership and humble leadership promote regeneration through growing others' skills and abilities as well as facilitating their inward socio-emotional growth.

Regeneration is also a central concept within servant leadership. Servant leaders' vision for a good and better society can only be achieved if they multiply their influence. As such, they build others with the intention that they are "more likely themselves to become servants" (Greenleaf, 2002, p. 27). To become servants, though, followers must experience regenerative growth. That is, they must grow as persons such that they, while being served, become healthier and wiser (Greenleaf, 2002). Consequently, regeneration is a core belief to servant-leaders that influences behaviors, and those regenerative behaviors are quite similar to those described above. By realizing their own limitations and humbly sharing their power, servant-leaders cultivate leadership capacity in others. They also cultivate followers' own desires for growth and development, through demonstrating deep care, concern, and compassion on a personal level.

This idea of regeneration is exemplified by the actions of Allwel, a small, licensed home-care-services agency operating in New York state. Allwel originally specialized in serving patients with traumatic brain injury when they opened in 2000, but has since broadened their focus. The company works to help ease the burdens of patients and their families, providing their patients with the resources and support they need to live with health and dignity. Allwel's approach to regeneration is a unique one, found in their emphasis on the continuous development of their employees. Beyond the standard trainings on proper patient care that would be expected of an organization such as this, Allwel features a unique training program in the form of their "Allwel U" that develops their employees in skills far beyond the scope of their jobs. Management at Allwel noticed that many of their employees struggled with the kinds of basic life competencies that others might take for granted: paying rent on time, budgeting their money, managing a bank account, or managing family conflict. They designed Allwel U. with these needs in mind. Beyond basic job training and more advanced management skills, they also teach their employees life skills to help them be more successful human beings, outside of work. According to management, this is a good investment: They say turnover dramatically decreases for employees who take advantage of this life-skills training, and that those employees become some of their best caregivers and strongest advocates in the community. In the words of the company's co-founder and president, Chris Brown-Hall:

> One of the ways that Allwel has grown over the years is that understanding and coming to learn that it's as important for us to care for our employees and our staff members as it is for us to care for our patients... a lot of times, our staff members are experiencing their own challenges at home or in their lives that may impact their ability to be successful employees and successful caregivers. We've pushed ourselves to pay attention to that and to seek out those opportunities where we can help support our employees and staff members in addressing their own challenges so that they can be that much more successful at work and that much more successful at providing the care that we've charged them with, in the homes of our patients. (Brown-Hall, 2017)

Interstate Batteries also puts regeneration in action through both regenerative skills and regenerative growth. The company models regenerative skills through its President's Intensive Leadership Orientation Team (PILOT). The team "serves to assist in the growth and development of the company's emerging leaders" ("Leadership", n.d.). In this way, the organization builds employees' leadership capacity and nurtures employee growth and development.

Beyond developing employees' skills and leadership capabilities, Interstate Batteries attends to employees' spiritual well-being through its Chaplain's Group. This group "exists to impact others with the love of Christ" ("Chaplain's Group", n.d.). It reflects the Chairman and former CEO Norm Miller's belief in "God's power to change lives because it was that power that turned his own life around after years of drinking as hard as he worked" ("Leadership", n.d.). The Chaplain's Group hosts inspirational speakers, offers opportunities to participate in mission-aligned community nonprofits, and provides a safe place to talk about life to all employees regardless of their individual spiritual beliefs. This forum illustrates how Interstate Batteries makes transparent and acts upon its values in a way that serves others. Furthermore, it offers a cogent example of demonstrating care, concern, and compassion for employees' socioemotional welfare and fostering an environment of understanding, acceptance, and personal development that leads to regenerative growth.

Summary
Although servant leadership has something in common with most approaches to relational leadership, it is distinct in key ways. These distinctions focus on deep convictions to nurture followers' personal freedom and growth and to express their humble, determined will to improve society. Servant leadership is a natural overflow of leaders' underlying beliefs and driving motivations. Consequently, it can only be sustained through embedding relational leadership's four core beliefs into the leader's self-concept. The four core beliefs thus become a measure of the extent to which leaders are, in Greenleaf's words, servants first.

What are some common misconceptions about servant leadership as practiced in organizational settings?

Greenleaf rejected attaching specific descriptions or definitions to servant leadership, likely in part because of his desire that it emerge naturally from a servant mindset, that the servant-leader be guided by doing as much good as possible without ascribing to certain decision rules or, in his words, "checklists" (Greenleaf, 1996). Whereas this may be excellent advice for those leading from their hearts, it's less useful to those of us attempting to understand exactly what servant leadership entails. And this decision by Greenleaf may have inadvertently led to the emergence of myths about servant leadership, which represent the idea in ways inconsistent with both Greenleaf's own writings and subsequent research.

The understanding of servant leadership provided here, based on influence and motivation in service to stakeholders, is suggestive of what servant leadership is. In seeking to understand exactly what something is, though, it is also important to clearly grasp what something *is not*. The existence of several myths about servant leadership suggest important starting points for establishing its boundaries. In this section, we review four myths about servant leadership, and explain how each is incompatible with the core ideas of this form of leadership.

1. Servant leadership is 'soft.'

Some individuals have suggested that servant leadership is a relatively soft form focused on being as nice as possible to followers. Dave Berkus (2016) forcefully makes this point as he argues that servant leadership "doesn't sound tough or forceful enough," before concluding that it creates "the perception of that leader being soft and lacking in strong leadership traits." Others argue that being nice is itself contradictory to leadership, citing research to claim that "real-world success comes from behaviors that are precisely the opposite of typical leadership prescriptions" (Pfeffer, 2015). Writers at *Forbes* (Ashgar, 2014) go even further as they claim that nice leaders finish last, whereas more narcissistic, self-centered leaders are the ones best positioned for success. Let's start with the last claim. The argument that self-centered, rather than other-centered, leaders are best positioned to succeed has been around for a while, at least since Milton Friedman argued that a profit focus was the only reasonable priority for modern businesses (Friedman, 1982). The *Forbes* piece, as do many others, draws upon a *Harvard Business Review* article by Michael Maccoby (2000) which proposes that narcissists are the "new and daring" leaders who tend to emerge as chief executives, and who match heroic myths regarding what good leadership is. However, Maccoby (2003) is much more nuanced in his conclusions than those who draw on him, noting that although the narcissists that tend to emerge as leaders have many strengths, they have just as many weaknesses, including sensitivity to criticism, poor mentoring skills, and relatively low levels of empathy and ethics. Subsequent empirical research on narcissistic leaders has presented a somewhat negative picture: whereas self-centered people do often become leaders, they do not typically enjoy long-term success (Judge, LePine, & Rich, 2006). In the short term, narcissists seem bold, charismatic, confident, and visionary. In the long-term, though, they tend to be revealed as fragile, self-centered, and exceedingly poor relationship managers. Arijit Chatterjee and Don Hambrick have devoted several years to studying narcissism in executive leadership in hundreds of companies, and have concluded that self-centered managers take more risks and make bigger moves, but don't drive greater performance; instead, they tend to ignore objective data in favor of seeking social praise (Chatterjee & Hambrick, 2007, 2011).

Of course, just because a self-centered narcissistic leader isn't ideal, that doesn't necessarily mean that the opposite type of leader is better. As Michael Fertik (2014) excellently pointed out in *HBR*, a problem can emerge if a leader is *too* nice. A leader whose every action is driven by maintaining the mood and ego of his or her followers is a "doormat," one who isn't ready or willing to push a team to higher levels of performance. And the servant leader, clearly, *isn't* that 'too nice' leader. Greenleaf wrote that the servant-leader has the long-term best interests of others at heart, which may conflict with making them feel good right now. The most successful developer of followers at AT&T, he wrote, didn't prioritize their happiness and the ease of their jobs, but rather worked to ensure they remained busy with challenging work. He was friendly, but "not folksy or chatty." He would even go so far as to knowingly help some of his more arrogant team members fail, so that he could help them learn from the experience (Greenleaf, 1998). The servant-leader must ask, "Am I willing to say, 'Do it now!' when it would be more pleasant all around if I said, 'Tomorrow is OK'?" (Greenleaf, 1996: p. 48).

The servant-leader builds strong relationships and cares for stakeholders. But the servant-leader is no pushover. In the drive to help others maximize their potential, servant-leaders push those followers, further and further, to surpass their self-perceived limitations. The servant-leader may act out of concern and care, but their actions are hardly those of a soft touch.

2. Servant leadership stands in the way of profit.

Given the servant leader's emphasis on stakeholder good—benefiting followers, customers, communities, and societies—it is not unreasonable to wonder where a business's profit focus comes into play. It is not uncommon to hear that servant leadership is therefore antithetical to the needs of a business. A focus on stakeholders and communities must come at the expense of revenues and profits, it's argued, and servant-leaders direct attentions and resources away from what a business needs (e.g. Andersen, 2009; Giampetro-Meyer, Brown, Browne, & Kubasek, 1998). If organizational concerns are secondary, then servant-leaders cannot be the most effective stewards of an organization.

These are at first glance compelling points, which have spurred some heated rebuttals from the servant leadership community which, we argue, risk creating a false dichotomy. For instance, an article covering servant leadership in *About Leaders* (McCuistion, 2018) argues that "leaders must choose between doing the right thing for employees over increasing the bottom line." The author may be on to something, but Greenleaf would argue that it's not quite so simple as choosing one over the other. This is put most clearly in his letter to a firm hoping to become a servant leadership organization, which he starts by advising them: "... the company is to be economically successful... The criteria for economic success are well established and the economic performance of the company as a whole is currently good. This is to be maintained." (Greenleaf, 1970, p. 172). Indeed, there's a reason that stewardship and conceptual skills of understanding the business are often listed as key dimensions of servant leadership (Liden et al., 2008; van Dierendonck & Nuijten, 2010): Without a meaningful focus on revenue and profit, an organization cannot be sustainable. And regardless of how much an organization serves today, there will be no organization serving tomorrow if it can't keep the lights on.

The argument of servant leadership, rather, is that profit is a key priority of an organization, but one of several. Further, profit may be best developed through active stakeholder involvement, engagement, and service. Professor Ed Freeman has argued consistently in his stakeholder theory of the organization that (a) serving customers, employees, and communities is a highly effective method to generate long-term financial success, and (b) serving those stakeholders is a valued end, in and unto itself (Freeman, 1984). Empirical research tends to back up these propositions, showing that stakeholder service pays off over time: Firms that focus broadly on stakeholder needs, rather than only stockholder performance, tend to experience greater return on investment (ROI) and growth (de Luque, Washburn, Waldman, & House, 2008). Executive servant leadership, in particular, is related to greater return on assets (Peterson, Galvin, & Lange, 2012), even when controlling for more charismatic, transformational leadership behaviors. Throughout organizations, servant leadership has been consistently related to employee and team effectiveness, engagement, commitment, well-being, and innovation, through over 50 studies published in peer-reviewed scientific journals (Lemoine et al., 2019), all of which are directly related to firm profitability.

3. Servant leadership is just being ethical.

Some advocates of servant leadership have attempted to simplify it by arguing that it's just about "doing the right thing" (e.g. Drucker, 2003; Hunter, 2018). But as argued above, "ethics" is a deceptively complicated term, and the servant-leader uses a very specific approach to ethics focused on stakeholder good. Beyond the definitional flexibility, this understanding of servant leadership is also problematic in that it encourages the two myths debunked above, as "ethics" doesn't necessarily involve profitability concerns or delivering difficult feedback to employees. Do servant-leaders attempt to be ethical by putting the needs of others first? Absolutely. But there's a good bit more to servant leadership than just ethics. Liden and colleagues (2008) developed the most validated and accepted structure of servant leadership in the academic research world, and they argued that ethical behavior—which they defined as characteristics such as honesty and fairness—was just one of seven dimensions of servant leadership. The others, reviewed earlier, include competencies less related to morality such as conceptual skills, empowering, and developing employees. Ethics, or at least a stakeholder-focused application of ethics, may indeed capture *part* of the servant leader, but not the whole.

4. Servant leadership is just about helping followers.

One of the more prominent myths among supporters of servant leadership, the idea that such leadership focuses solely on putting followers first, is not entirely accurate. From Wikipedia to the Society for Human Resource Management, servant leadership is often described as simply involving serving followers and serving their needs (which likely contributes to the myths above that servant leadership is anti-profit and too nice). Of course, servant-leaders do prioritize helping and developing followers to be the best they can be, but just focusing on the followers alone misses what is arguably Greenleaf's most important point about servant leadership.

In the first section of the first essay on servant leadership that Greenleaf released, he asked how many reasonably effective and moral leaders, "... having taken their firm stand against injustice and hypocrisy, find it hard to convert themselves into *affirmative builders* of a better society. How many of them will seek their personal fulfillment by making the hard choices and by undertaking the rigorous preparation that building a better society requires?" (Greenleaf, 1970: p. 24). The juxtaposition of the terms "servant" and "leader" was not meant simply to imply that a leader should serve followers, but instead that the best leader would be driven by a desire to serve, as idealistic as it sounds, all mankind. This naturally includes followers but is not limited to them. Rather, the servant-leader hopes to use their position of authority to leave the world a better place than he or she found it. As a young man, Greenleaf abandoned his early interests in mathematics and engineering to focus on leadership development after hearing specifically not of the impact leaders could have on *followers*, but their potential effects on society. He writes that this conversion took place, and the seeds for servant leadership planted, when his Professor Helming of Carleton College remarked that the world could not improve "unless there are people inside these institutions who are able to, and who want to, lead them into better performance for the public good." This idea of 'better performance for the public good' sums up servant leadership remarkably well: The organization will perform at high levels, and as it does so, it will create benefits for wider communities of stakeholders.

And effective servant leadership does indeed seem to have an impact outside of work teams. Customer service is one practical outcome of this focus, and research indicates that teams and individuals led by servant-leaders tend to place higher priorities on meeting customer needs, going above and beyond expectations to guarantee customer happiness and loyalty (e.g. Chen, Zhu, & Zhou, 2015; Jaramillo, Grisaffe, Chonko, & Roberts, 2009). Rather than caring only for a small group of followers, effective servant-leaders build cultures around moral character (Verdorfer, Steinheider, & Burkus, 2015) and service to others (Liden, Wayne, Liao, & Meuser, 2014). Furthermore, their followers subsequently start acting as servant-leaders themselves, regardless of whether or not they hold leadership positions (Lemoine & Blum, in press; Ling, Lin, & Wu, 2016). To our knowledge, servant leadership is the only form of leadership that has been scientifically demonstrated to include a focus on creating value for the community, and to have subsequent positive effects on community citizenship (Liden et al., 2008).

Altogether, the evidence suggests that servant-leaders do indeed prioritize service to followers, but that's only one of several stakeholder groups. Drawing from the work of Larry Spears, the former CEO of the Greenleaf Center for Servant Leadership, *Entrepreneur* listed six main principles of servant leadership, and one of them was "Building community." They quote the CEO of Unilever, one of the largest consumer-goods firms in the world, as stating that, "You can put yourself to the purpose of others, and in doing so, you can be better off" (Smale, 2018).

How can servant leadership be better infused into today's organizations?

As the preceding sections explained, servant leadership can only be infused into organizations to the extent that leaders actually believe its underlying precepts: pursuing the greatest good (particularly championing the plight of the powerless), empowering others, creating self-transcendence, and enabling regeneration unequivocally benefit others and build a good and better society. All of these beliefs combine to produce a sustaining desire, drive, and determination for servant-leaders to serve, and "to serve first" (Greenleaf, 1970, p. 27). This selfless conviction inoculates servant-leaders from the temptation to serve followers as a means to an end. Instead, they serve followers for their benefit, regardless of whether their followers reciprocate. Servant-leaders genuinely care about their followers and believe in the transformative power of serving others. Servant leadership is an expression of the heart. It is an end in itself. Once leaders buy into the beliefs that undergird servant leadership, they can embed servant leadership into organizations through three intersection points: organizational culture, leader time horizons, and flourishing human resource (HR) practices.

Intersection Point #1 – Organizational Culture

Leaders have an indelible role in fashioning their organization's culture. Research indicates that servant leadership produces a service climate and a fairness climate (Walumbwa, Hartnell, & Oke, 2010) as well as a serving culture within their workgroups (Liden et al., 2014). These social contexts motivate followers to go above and beyond to help their organization (Ehrhart, 2004), serve their customers (Chen et al., 2015), and contribute to the community by volunteering for community activities outside of work (Liden et al., 2008). In addition to empirical evidence, anecdotal examples illustrate how servant leadership beliefs can be embedded into an organization's culture. Consider the case of the PPC Partners companies, a 100% employee-owned holding company managing four of the largest and most successful electrical contractors in the U.S. The dominant goals at PPC Partners reflect servant leadership's ethos:

> "Ask any leader at PPC Partners what the single, most important goal of the company is and the answer may surprise you. It is not profit, market share, or innovation, though they certainly matter. The answer is developing people to their highest potential. That is how the company prospers long-term." (*PPC Partners: The Power to Serve*, 2011, p. 92)

Starbucks' culture also illustrates how servant leadership principles can be integrated within the organization. The leadership team at Starbucks has built a culture of community welfare through its efforts to improve sustainability, strengthen communities, and create mechanisms for social mobility for vulnerable members of the community. As a testament of the employment opportunities it creates for those within the community, Starbucks has hired over 71,000 Opportunity Youth (people aged 16 to 24 who are out of work and not in school), 1,600 refugees, and over 22,000 veterans and military spouses (Starbucks Corporation, 2019).

Intersection Point #2 – Leader Time Horizons

In addition to embedding core servant leadership beliefs into an organization's way of doing things, servant leadership can be infused into organizations by encouraging leaders to pursue higher-order goals by extending their time horizons. Seldom do quick fixes or short-term solutions exist to attain stakeholders' higher-order needs or an organization's higher-order goals (e.g., industry, community, or societal impact). Instead, higher-order goals are often achieved by shifting a leader's mindset to a long-term orientation. Investing in follower growth may pay short-term dividends, but the benefits accrue exponentially over the long term (for the organization and beyond). Leaders should be encouraged to transcend the allure of reacting to achieve immediate results by thoughtfully developing a relational strategy to build followers' current and future competencies. For example, leaders who consistently express care and empathy toward their followers may reap immediate relational dividends but may also, and more importantly, shape followers' behaviors toward their colleagues, customers, children, and others with whom they come in contact. A long-term view of relational investment promises to reap munificent economic and social benefits. Moreover, this long-term focus produces a growth mindset in which leaders are free to enrich the lives of people with whom they come into contact and leave others better off because of their influence.

Might employees take advantage of selfless giving? Consider PPC Partners' perspective when key employees left the company to start their own business. Leaders at PPC Partners thought to themselves: "They may be more effective working for themselves than they can be working with PPC. If we are practicing servant leadership, we might want to help them get into business and do business with them" (*PPC Partners: The Power to Serve*, 2011, p. 161). Ultimately, personal outcomes are inconsequential. It's societal benefit that matters most. Servant-leaders believe that societal benefit leads to organizational success, and the research indicates that this belief is accurate (de Luque et al., 2008).

Intersection Point #3 – Flourishing Human Resource (HR) Practices

Servant leadership can be infused into organizations through attention to organizational HR policies and practices that promote equal opportunities, employee safety, and employee growth. Organizations should equip leaders to develop competencies related to ethical decision making and investing in followers' growth. As noted earlier, servant-leaders behave ethically by serving the needs of multiple stakeholders. As such, organizational policies, practices, procedures, and norms should be aligned with this underlying ethic. If norms prevent followers from flourishing and realizing their potential, a true servant-leader will strive to change those norms so that they help followers without hurting other stakeholders. Let us consider three HR practices that promote equal opportunities, employee safety, and employee growth, respectively.

Equal opportunities. Starbucks' commitment to pay, gender, and racial equality within the organization imbues servant leadership's emphasis on respect and inclusion. In 2017, Starbucks reported that the organization has reached 100% pay equity for employees of all genders and races (Starbucks Corporation, 2019). Starbucks is currently taking strides to ensure that all races and genders are well-represented in top management. The organization aims to have 50% of all senior leadership positions occupied by women. It also pledges to increase the racial diversity of its senior leaders by 50% (Starbucks Corporation, 2019). Starbuck's commitment to high ethical and moral standards extends to their practices and procedures for producing beverages. To date, over 99% of coffee and 95% of tea sold by the organization is verified as ethically sourced under C.A.F.E. Practices (Starbucks Corporation, 2019).

Employee safety. Servant-leaders also safeguard employees' well-being by adopting policies and procedures that keep employees safe. "Safety" is one of the few keywords included at the heart of PPC Partners' mission statement: "The mission of PPC is to provide technically advanced building services, equipment services, and on-site electrical construction while maintaining a safe, high quality, low cost advanced service delivery system" (PPC Partners, 2018). Richard Pieper, the founder and former head of PPC Partners, explains that safety is a core value at PPC Partners not because it will bring more business for the company over the long term or because it is a norm in the industry, but because "it's the right thing to do…our approach [to safety] has always been a moral one" (*PPC Partners: The Power to Serve*, 2011, p. 155).

Todd Cook, safety manager at PPC Partners, similarly notes that safety makes business sense because it helps employees get back to work sooner should an accident occur: "Think about a person who has an injury…when people are left at home, often alone, they may think that their company doesn't care about them. I think it's our moral obligation to get people back to productive work as soon as we can" (*PPC Partners: The Power to Serve*, 2011, p. 157). Such a strong emphasis on safety not only serves employees' best interests, but it also affects the industry in two ways. First, PPC Partners asks its subcontractors to fully comply with PPC Partners' safety standards and expectations. Subcontractors would be denied new work by PPC Partners if they did not commit to equally high levels about safety. This point illustrates that a company's ethical norms can extend beyond their organizational boundaries to other organizations with which it is connected. Their ethical standards thus have a magnified positive impact on employees within their larger realm of influence. Second, this emphasis on safety produced markedly low accident rates and helped PPC earn some of the biggest contracts in the industry (*PPC Partners: The Power to Serve*, 2011). This sequence of events bolstered the company's profitability.

Employee growth. Servant leadership can be instilled within an organization by adopting practices that help followers grow and succeed by providing professional and socioemotional resources (see regenerative skills shown in Figure 1). Growing others' skills encompasses building others' leadership capacity and multiplying one's leadership influence through mentoring. PPC partners illustrates these concepts through offering employees continuous education within the organization and incentivizing them to continue their formal education. Moreover, people must successfully mentor a subordinate to be their successor if they desire to advance to a higher managerial position. As such, organizational policies and practices support servant leadership principles related to building employees' leadership capacity and the organization's leadership capacity (through mentoring).

Organizations can also strengthen employees' socioemotional resources. Leader integrity is an integral mechanism through which leaders build trust with stakeholders and contribute toward their stakeholders' socioemotional well-being. Followers evaluate leaders' integrity by examining the alignment between their words and actions. Integrity is paramount for servant leaders. According to Richard Pieper, servant-leaders have "radical integrity in all they do…it is the heartfelt words, action and empathy of another that raises up society, an organization, a community, a family or an individual" (Jagler, 2017). In April 2018, Starbucks' Chief Executive Officer, Kevin Johnson, modeled integrity through his response following a national controversy in which two black men were arrested while waiting for a meeting at their local Starbucks in Philadelphia (Stevens, 2018). Regarding the incident, Johnson remarked, "We work to create a warm welcoming environment for all customers … We failed to do that on that day. It was an opportunity for us to step back and learn and acknowledge that we can be better" (Haddon, 2019). Johnson responded to the incident by closing 8,000 Starbucks stores in the United States on May 29[t], 2018 and providing 175,000 employees with anti-bias and inclusion training (Starbucks Corporation, 2019). These actions signaled an alignment between the leader's espoused values and his commitment to enact behaviors that reflect those values.

Conclusion

Servant leadership is a powerful concept that has transformative relational potential. Servant-leaders are visionaries who are unconstrained by short-term worries and others' actions. They are free to impact society for the better because they buy into four relational pillars: morality, empowerment, self-transcendence, and regeneration. Their influence multiplies because they grow healthier, wiser, and freer people. After all, "growing and building" is the hallmark of servant leadership: "For the servant who has the capacity to be a builder, the greatest joy in this world is in building" (Greenleaf, 1977, p. 261). Why settle for bigger buildings when you can invest in building better lives and molding the hearts and minds of future generations? How will you steward your influence? Will it leave a legacy that outlives you?

Chapter 5 References

Adubato, S. (2017, January 16). *M&T bank focuses on community development* [Video file]. Retrieved from https://www.youtube.com/watch?v=m8f_A8AxA10

Allen, E., & Williams, J. (2019). Employee engagement+ social good= a winning combination. *Journal-American Water Works Association, 111*(1), 52-55.

Ajzen, I. (1991). The theory of planned behavior. *Organizational Behavior and Human Decision Processes, 50*(2), 179-211.

Andersen, J. A. (2009). When a servant-leader comes knocking. *Leadership & Organization Development Journal, 30*(1), 4-15.

Ashgar, R. (2014, November 19). You're Too Nice To Be A Great Leader (And That's Okay). *Forbes.* Retrieved from https://www.forbes.com/sites/robasghar/2014/11/19/youre-too-nice-to-be-a-great-leader-and-thats-okay/#69bef9f97112

Avolio, B. J., Gardner, W. L., Walumbwa, F. O., Luthans, F., & May, D. R. (2004). Unlocking the mask: A look at the process by which authentic leaders impact follower attitudes and behaviors. *The Leadership Quarterly, 15*(6), 801-823.

Berkus, D. (2016). Is 'servant leadership' too soft for today's workforce? *Berkonomics.* Retrieved from https://berkonomics.com/?p=2662

Blanchard, K., & Broadwell, R. (2018). *Servant leadership in action: How you can achieve great relationships and results.* Oakland, CA: Berrett-Koehler Publishers.

Brown, M. E., Treviño, L. K., & Harrison, D. A. (2005). Ethical leadership: A social learning perspective for construct development and testing. *Organizational Behavior and Human Decision Processes, 97*(2), 117-134.

Brown-Hall, C. (2017). Our Dedicated Team. Retrieved from https://allwelcares.com/about_home_care/our-caregivers/.

Chaplain's Group. (n.d.). Retrieved from https://www.interstatebatteries.com/about/chaplains-group

Chatterjee, A., & Hambrick, D. C. (2007). It's all about me: Narcissistic chief executive officers and their effects on company strategy and performance. *Administrative Science Quarterly,* *52*(3), 351-386.

Chatterjee, A., & Hambrick, D. C. (2011). Executive personality, capability cues, and risk taking. *Administrative Science Quarterly,* *56*(2), 202-237.

Chen, G., Sharma, P. N., Edinger, S. K., Shapiro, D. L., & Farh, J. L. (2011). Motivating and demotivating forces in teams: Cross-level influences of empowering leadership and relationship conflict. *Journal of Applied Psychology, 96*(3), 541.

Chen, Z., Zhu, J., & Zhou, M. (2015). How does a servant-leader fuel the service fire? A multilevel model of servant leadership, individual self identity, group competition climate, and customer service performance. *Journal of Applied Psychology, 100*(2), 511-521.

Collins, J. (2001). *Good to great: Why some companies make the leap... and others don't.* New York: Harper Business.

Conger, J. A., & Kanungo, R. N. (1998). *Charismatic leadership in organizations.* Thousand Oaks, CA: Sage Publications.

DardenMBA (2015, November 15). *Inspiring Leaders: Robert G. Wilmers, M&T Bank Corporation* [Video file]. Retrieved from https://www.youtube.com/watch?v=miBPl5aXd10

Deci, E. L., & Ryan, R. M. (2000). The" what" and" why" of goal pursuits: Human needs and the self-determination of behavior. *Psychological Inquiry, 11*(4), 227-268.

de Luque, M. S., Washburn, N. T., Waldman, D. A., & House, R. J. (2008). Unrequited profit: How stakeholder and economic values relate to subordinates' perceptions of leadership and firm performance. *Administrative Science Quarterly, 53*(4), 626-654.

Drucker, P. F. (2003). *The Essential Drucker.* New York: HarperCollins.

EA Engineering, Science, and Technology, Incorporated. (2017). *Memorandum: 2017 company goals.* Hunt Valley, MD: Ian MacFarlane.

Ehrhart, M. G. (2004). Leadership and procedural justice climate as antecedents of unit-level organizational citizenship behavior. *Personnel Psychology, 57*(1), 61-94.

Fertik, M. (2014, April 07). The Problem With Being Too Nice. *Harvard Business Review.* Retrieved from https://hbr. org/2014/04/the-problem-with-being-too-nice

Freeman, R. E. (1984). *Strategic management: A stakeholder approach.* Boston, MA: Pitman.

Friedman, M. (1982). *Capitalism and freedom.* Chicago, IL: University of Chicago Press.

George, B. (2010). *True north: Discover your authentic leadership.* San Francisco, CA: John Wiley & Sons.

Giampetro-Meyer, A., Brown, T., Browne, M. N., & Kubasek, N. (1998). Do we really want more leaders in business? *Journal of Business Ethics, 17*(15), 1727-1736.

Glynn, M., & Epstein, J. D. (2017, December 17). End of an era: M&T's Robert Wilmers, force in community, dies at 83. *The Buffalo News.* Retrieved from https://buffalonews. com/2017/12/17/mt-chairman-wilmers-has-died/

Greenleaf, R. K. (1970). *The servant as leader.* Newton Centre, MA: The Robert K. Greenleaf Center.

Greenleaf, R. K. (1977). *Servant Leadership: A journey into the nature of legitimate power and greatness.* Mahwah, NJ: Paulist Press.

Greenleaf, R. K. (1996). *On becoming a servant leader: The private writings of Robert K. Greenleaf.* San Francisco, CA: Jossey-Bass.

Greenleaf, R. K. (1998). *The power of servant leadership.* San Francisco, CA: Berrett-Koehler.

Greenleaf, R. K. (2002). *Servant leadership.* South Orange, NJ: Greenleaf Institute for Servant Leadership.

Gold Standards. (n.d.). Retrieved from http://www.ritzcarlton.com/ en/about/gold-standards

Haddon, H. (2019, October 10). Meet the Starbucks CEO who has to follow Howard Schultz. *The Wall Street Journal.* Retrieved from https://www.wsj.com/articles/meet-the-starbucks-ceo-who-has-to-follow-howard-schultz-11570708802

Hennick, C. (2019). Emphasis on the public good. *Engineering Inc., 2-5.* Retrieved from https://www.acec.org/publications/engineering-inc/

House, R. J. (1977). A 1976 theory of charismatic leadership. In J. G Hunt and L. L. Larson (Eds.), *Leadership: The cutting edge.* Carbondale, IL: Southern Illinois University Press.

Hunter, J. (2018). Jim Hunter - Servant Leadership Interview Series. In B. Lichtenwalner (Ed.).

Jagler, S. (2017, April 8). Pieper is the ultimate servant leader. *Milwaukee Journal Sentinel.* Retrieved from https://www.jsonline.com/story/money/columnists/steve-jagler/2017/04/08/jagler-pieper-ultimate-servant-leader/100173526/

Jaramillo, F., Grisaffe, D. B., Chonko, L. B., & Roberts, J. A. (2009). Examining the impact of servant leadership on sales force performance. *Journal of Personal Selling & Sales Management, 29*(3), 257-275.

Judge, T. A., LePine, J. A., & Rich, B. L. (2006). Loving yourself abundantly: Relationship of the narcissistic personality to self- and other perceptions of workplace deviance, leadership, and task and contextual performance. *Journal of Applied Psychology, 91*(4), 762-776.

Leadership. (n.d.a). Retrieved from https://www.interstatebatteries.com/about/leadership/chris-willishttps://www.interstatebatteries.com/about/leadership/chris-willis

Leadership. (n.d.b). Retrieved from https://www.interstatebatteries.com/about/leadership/norm-millerhttps://www.interstatebatteries.com/about/leadership/norm-miller

Lemoine, G. J., & Blum, T. C. (in press). Servant leadership, leader gender, and team gender role: Testing a female advantage in a cascading model of performance. *Personnel Psychology.* doi:10.1111/peps.12379

Lemoine, G.J. & Blum, T.C. (2020). Leadership and servant leadership: Understanding both by bridging the past and present. In Burkhardt, J.C. & Joslin, J.Y. (Eds.), *Inspiration for servant leaders: Lessons from fifty years of research and practice* (pp. 3-45). Atlanta, GA: Greenleaf Center for Servant Leadership.

Lemoine, G. J., Hartnell, C. A., & Leroy, H. (2019). Taking stock of moral approaches to leadership: An integrative review of ethical, authentic, and servant leadership. *Academy of Management Annals, 13*(1), 148-187.

Liden, R. C., Wayne, S., Liao, C., & Meuser, J. (2014). Servant leadership and serving culture: Influence on individual and unit performance. *Academy of Management Journal, 57*(5), 1434-1452.

Liden, R. C., Wayne, S. J., Zhao, H., & Henderson, D. (2008). Servant leadership: Development of a multidimensional measure and multi-level assessment. *The Leadership Quarterly, 19*(2), 161-177.

Ling, Q., Lin, M. Z., & Wu, X. Y. (2016). The trickle-down effect of servant leadership on frontline employee service behaviors and performance: A multilevel study of Chinese hotels. *Tourism Management, 52*, 341-368.

Luthans, F., & Avolio, B. J. (2003). Authentic leadership development. In K. S. Cameron, J. E. Dutton, & R. E. Quinn (Eds.), *Positive Organizational Scholarship* (pp. 241-258). San Francisco, CA: Berrett-Koehler Publishers.

Lutz, A. (2014, October 13). Nordsrom's employee handbook has only one rule. *Business Insider.* Retrieved from https://www.businessinsider.com/nordstroms-employee-handbook-2014-10

Maccoby, M. (2000). Narcissistic leaders: The incredible pros, the inevitable cons. *Harvard Business Review, 78*(1), 68-78.

Maccoby, M. (2003). *The Productive Narcissist: The Promise & Peril of Visionary Leadership.* New York, NY: Broadway Books.

Maxwell, J. C. (2011). *The 5 levels of leadership: Proven steps to maximize your potential.* New York, NY: Hachette Book Group.

McCuistion, D. (2018, July 3). The Courage of Servant Leadership. *About Leaders.* Retrieved, from https://aboutleaders.com/courage-servant-leadership/#gs.IQ5v7JI

Our Culture. (n.d.). Retrieved from https://www.interstatebatteries.com/about/our-culture

Owens, B. P., Johnson, M. D., & Mitchell, T. R. (2013). Expressed humility in organizations: Implications for performance, teams, and leadership. *Organization Science, 24*(5), 1517-1538.

Peterson, S. J., Galvin, B. M., & Lange, D. (2012). CEO servant leadership: Exploring executive characteristics and firm performance. *Personnel Psychology, 65*(3), 565-596.

Pfeffer, J. (2015, August 7). Everything we bash Donald Trump for is actually what we seek in leaders. *Fortune.* Retrieved from http://fortune.com/2015/08/07/donald-trump-leadership-lessons/

PPC Partners. (2018). Who we are. Retrieved from http://ppcpartners.com/

Schein, E. H., & Schein, P. A. (2018). *Humble leadership: The power of relationships, openness, and trust.* Oakland, CA: Berrett-Koehler Publishers, Inc.

Shamir, B., & Eilam-Shamir, G. (2018). "What's your story?" A life-stories approach to authentic leadership development. In I. Katz, G. Shamir, R. Kark, & Y. Berson (Eds.), *Leadership Now: Reflections on the Legacy of Boas Shamir* (pp. 51-76). Bingley, WA: Emerald Publishing Limited.

Shamir, B., House, R. J., & Arthur, M. B. (1993). The motivational effects of charismatic leadership: A self-concept based theory. *Organization Science, 4*, 577-594.

Smale, T. (2018, January 24). 'Servant Leadership' and How Its 6 Main Principles Can Boost the Success of Your Startup. *Entrepreneur.* Retrieved from https://www.entrepreneur.com/article/307923

Spreitzer, G. M. (1995). Psychological empowerment in the workplace: Dimensions, measurement, and validation. *Academy of Management Journal, 38*(5), 1442-1465.

Starbucks Corporation. (2019, August 13). *2018 Starbucks Global Social Impact Report* [Press release]. Retrieved from https://stories.starbucks.com/stories/2019/2018-starbucks-global-social-impact-report/

Stevens, M. (2018, April 15). Starbucks C.E.O. apologizes after arrests of 2 black men. *The New York Times.* Retrieved from https://www.nytimes.com/2018/04/15/us/starbucks-philadel-phia-black-men-arrest.html

Uhl-Bien, M. (2006). Relational leadership theory: Exploring the social processes of leadership and organizing. *Leadership Quarterly, 17*, 654-676.

van Dierendonck, D., & Nuijten, I. (2010). The servant leadership survey: Development and validation of a multidimensional measure. *Journal of Business and Psychology,* 1-19.

Verdorfer, A. P., Steinheider, B., & Burkus, D. (2015). Exploring the socio-moral climate in organizations: An empirical examination of determinants, consequences, and mediating mechanisms. *Journal of Business Ethics, 132*(1), 233-248.

Walumbwa, F. O., Hartnell, C. A., & Oke, A. (2010). Servant leadership, procedural justice climate, service climate, employee attitudes, and organizational citizenship behavior: A cross-level investigation. *Journal of Applied Psychology, 95*(3), 517.

Waldman, D. A., & Yammarino, F. J. (1999). CEO charismatic leadership: Levels-of-management and levels-of-analysis effects. *Academy of Management Review, 24*(2), 266-285.

Zhang, X., & Bartol, K. M. (2010). Linking empowering leadership and employee creativity: The influence of psychological empowerment, intrinsic motivation, and creative process engagement. *Academy of Management Journal, 53*(1), 107-128.

Chapter 6

Servant Leadership in Practice: A Lived Example

Ashleigh E. Bell

WHAT DOES SERVANT LEADERSHIP LOOK LIKE IN PRACTICE? What impact do servant-leaders have on the organizations they serve and lead? This chapter tells the story of how one servant leadership practitioner discovered servant leadership, how he lives it out, and how his servant-first practices have created opportunities for his employees and broader community throughout the course of his robust career.

There is a reluctance it seems to identify oneself as a servant leader. It may appear to be immodest or over reaching. But individuals who seek to respond to the challenge described by Robert Greenleaf have not only a right but perhaps some responsibility to articulate their desire to lead in a way that is consonant with the ideals Greenleaf promoted. If followers are to know what to expect and if the leader truly wishes to be held fully accountable for her or his actions, stating a high standard is entirely consistent with the concepts described in this book.

Setting a high bar also has the effect of inspiring others towards their own expressions of greatness. Particularly within the context of a long-standing organization, the commitments made by highly visible executives—when they are consistently backed up with action—lift the sights and clarifies what is expected of all others and at all levels. For a non-profit organization, a government agency, an educational institution or a company in a competitive business environment to grow into a servant led success, the leader may be self-effacing in many ways but must be bold in espousing the core values of the organization.

There are many individuals, some well known and many still not celebrated, that have committed themselves to meeting "the difficult test" that Greenleaf specified in his essay, "The Servant as Leader," and repeated many times in the years of his speaking and writing. Examining one could do a disservice to others if in any way it diminishes their efforts. But leaving the discussion of servant leadership without pointing out that this concept can be realized (by mere mortals no less!) would run the risk of suggesting that the concept is beyond us all. It is not, as the example offered here attests.

Challenge and formation

Richard Pieper became the president of his family's company, Pieper Electric, at the age of 24 and over many years has grown the business to become one of the top electrical contracting firms in the United States. Today, the company is known as PPC Partners, employing approximately 1,600 people across nine states (Jagler, 2017). "Dick" Pieper currently serves as the non-executive chairman of the Milwaukee-based company while leading a number of philanthropic ventures in his community. This chapter is based on an interview I sought with Mr. Pieper. In March 2019, we spoke together about his experiences and his evolution as a leader of a major business and in his community. As you will discover, our rich and wide-ranging discussion was full of surprises and offered evidence of his deep commitment to servant leadership.

Pieper emerged as an entrepreneur early in his life, embracing a range of opportunities to learn all while serving others from a very young age. During World War II, he sold supplies necessary to make soap by scraping the fat off of grills, collecting it in cans to sell to the butcher. At the same time, he supported a sick family member by selling the crafts she made in order to help pay for her medical care. Throughout his childhood, Pieper participated in the Boy Scouts and first belonged to a troop that did not have a trained leader. Despite the lack of structure, Pieper excelled and served as an assistant scoutmaster before finishing grade school. Later, as a college student, Pieper took on several leadership roles including being the president of his fraternity, vice president of the fraternity counsel, and chairman of elections among other roles. Although Pieper attended classes and worked toward a technical degree, his focus was on organizing and leading people. These early experiences foreshadowed the work that he would do over the course of his career, leading and mentoring others and creating the conditions where all members of a community can thrive.

When Pieper, in his early twenties, purchased his family's business from his father, he became increasingly involved in the Young Presidents' Organization (YPO), a network of young chief executives that presented Pieper with a range of learning experiences. Through YPO, he had the opportunity to travel to Turkey to consult with an international engineering company with a goal to help improve the company's culture. During this time, Pieper observed that the company was centered around the organization's leader with little regard for or consideration of other employees. He recalled conversations in which the boss asked for team members' input with the clear expectation that they would nod along in agreement and withhold their own independent ideas and contributions. Pieper reflected: "The people were serving the boss and I was serving the people. I reversed the culture, respecting the people who were doing the work." Pieper knew this culture needed to change in order to best serve the company's goals as well as the experiences of the employees. To do this, Pieper advocated for a new style of management that elevated the voices and experiences of employees at all levels of the company. Within his first two weeks, Pieper worked with the leader to implement these new practices. Thirty years later, he returned to the same company and the current employees shared that the management practices Pieper helped implement are still embraced to this day.

Through his work in Turkey, Pieper sought to put the employees first and create structures and systems that would leave them more autonomous and help the company to thrive. Around this same time, Robert Greenleaf began to publish his thoughts on leadership. Although Pieper had not yet been introduced to Greenleaf's teachings, he had already begun to model a number of servant leadership principles in his work, as suggested above. In the 1995 book, *Introduction: Servant Leadership and The Greenleaf Legacy*, Larry Spears describes the essence of Pieper's experience in Turkey. He states: "Servant leadership advocates a group-oriented approach to analysis and decision making as a means of strengthening institutions and improving society...Some people have likened [servant leadership] to turning the hierarchical pyramid upside down" (p. 8).

Discovering Greenleaf

Shortly after Greenleaf published his first book, Pieper was given a copy by a colleague. Reading Greenleaf's manuscript, he thought, "This is exactly what we think we're doing [at Pieper Electric]!" After that, he got a book for each member of his executive team and underlined key takeaways to emphasize the philosophical alignment to their current culture. Greenleaf's writings resonated with the group and they agreed that servant leadership captured their work together at Pieper Electric. Despite their initial enthusiasm, the book was put back on the shelf and servant leadership was not explicitly discussed again among the company's leadership until much later.

During this time, Pieper and his wife, Suzanne, were planning for the future and decided that they would not give their assets to their children; instead, they committed to investing back into the community. Pieper recognized that his company was his greatest asset, so he and his executive team agreed to sell the company to their employees at face value. In order to maximize the impact of this action, Pieper researched other companies that were employee owned. In the course of this research, Pieper connected with Jack Lowe, the leader of TD Industries based in Dallas, Texas. At the time, Lowe was the chairman of the Greenleaf Center for Servant Leadership and encouraged Pieper to get involved. Remembering his previous conversations about Greenleaf with his company leadership, Pieper was eager to learn more. Soon Pieper found himself inviting other business leaders to Greenleaf Center meetings and speaking about his work. Excitement surrounding Greenleaf's work spread quickly among Pieper's colleagues and associates.

Embracing servant leadership

After attending a meeting at the Greenleaf Center, Pieper recalled thinking, "This is a great place to be fed on the principles that we believe in." In other words, the community of practice that came together through the Greenleaf Center provided resources and materials that validated and strengthened the management style and culture that already existed at Pieper's organization, which by this point had grown to include a holding company, called PPC Partners. Around the time the company was being converted to employee ownership, Pieper and members of his executive team attended a number of meetings at the Greenleaf Center. Together they became more committed to formally integrating Greenleaf's teachings with their company's culture and goals. Pieper explained that learning more about Greenleaf's writings enhanced the learning processes and systems that existed at PPC Partners, adding supplemental materials, a depth of detail, and structure that did not previously exist.

Pieper emphasized that learning about Greenleaf's work did not directly change the practices of his company. Instead, they provided a formal body of knowledge that, according to Pieper, grounded their work together. His team already had a strong culture that emphasized self-improvement and Greenleaf provided tools that allowed for further learning and development. Peiper went on to say that, "Greenleaf created a reference, a body of knowledge, a source that we could weave through the company that is well-founded."

As Pieper continued to describe the seamless alignment between his company's practices and Greenleaf's texts, he pointed out that Greenleaf talks about the "natural feeling" that people have which directs them to serve as they lead. Greenleaf stated: "The servant-leader is servant first… It begins with the natural feeling that one wants to serve, to serve first" (Greenleaf, 1977). Pieper shared that the people in his company had that natural feeling in common to serve their team and community. He went on to describe it by saying, "That natural feeling lead us—when you come into situations, you naturally want to help, naturally want to serve. And the fact that you have somebody to share that with, expands it. It's a natural thing." This sentiment remains core to Pieper's work and is celebrated on the company's website, which proudly states, "Our people are our power. People are our most valuable asset. We invest in their future. Our people grow in a unique culture of entrepreneurship, empowerment, servant leadership, lifelong learning, quality, safety and high ethical standards" (Our People, n.d.).

Serving his community

In *Reflections on Leadership,* Spears (1995) identifies ten "critical characteristics of the servant leader": listening, empathy, healing, awareness, persuasion, conceptualization, foresight, stewardship, commitment to the growth of people, and building community (pp. 4-7). Pieper exemplifies many of these key characteristics, especially a commitment to the growth of people and building community. In addition to his work with PPC Partners, Pieper has spearheaded the development of a range of resources to serve his local community in his home state of Wisconsin.

Over the years, Pieper has built an infrastructure and many separate communities of practice that foster the development of other professionals looking to embrace the principles of servant leadership in their work. He organized the Wisconsin Servant Leadership (WSL) group which aims to "lift the capacity of others" by offering events, workshops, roundtable discussions, resource sharing and more (Servant Leadership - Lead by Serving, n.d.). Local practitioners can attend in-person offerings while remote community members have access to a wealth of resources through the WSL website and newsletter.

Pieper also invested in the Wisconsin Character Education Partnership (WCEP) with the mission of "promoting the intentional proactive effort by educators to instill in all Wisconsin's students, core universal ethical values such as integrity, honesty, fairness, responsibility, and respect for themselves and for others through character education" (Wisconsin Character Education Partnership, n.d.). WCEP empowers teachers and administrators to lead *and* serve the next generation of young leaders by creating a positive school environment built on a foundation of goodness and integrity (Wisconsin Character Education Partnership, n.d). In addition to WSL and WCEP, Pieper and his family's foundation support a number of other philanthropic causes.

Reflection and example

Reflecting on Pieper's story, I cannot help but think of my own. I began my professional journey as a middle-school teacher in post-Hurricane-Katrina New Orleans, Louisiana. As an educator, I have always considered myself in service to my students and the communities that raised them. I learned about Greenleaf's writings years after my time in New Orleans and I had a similar reaction to Pieper. Discovering servant leadership and Greenleaf's teachings did not change my values or the way I see myself as a leader; however, learning about the principles of servant leadership provided me with a more concrete framework to reflect on my practice and the impact that I have on those I serve. Pieper's experience spreading the teachings of Greenleaf and bringing his colleagues along on his journey to learning about servant leadership opened my eyes to the possibilities of helping foster the growth of my colleagues as much as my students.

Like Pieper, I came to servant leadership after some of my more formative developmental experiences as a leader. Looking back on our conversation, it's easy to notice the many differences between Pieper's path and my own; however, our conversation pushed me to consider the ways that I can expand my impact by empowering other servant leaders. As Spears (1995) wrote, "Servant-leadership crosses all boundaries and is being applied by a wide variety of people working with for-profit businesses, not-for-profit corporations, churches, universities, and foundations" (p. 8). This was reflected throughout my conversation with Pieper.

While this chapter provides a unique and powerful example of servant leadership in practice, it is important to note that this is one example among many. Leadership is not a "one-size-fits-all" phenomenon and in many ways, it looks different on everyone. As an educator and servant leadership practitioner myself, I encourage my students to find their own authentic voice and brand of leadership. Observing others and learning about their journeys helps us to experiment with new styles of leading and consider what feels most natural.

The range of anecdotes, organizations, and individuals illustrated throughout this book provide snapshots of servant leadership in practice. As modern organizations evolve in response to shifts in our culture and society, so do our observations of the principles of servant leadership. Learning about Mr. Pieper's journey and development as a servant-leader and champion of servant leadership allowed me to reflect on my own practice and goals for the legacy that I—and no doubt many others—hope to leave behind.

As you reflect on this chapter, consider what aspects of Pieper's development as a leader and commitment to serving others most resonate with you. If you identify as a servant leader, how do you embrace Greenleaf's teachings as you seek to serve your colleagues or community? If you don't identify as a servant leader, why not? What facets of servant leadership do you observe in your current team or within your organization? Finally, what examples of servant leadership do you observe in today's rapidly evolving, tumultuous political climate? What would you like to see change and how can you serve others in pursuit of this change? I hope that through considering these questions you will deepen your self-awareness and curiosity as a leader by reflecting on the ways in which we work together and serve our broader community.

Chapter 6 References

Greenleaf, R. K. (1977). *Servant leadership: A journey into the nature of legitimate power and greatness.* New York: Paulist Press.

Jagler, S. (2017). Jagler: Pieper is the ultimate servant leader. *Journal Sentinel.* Retrieved from https://www.jsonline. com/story/money/columnists/steve-jagler/2017/04/08/ jagler-pieper-ultimate-servant-leader/100173526/

Mission, Vision & Strategies. (n.d.) Retrieved from https://wicharacter.org/about-us/our-strategies/

Our People. (n.d.) Retrieved from http://ppcpartnersinc.com/ our-people/

Servant Leadership - Lead by Serving. (n.d.) Retrieved from http:// srpieperfamilyfoundation.com/servant-leadership/.

Spears, L. C. (Ed.). (1995). *Reflections on leadership: How Robert K. Greenleaf's theory of servant-leadership influenced today's top management thinkers.* New York, NY: John Wiley & Sons, Inc.

Wisconsin Character Education Partnership. (n.d.) Retrieved from http://srpieperfamilyfoundation.com/character-education/

Conclusion

Prophecy and Disruption

John C. Burkhardt & Jessica Y. Joslin

ROBERT K. GREENLEAF PUBLISHED HIS FIRST ESSAY, "THE Servant as Leader" (1970), fifty years ago. As often observed his perspectives on leadership and on organizational life were in sharp contrast with many of those that preceded him. His essay and subsequent writings were drawn around something that seemed a contradiction, not only illustrated with his titling of the original essay, but one that begged translation both fundamentally and conceptually. Even as his writings have been shared across the world and adopted in many different contexts, the enigmatic relationship between "servant" and "leader" continues to challenge practitioners and scholars alike. This recognition of paradox is not a consequence of ideas that lack clarity nor importance. On the contrary, in common with many comparably profound insights, Greenleaf's description of the servant as leader at times hovers over both scholars and practitioners, where great ideas are acknowledged, but seem often to be just beyond reach.

The dilemma set forward by Greenleaf still puzzles many of us. While his basic concept may prove timeless, it is equally true that the context in which he espoused it has changed dramatically. He wrote at a dramatic moment in our social and political history. Hierarchies were questioned and authority challenged internationally, on our campuses, in our communities, and on the streets. Civil rights were forcefully asserted on behalf of individuals and groups that had been denied opportunities, denied rights, and often denied their very lives for hundreds of years. Our view of poverty, wellness, equity, and justice was reconsidered. The technologies that shape our world in the 21st century and would fundamentally affect every relationship in our lives were, at that time, not even available in dreams. Our understanding of merit and potential, which seemed to be inextricably tied to our perceptions of an eligibility to lead, were beginning to widen. Notably, given the context of Greenleaf's work, our organizations were rapidly changing in size, structure, complexity, and purpose. Indeed, Robert Greenleaf was writing in the midst of an era of what would prove to be relentless, accelerating, and logarithmic change. We are still caught up in it.

Many social historians suggest that we may have been misled into thinking that the world would return to "normal" following two massive wars. Any realization of "normal" became increasingly elusive and indeed neither fair, attractive, nor satisfactory for many. In the end (if we are near the end), "normal" proved impossible for any of us. Because Greenleaf and his concept of servant leadership was ushered out of a specific and disrupted context, and because he took as his subject the character and role of leaders within typical organizational settings of the later 20th century, it is especially appropriate that we reexamine his seminal contributions in the very different contemporary environment we inhabit.

That is the primary reason behind the conception of this book. It may be equally important to know how we wrote it.

We set out to organize our efforts in a way that honored the great insight and unusual vision that Greenleaf demonstrated. We organized with a commitment to benefit from the differences we enjoy because of the ways our worlds have changed in the last fifty years. In terms of theme, substance, and the representation of perspective, we approached the selection of authors, their interactions, and the entire editing process with a goal of bringing new people and ideas into contact with one another and ultimately our readers. To further this commitment, we made use of communications technologies that were not available in 1970, we worked asynchronously, we shared documents in the cloud, we took the luxury of innumerable drafts and revisions, and we anticipated that the finished product would not need to be typeset or bound but could be produced in multiple forms, circulated around the world within a few minutes of our final key strokes. Sadly, none of this accelerated our completion of the book and may have even delayed it. We did meet our goal of recognizing Greenleaf's 50-year anniversary of his original essay (albeit barely).

Amidst all that has changed, perhaps the most important difference we can identify from 1970 to 2020 would be the new attitudes and remarkable new benefits of increased diversity and greater inclusion within our organizations and institutions. Still very fragile and incomplete, comparing then and now does give reason for some hope. Greenleaf wrote of organizations as they were structured and populated in a male-dominated, white, and restricted society. Directly and indirectly those structures still influence us but, like many of our businesses and institutions, we knew we could benefit from the wisdom and experiences of a larger and more diverse group of authors positioned to reflect upon leadership and organizations in a decidedly different society. As this book reflects, many of Greenleaf's concepts resonate even more deeply in this world than the one he left— even if our organizations are not in all cases healthier, safer, or more just than those of half a century ago, as he might have hoped.

This book might have been written by sociologists, cultural historians, or even futurists. We adopted an organization for the book as it could be shaped by teams of established and emerging scholars within the field of leadership, itself a field of study that incorporates many different disciplines. Each of these diverse teams responded in different ways to the challenge of describing how servant leadership has been understood and used in the past and how it is being understood and applied today. Had we not made a commitment to organize the writing process as a true and inclusive collaboration—had we adopted the more common editorial approach of simply letting each author submit an independent chapter and then bound them as a collection—the organization of chapters and the selection of authoring teams might have resulted in an abundant but otherwise incomprehensible dispersal of ideas rather than a new, curated work of scholarship.

To ensure that the goal of meaningful coherence could be met (and without implying that there is only one conclusion to be drawn across all of these chapters) it has now been left to the book's editors to highlight and synthesize the many topics that have been explored in this text, discuss how they have contributed to the rich literature on servant leadership, and to suggest how these ideas might be applied in the practice of leadership. In doing so, we must offer some challenges that emerge from the book when it is considered as a completed volume. We accept this role with the humility and responsibility of the community "clerk," known in the Quaker tradition (with which Greenleaf personally affiliated) serving as a voice given to keep track and when asked to summarize a discussion among a "society of friends." This is our role in this chapter: to reflect on what has been said in the preceding pages and to assign it its appropriate stature.

In their opening chapter, Lemoine and Blum begin the discussion with a detailed look and a critical assessment of the research conducted about servant leadership over the last several decades. Introducing one of the consistent themes of past research, one that is taken up in subsequent chapters of this book, they reveal the struggles associated with efforts made to clarify how the concept has been operationalized. They offer a short, recent-history lesson on this theme. Though servant leadership (as a named concept) has been around for several decades, there was a resurgence of interest in the topic after the 2008 financial crisis, consistent with other recent times when corporate scandal and mismanagement have shown up in the news. These scandals highlight the disturbing frequency and apparent ease with which those in power abuse those they lead, often taking advantage of personal and public trust. Servant leadership is often viewed as a potential salve to this mismanagement because it, as Lemoine and Blum suggest, provides a "different lens of leadership which emphasizes cooperation and care for stakeholders over power and short-term gains."

This growth of interest in servant leadership, perhaps sparked by the realization that leaders and leadership may be failing us in our organizational, institutional, community, and civic lives, has resulted in increased formal research on the topic over the last decade and has drawn in scholars from several academic fields. The research consistently shows that servant leadership is related to a number of positive outcomes for leaders themselves, for their followers, and their shared endeavors. However, Lemoine and Blum argue that, somewhat surprisingly, lacking from this increasing body of servant leadership literature is a clear agreement on what exactly they and others are studying. In short, there is evidence for effect but still a lack of specificity as to the nature of the cause. Lemoine and Blum suggest that this lack of agreement is problematic because it makes it difficult to assess and further grow the literature base if it remains unclear that researchers are examining the same topic. This does not mean that the concept is invalidated, however, only challenging.

In pursuing a more cohesive definition of servant leadership, Lemoine and Blum draw upon three sources: 1) components of servant leadership agreed upon by experts, 2) Greenleaf's writings, and 3) the broader leadership literature. Ultimately, they put forward this definition:

> Servant leadership is composed of influence behaviors, manifested humbly and morally within relationships, oriented towards continuous and meaningful improvement for all

stakeholders. These stakeholders include, but are not limited to, those being led, communities, customers, and the leader, team, and organization themselves.

This definition can be a helpful contribution to the servant leadership literature. The emphasis on improving the experience for stakeholders from across an organization distinguishes servant leadership from some other leadership philosophies. Lemoine and Blum are careful to note that the term "stakeholders" extends beyond those who are directly involved in the day-to-day operations of the organization and is enlarged to include the communities that they serve. While the language of "stakeholders" may seem too close to market economics (as opposed to a more humanistic tradition) this phrasing does offer focus and brings attention to the fact that servant-leaders have a responsibility to be good stewards of both their organizations and the broader community. (We will return to this point at the end of this chapter).

As the first chapter by Lemoine and Blum looks back and uses existing literature to frame a future research agenda, the next team of authors examined servant leadership from a specific methodological tradition and suggested how this might move us forward in our understanding and practice. In considering the questions servant leadership research should tackle next (especially from a quantitative analytic standpoint), Xu, Zhong, and Liden's article provides an exemplary starting point.

Xu, Zhong, and Liden point out that it is important to know more about the applicability of servant leadership across different countries and cultures, and assert that comparative research is especially needed in this regard. At the time of their writing, research has shown positive results in the U.S. and a handful of other parts of the world; more international and cross-cultural research is needed. Their analysis is based on strong empirical work, much of it grounded in Liden's scales of leadership behavior that have advanced quantifiable assessments within and across organizations. As the authors of this chapter point out, further comparison studies would help us to better understand the differences in servant leadership practices across the globe, and to learn alongside and from international servant leadership partners. We are fortunate that this very theme is addressed in a subsequent chapter in this book by Overton and Carter.

Xu, Zhong, and Liden offer a number of helpful recommendations for practitioners. They suggest that servant-leaders should work to "maximize the benefits of servant leadership" and ensure that it touches as many parts of an organization as possible. Servant-leaders should take care in "*selecting* and *cultivating* servant leaders" (italics in original). Current research on the characteristics of successful servant leadership offers helpful suggestions for selecting servant individuals to serve as leaders. For example, we know that narcissism is not a trait that is often found in successful servant-leaders (although it is one that is typically found in the traits of otherwise promising leadership candidates), and should be screened for in cultivating others to share in the practice of this particular expression of servant based leadership.

It is also important to develop what Xu, Zhong, and Liden call a "servant culture" within an organization. This is not itself an easy task, and it should be recognized that the authors' suggestion requires a conceptual leap from an individualistic relationship between leaders and followers and that of the leader as ecologist. Research has shown that servant leadership can be taxing on leaders, and Xu, Zhong, and Liden recommend that "organizations continually help to replenish leaders' tangible and intangible resources, so that they can sustain their servant leadership behaviors." For example, organizations can periodically give official recognition that rewards exemplary servant leaders. This finding reminds us that building a servant culture within an organization is not something that can be accomplished through one training or conversation, but is the result of continued investment in the organization, its people, and fellow servant leaders. Servant-leaders risk becoming isolated if they do not take the time to celebrate, care for, and support one another.

As the authors suggest, while current research on servant leadership has shown that it holds tremendous promise for organizations, we know little about how it arises within organizations. Xu, Zhong, and Liden point out that we also need to know more about what they call the "potential dark sides of servant leadership." A number of theoretical papers have touched on the possibility of harm that servant leadership can cause to its practitioners, including the possibility of burnout. However, there are few empirical studies that examine these phenomena that could help practitioners identify factors that could be employed to help buffer potential harm. It is important that as we encourage the development of servant leadership practice, we do so in ways that are sustainable for individual practitioners and the organizations they lead. Learning more about any "dark sides" would help ensure that practitioners have the support and tools they need to ensure the long-term development and sustainability of servant leadership within organizations.

A significant strength of servant leadership research is that it originates from a range of methodological, epistemological, and disciplinary perspectives and backgrounds. The wider and more diverse set of studies and methods employed in servant leadership research is, the better chance we have of improving servant leadership practice in the most informed and comprehensive way possible. Song and Ferch's chapter discusses the ways that qualitative servant leadership research continues to help us better understand the concept and offers valuable insights as to how to best prepare and support emerging servant leaders. While they commend the breadth of methodologies employed in servant leadership research, they argue convincingly that qualitative research is uniquely suited to this topic:

Qualitative researchers, in embracing formlessness, forgo the tendency to become too dependent on rationalism and the over-expressed linear mindset often associated with a leader-first mentality. Hyper-rationalism tends toward black and white thinking and calcification.

In making a carefully considered connection between servant leadership practice and methodology, Song and Ferch present a challenge for servant leadership researchers: As we study servant leadership, how can we best ensure that our research practices and methodologies reflect a servant-first perspective? This is not to suggest that any particular methodology should be the exclusive choice for framing servant leadership research, but that as leadership researchers/practitioners, we too need to continually invest in and reflect upon our own servant leadership practice.

In approaching their thought-provoking chapter, Song and Ferch focus attention on six particularly important qualitative-research articles and discuss what could be learned from the diverse set of topics addressed by their authors. The works they reviewed engaged several important themes. For example, Campbell (2017) looked at the importance of forgiveness and reconciliation as servant leadership practice, and the role that these elements can have in collective healing to address past injuries perpetuated by organizational leadership and resulting from accepted cultural practices. Song and Ferch's chapter reminds us that servant leadership research is made stronger when it includes research from scholars with a range of methodological and epistemological perspectives. The qualitative research they highlight helps us to take crucial close look at particular elements of servant leadership practice and what we can learn from those living it out in the world.

That close look is exactly what Ashleigh Bell brings us in her conversation with Richard Pieper. Her interview gives us an example of one dedicated servant leadership practitioner, his story of coming to servant leadership, and how he has translated servant leadership theory and research into his professional life. Pieper is a very accomplished professional who became president of his family's company, Pieper Electric, at the young age of 24. Greenleaf's works aligned closely with his own goals, and helped drive his commitment to nurturing a servant leadership culture and sharing the practices of servant leadership with others. As discussed by several authoring teams, one important element of servant leadership is the importance of considering both those within the organization and members of the surrounding community. Pieper took this charge to heart, shifting the company to employee ownership and recognizing, as declared within company materials, that "Our people are our power. People are our most valuable asset. We invest in their future" (Our People, n.d.). He is a committed philanthropist and is actively invested in spreading servant leadership practice and scholarship, so others can learn about the practice and bring it to their organization. Indeed, he is an exemplary model of servant leadership in action.

The decision to include a chapter that examined servant leadership as a journey was made entirely out of respect for Greenleaf's repeating narratives over the course of his career and as reflected in his writing through the end of his life. As a group of authors, we felt that we must find an appropriate way to recognize the developmental path that many servant-leaders describe. Even though this chapter differs in form from others in the book, it clearly has its place. Servant-leaders are people responding to the challenges of complicated lives. Their problems are not entirely different nor are they blessed with saintly grace (or destined for martyrdom) as they lead and serve in contemporary organizations. Richard Pieper seems to exemplify an individual striving to meet the "true test" penned by Greenleaf in his essays 50 years ago.

Hartnell, Lemoine, Ghahremani, and Stolter look at how servant leadership applies to modern organizations a half century after the term was coined. In particular, they are interested in how servant leadership is distinct among other relational leadership styles and how it manifests in organizations. Though servant leadership overlaps with other relational leadership practices in many ways, it differs through its "focus on deep convictions to nurture followers' personal freedom and growth, and to multiply their humble, determined will to improve society." The authors remind us that being a servant-leader and building a servant-leader culture within an organization is an extraordinarily difficult task and involves a vision with a scope that stretches beyond the walls of a given organization. To face this challenge, a skilled servant leader, according to this team of authors, must have a particular strength of "foresight and insight" on which they build upon what has been done in the past, address observed mistakes, and make intentional choices going forward.

Hartnell et al. were aware that servant leadership practitioners (and those that observe them) can often encounter a number of misconceptions about servant leadership that threaten to undermine its ability to spread throughout an organization. For example, it is often assumed that servant leadership is "soft," in that it does not maximize tangible goals or relate to profit, or that it is simply a way of being an ethical human being and is not, in fact, a grounded and well-researched leadership strategy. The authors take on these and other misconceptions one by one. They point out that to suggest that servant leadership is "soft" ignores the fact that servant-leaders are charged to focus on helping others to grow, challenging them to work past any self-imposed limitations. Hartnell et al. recognize that the notion that servant leadership may stand in the way of profit may at first seem compelling, because supporting one another may appear to distract from achieving apparent productivity in other areas. However, while profit is an important goal of a company, it should only be one of many. To suggest that being profitable is at odds with caring for stakeholders is both short sighted and a false dichotomy. In fact, there are numerous academic studies that highlight the fact that servant leadership has been shown to improve team effectiveness, organizational innovation, and other positive outcomes that are linked to profitability.

Given the many challenges and misconceptions about servant leadership that exist, Hartnell and his colleagues argue that it is important that servant-leaders be deeply committed to integrating the practice into their organizations. In addition to a strong drive, servant-leaders must be dedicated to the principles that undergird servant leadership, which they define as, "pursuing the greatest good (particularly championing the plight of the powerless), empowering others, creating self-transcendence, and enabling regeneration unequivocally benefit others and build a good and better society."

Overton and Carter's chapter challenges us to consider the relationship of servant leadership to culture, and to consider how servant leadership arises and is practiced in various cultural settings. They acknowledge that there are many definitions of culture, yet "a central theme of these definitions is a focus on the attitudes and knowledge that a group of people come to know or absorb through living within a particular historic, geographic, social, and political environment." Overton and Carter add that "culture, as we understand it, is all of those things we often unknowingly or unconsciously take on and act out of based on the social environments we are born into or adopt." They acknowledge that Greenleaf was obviously and quite deeply rooted in particular aspects of American culture and at a certain time, and his ideas about servant leadership arose from within that personal and cultural space.

Overton and Carter recount that specific challenges to servant leadership's applicability to other cultures were raised quickly after Greenleaf's works were published. Many African Americans objected to the use of the word "servant" as being painfully referential to the history of enslaved populations at a time when these very groups were seeking greater justice and demanding access to positions of power from which they had long been excluded. While many African Americans are exemplary servant leaders, this history highlights the fact that servant leadership is not always seen and interpreted in the way that Greenleaf intended. Accordingly, it is incumbent upon those invested in servant leadership to remain sensitive to the fact that the practice is not seen or heard the same way by all communities, and to educate themselves on various cultural practices that may be different from their own.

Overton and Carter point out that there is a growing research base that can teach us more about the relationship between servant leadership and culture. While there is much more to learn, they invite us to find hope in the fact that as this conversation grows, new scholars are drawn to the discussion. With this observation, the authors invite us to step back and look at who has engaged in servant leadership research to this point: What identities do they hold? What countries and regions do they represent? Following these questions, we should ask: Who is not included in this group and why might they be left out? As we seek to expand how we understand who is considered a servant-leader (and what it is to be a servant leader), we should also challenge ourselves to invite more people to engage in this research and consider what barriers we might, consciously or otherwise, be putting in their way.

The authors in this volume have brilliantly identified the strengths of previous research about servant leadership and offered ideas of where it should be further stretched and challenged. As editors of this volume, we have suggestions to add that we hope will aid in the effort to grow research in this field and invite new scholars into this conversation.

Integration of new disciplinary perspectives.

More research and better theory are needed to understand what it means to serve others and what this actually looks in light of what we have learned from feminist theory, critical race theory, disability studies, and other critical fields of study. These areas of scholarship have helped us to understand the history and concerns of individuals with a range of identities and highlight how the needs of people with marginalized identities continue to be dismissed and ignored within many organizations. They make use of new tools of inquiry and they are based on quite different assumptions about individuals, organizations, and society than those that dominated leadership and organizational literature at the time of Greenleaf's writing. In this respect, we applaud the insights offered in the chapter by Song and Ferch which points to the importance of using a range of lenses and methods to examine the broad and the nuanced aspects of this subject matter. Clearly, making a commitment to serve others should involve learning about how individuals of a range of intersectional identities have been marginalized within a given organization (and across society at large) and seek to address any perspectives within an organization that limit inclusion.

Accepting the challenge of Greenleaf's full definition of servant leadership

While Robert Greenleaf's works often focused on the relationship between leaders and the followers with who they directly interacted, he also challenged leaders to ensure that their efforts were working to serve the least privileged of society, or at the very least not causing them additional harm. It is no less important that servant-leaders adhere to this aspect of the "true test" which Greenleaf consistently cited as it is that servant-leaders treat their immediate followers with care and respect. While no one familiar with Greenleaf's works could reasonably argue that discrimination is compatible with the values of servant leadership which he espoused, he additionally bespoke leaders to give attention to the impact of their own work and that of their organizations on the world around them.

As editors, we contend that organizations (and leaders) that are committed to servant leadership must undergo the hard work needed to challenge discriminatory and biased practices both within their organizations and in the society that surrounds them. Servant-leaders must, as a very basic starting point, ensure that diversity, equity, and inclusion are core values fundamentally inseparable from servant leadership practice. Further, the circumstances we face today and into the future call on leaders to respond to challenges that might not have seemed nearly as urgent when Greenleaf wrote about servant leadership fifty years ago. Organizations and those who influence their actions must make affirmative commitments to a sustainable, safe and equitable world. As Greenleaf wrote in one of his final essays, "The quality of a society will be judged by what the least privileged in it achieves."

Further investigation into the stakeholder theory of servant leadership

Greenleaf wrote his essays before the concept of stakeholders (as distinguished from the term "shareholders") had grown in recognition and popularity. He was not indifferent to the underlying idea by any means. Greenleaf does approach this consideration in what is perhaps his second most cited essay, "The Institution as Servant" (1972), although the context adopted for that piece was largely shaped by the responsibilities of leaders within public and non-profit settings. Lemoine and Blum's chapter posits a definition of servant leadership which encompasses the broad range of stakeholders to whom a servant-leader should be committed and the responsibility that a leader has beyond the walls of the organization and into the community itself. This perspective has both merit and currency. Additional research is needed to examine how individual servant-leaders understand who is included in their list of stakeholders and how that understanding shapes how they serve directly and indirectly. Companies and organizations often provide tremendous benefit to their communities through the creation of jobs, philanthropic efforts, and through a number of other means. However, we are also aware of the many ways that organizations, while pursuing their own interests or even the economic security of their employees and investors, can cause significant harm. We believe that part of being a responsible servant-leader includes doing everything possible to address and mitigate potential harm to communities, and for taking responsibility to address harm when it occurs. This expectation is consistent with Lemoine and Blum's definition of servant leadership (and that of many others) that it is important for servant-leaders to focus on long-term goals over short-term gains. We believe that focusing on the long term means ensuring that the organization and the surrounding environment will be healthy and safe for future generations.

More carefully considering differences in cultural contex

The chapter authored by Overton and Carter pushed the original thoughts of Robert Greenleaf to new levels of application. As this volume has demonstrated repeatedly across the contributions of its many teams of collaborators, much has changed in the world over 50 years, and much keeps changing. Exploring how Greenleaf's essays fit with the circumstances found in new organizational, community, and societal environments is simply critical, especially if this powerful concept is to be extended in use in the decades that follow. Few important ideas are confined within a single culture or stifled within the bounds of their original language. Indeed, Greenleaf's simple essay of 50 years ago has been translated into more than 20 languages and inspired academic institutes and communities of practice in dozens of countries. In each of these settings, the paradoxes of Greenleaf's seminal ideas are discussed, altered and refitted. Real progress will occur when the lessons of these many different settings are compared, and become the source of even greater wisdom and practical application.

Meeting the "true test" of full inclusion

Beginning in the late 20th century, many disability-rights activists began using the phrase, "nothing for us without us" (Charlton, 2000). This saying, like many used in social movements, has a complex and rich history that has echoes in other calls for inclusion, justice, and access to power. These activists suggested that those who were involved in disability-access work were not doing so effectively unless they included those with disabilities in their efforts. We believe the same principle applies practicing servant leadership within organizations. It is important that organizations invested in servant leadership consider who is and who is not present and fully heard when decisions are being made about an organization's plans to invest in those they serve. Inviting stakeholders from all levels within an organization to the table helps ensure that servant leadership endeavors will have their intended outcome and not result in something for the people of the organization that is created without their input. We anticipate that these conversations will result in fresh insights regarding how the organizations servant-leaders can best care for and support one another, and their community, and inspire increased interest in servant leadership.

—

Among Robert Greenleaf's last works was a deeply personal essay entitled, "Old Age: The Ultimate Test of Spirit" (1987). As something of an addendum to this reflection, he included two additional compositions, each written on different subjects and addressed to the community of the Society of Friends. Except for the fact that they appear as the final pages of Greenleaf's directly attributed works, they might be easily ignored as nothing more than marginal ideas. They offer us jewels of thought.

In one of these pieces, Greenleaf quotes Albert Camus, whose lovely metaphor describing the origination and life of great ideas ("coming into the world as gently as doves") provided the invocation offered at the beginning of the Forward of this volume. If it bears repetition, we would send you back to the first pages of this volume and allow you to judge whether or not we came at all close to meeting our aspirations for this book.

There is yet another precious insight found in Greenleaf's final work, this one apparently original. In the "Friends Journal," published in September 1975, he wrote:

> There is a theory of prophesy which holds that prophetic voices of great clarity, and with a quality of insight to that of any age, are speaking cogently all of the time. Women and men of stature equal to the greatest of the past are with us now addressing the problems of the day and pointing to a better way and to a person better able to live fully and serenely in these times.

To this we can only say: "Let them speak loudly...and now."

Conclusion References

Campbell, A. (2017). Forgiveness and reconciliation as an organizational leadership competency within transitional justice instruments. *The International Journal of Servant-Leadership, 11*(1), 139-186.

Charlton, J. I. (2000). *Nothing about us without us: Disability oppression and empowerment.* Berkeley and Los Angeles, California: University of California Press.

Greenleaf, R.K. (1987). Old age: The ultimate test of the spirit. Indianapolis, IN: The Robert K. Greenleaf Center.

Greenleaf, R.K. (1972). The institution as servant. Indianapolis, IN: The Robert K. Greenleaf Center.

Greenleaf, R. K. (1970). The servant as leader. Newton Centre, MA: The Robert K. Greenleaf Center.

Our People. (n.d.) Retrieved from http://ppcpartnersinc.com/our-people/

About the Authors

Ashleigh E. Bell is an educator and practitioner with a range of experience in program development, facilitation, and curriculum design with a track record of empowering and elevating underrepresented groups in engineering, entrepreneurship, and leadership in higher education. Ashleigh has coached and created learning opportunities to prepare undergraduate and graduate students - particularly those from underrepresented backgrounds - for successful careers. Ashleigh received her master of arts degree in higher education from the University of Michigan and a bachelor of arts degree from Duke University.

Terry C. Blum is the founding director of Georgia Tech's Institute for Leadership and Entrepreneurship that develops individual and organizational leadership capabilities for economic growth, social responsibility, and environmental sustainability. She earned a Ph.D. from Columbia University and has published on topics related to the organization of and innovation in health services related to behavioral health care.

John C. Burkhardt is the founding Director of the National Forum on Higher Education for the Public Good (National Forum). John currently holds an appointment as professor of clinical practice at the Center for the Study of Higher and Postsecondary Education at the University of Michigan. Prior to establishing the National Forum, John was program director for leadership and higher education at the W.K. Kellogg Foundation. John's research focuses on leadership and transformation, organizational culture, and the role of philanthropy in U.S. society and higher education.

Alan Carter, Sr. is a serial entrepreneur with over four decades of venture creation experience in divergent market segments, including retail building materials, radio broadcasting, voice messaging franchising, and K-12 educational services. He is currently a candidate for his Ph.D. in Ethical and Creative Leadership at Union Institute & University. Mr. Carter and his wife, Eve, live in the Shenandoah Valley of Virginia and are owned by two charmingly persistent cats.

Shann Ray Ferch, Ph.D. is Professor of Leadership Studies with the internationally recognized Doctoral Program in Leadership Studies at Gonzaga University, and the Editor of The International Journal of Servant-Leadership. Dr. Ferch's work regarding leadership, organizational culture, and the human will to forgive and reconcile has appeared in scientific journals and other scholarly venues internationally, and he has served as a visiting scholar in Africa, Asia, Europe, and South America.

Hamed Ghahremani is an Assistant Professor in the Department of Management and Marketing at the University of New Orleans. He received his Ph.D. in Organizational Behavior and Human Resource Management from the University at Buffalo (SUNY). Hamed's research interests include the intersection of leadership, ethics, and teams.

Chad Hartnell is an Assistant Professor in the J. Mack Robinson College of Business at Georgia State University. He studies elements of the social context and their influence on organizational, team, and individual effectiveness. In particular, Dr. Hartnell researches leadership, organizational culture, and the interplay between them.

Jessica Y. Joslin is the Director of Dialogue Initiatives and Diversity Education at the University of Illinois at Chicago. She received her Ph.D. in Higher Education from the University of Michigan, and holds additional degrees from Harvard University and Northwestern University.

G. James Lemoine is an Assistant Professor at the School of Management at the University at Buffalo (SUNY), and a researcher with the UB Center for Leadership and Organizational Effectiveness. He primarily studies issues related to leadership, ethics, creativity, research methods, and how they do and don't play nicely together. Dr. Lemoine also serves as a trustee for the Greenleaf Center for Servant Leadership.

Robert C. Liden (Ph.D., University of Cincinnati) is Professor of Management and Associate Dean for doctoral programs in the College of Business Administration at the University of Illinois at Chicago. His research focuses on interpersonal processes as they relate to such topics as leadership, groups, and career progression.

Betty J. Overton has spent her career working in higher education and in philanthropy. She is a former faculty member in the Center for the Study of Higher and Postsecondary Education at the University of Michigan, served as Provost and Vice President for Academic Affairs at Spring Arbor University, and spent ten years as a program director at the W.K. Kellogg Foundation. Presently, she is on the faculty at Union Institute and University, teaches at Hope Africa University in Burundi, and acts as Senior Associate with the National Forum on Higher Education for the Public Good at the University of Michigan.

Jiying (Jenny) Song, Ph.D., PMP, is an Assistant Professor of Business and Economics at Northwestern College and the Associate Editor of The International Journal of Servant-Leadership. After receiving her Master of Engineering in China and working in the field of IT for 14 years, she came to the United States and earned her Master of Divinity from George Fox University and Ph.D. in Leadership Studies from Gonzaga University.

Derek J. Stotler is a Ph.D. Candidate in the J. Mack Robinson College of Business at Georgia State University. His research focuses on leadership, leader emergence, and work-family balance.

Haoying (Howie) Xu is a Ph.D. Student in the Department of Managerial Studies at the University of Illinois at Chicago. His research focuses on leadership, idiosyncratic deals, groups, and volunteering.

Meng Zhong is a Doctoral Candidate in Organizational Behavior and Human Resource at the University of Illinois at Chicago. His research focuses on performance feedback, interpersonal interactions, and time perspectives in the workplace.

www.ingramcontent.com/pod-product-compliance
Lightning Source LLC
Chambersburg PA
CBHW021920190326
41519CB00009B/865